# HOUSEHOLD, VILLAGE AND VILLAGE
# CONFEDERATION IN SOUTHEASTERN EUROPE

PAUL H. STAHL

Translated by Linda Scales Alcott

EAST EUROPEAN MONOGRAPHS

DISTRIBUTED BY COLUMBIA UNIVERSITY PRESS, NEW YORK

1986

DR
24
.S72
1986

# CONTENTS

# PREFACE

Studies of the traditional social structures and the property systems of the populations of south-eastern Europe increased following World War II. Information about the southern Slavs was gathered during the 19th century; the Romanians and the Albanians were studied more thoroughly later, in the 20th century; the Greeks, who present a great variety of forms, have also begun to be more well known. This research allows me to put forward this first comparative presentation. We are far from having exhausted the subject and I myself have omitted certain aspects which still merit detailed studies, the system of the villages forming the former Austrian *Militärgrenze,* for example, or the organization of various minority groups (Turks, Tatars, Tziganes).

Everywhere, lords existed, lords who were descended from the dominating ethnic group of a particular region, or belonging to a different ethnic group (the case, for example, of the Turkish *beys* living among the Slavs, Hungarian lords living among the Romanians, or Italian lords living among the inhabitants of the Greek islands); but the relationships between the peasants and the lords extend beyond the scope of this present study. The period covered is essentially that one where information of an historic nature (taken from historic documents) joins direct observation. That period occurs, for the vast majority of the populations of south-eastern

Europe, in the 19th century, and at the beginning of the 20th century, a period when the new social sciences, based on direct observation, make themselves known (sociology, ethnology, the history of popular art, and anthropological geography).

The resemblances between the groups of different origin are numerous; the differences are not less. Sometimes, these differences are quite simply, I believe, the result a varying rate of development, as is the case for the tribal regions which, in reality, conserve forms of life formerly known by all for the longest period of time. The relationships with other European populations are also important; they will be treated in another study.

Paul H. Stahl

# CHAPTER 1

## THE ROMANIANS

The house is the obvious, most preceptible expression of the birth of a new household, a fact which has remained valid for Romanian villages up to the twentieth century. A marriage was not even celebrated if the engaged couple did not have a house except in a case where a peasant was established as a tenant of another peasant (Rădulescu, 1940), p. 23. Even in our day, in collectivized villages, the right to individual property includes the place to construct a house and the house itself, built by the newly married couple and their parents.

In the past, an outsider could neither own arable land nor a house in the community village since doing so would have signified having the right to all community property. In Maramureș when a house was sold, it had to be expressly declared that the adjoining forest to the house was not included in the sale in order to avoid losing it. (Stahl H.H. 1930, pp. 203-204). The same was true in southern Transylvania where each inhabitant who bought a piece of property "obtained some possessions in all parts of the village territory" (Comănescu, 1885, p. 10).

A 1718 document clearly expresses this situation: "Having nothing with which to pay him, I gave him three house plots in the village of Lățcani, on the Moldava river, in the Suceava region; but these plots,

1

which I own with my brothers, I give, with haymaking rights, and rights to the fields, the forest and the ponds, including a ford for the mill and all its revenue" (Mihordea, Constantinescu, Istrati, 1966, II, p. 134).

This situation ensues from the former community organization of the villages and from the character of peasant economy; in fact, each household developed an activity which was supposed to assure it everything needed for its existence. Each one practiced agriculture, animal breeding, needed wood, water and so forth; consequently everyone had to have access to all economic categories of the territory. Once admitted into a community, the newcomer will claim and fairly easily obtain a series of rights permitting him to lead a normal life.

This was true even for enslaved villages. Thus, Iosif Jivan (1937, p. 439), in describing a village in Transylvania, distinguishes three categories of serfs ('iobagi'): 'serfs with land, who had a property in the village itself and some rights to the arable lands and the meadows; serfs with a house, who had some rights to a location in the village where they could construct a house; finally, serfs without a house who, while at the same time having a house site in the village, were living in houses put at their disposition by the lord."

The location which best suited the new household, inhabited by the new couple, was chosen as near as possible to the parents of the boy; therefore, in villages where the population was less and the ground sufficient, a separate group was able to be established which formed a new hamlet, inhabited after a certain number of years by a related group (Stahl H.H., 1959, pp. 152 sq.). The settlement thus takes on a scattered, characteristic nature found in various places in Romania (Mihăilescu, 1935 et 1937). The memory of these installations was still vivid among the peasants: "When a hamlet composed of three or four houses appeared, a lineage also appeared. Each peasant constructed houses for his children around the old house, depending on the amount of available land. When the family became too large, some simply moved away" (Iordache, 1977, pp. 25-26). Henri H. Stahl formulates the rule in the following manner: "Any restricted social group, having a stable, isolated location, without migrations, practicing the exclusion of persons who are not indigenous in order to defend its heritage, having endogamous customs, ends up transforming itself into a group of relatives" (Stahl H.H., 1959, p. 154). The regions of the Apuseni mountains furnish us with numerous examples.

In the 1950's, I had already studied people who were established on their lands, who had their private cemetery and a clear perception of forming a lineage known to its neighbors under a patronymic. Lucia Apolzan gives a list of the lineages forming separate hamlets in this same region, the hamlet bearing, from all evidence, in the majority of cases, the name of the principal group which inhabited it (Apolzan, 1943, p. 152). "There was only one related group here (affirmed by a peasant in the 1930's). There were several brothers who shared the lands. There was not one outsider, only our family members" (Apolzan, 1943, p. 154).

In enslaved villages, the lord himself determines the sites where the newly-weds must settle (Emerit, 1937, p. 282). When the State enacts agrarian reforms and accords properties to the peasants, it accords them lands upon which to construct houses. These grounds, equal and parallel among themselves, were situated perpendicular to a straight road, often to newly marked out streets. Thus, the villages of the new owners acquired a regular, geometric structure which distinguishes them from others.

But beginning with the second generation, the plots become unequal due to the unequal number of children born in the families. The plans of the village of Ruşeţu, situated into the plain of Bărăgan, are characteristic from this point of view; here one can see the original parcels and their divisions among the heirs after a certain number of years (Stahl H.H., 1937; Haufe, 1937).

Since it is in the large plains that most of the land to be divided among the peasants was found, and since it is always in this area that rectangular properties and streets in straight lines were most easily traced, nearly all the geometric villages are located there. In the colonization operations carried out in the 18th and 19th centuries by the Austrians, in the Banat, the state constructed even the houses and set each family up in a house, which thus became the symbol of the existence of a household. Francisc Griselini (1926, p. 183) published in 1780 his observations on the installation of the settlers by the Austrian State and cites the endowment of the peasants in houses by the state. At the same time, they received some land, livestock, grains, tools. The Russians also constructed villages, even some cities, of the geometric type in the Romanian regions occupied in a stable or temporary manner; this is true of Bessarabia, or of certain parts of Bărăgan. Thus, the presence of geometric type villages (Mihăilescu, 1935) indicates the presence of settlers.

The obligation to construct a house fell, as a general rule, on the boy's family. Here is an example, as it was studied in Nerej: "When the father considers that his son or his daughter has attained the age of reason—even if no marriage is in sight—he calculates, taking into account each of his children, the share which passes to him from each part of his assets. He builds a house for the child concerned and puts him in possession of everything. Thus, as far as males are concerned, generally the accomplishment of their military service is considered an obvious sign of maturity. During the month of our research in Nerej, we were able to observe three cases where the fathers, having defined the assets which each child would inherit, were in the process of building houses for their young boys, at that time servicemen, not one of whom was married" (Costa-Foru, 1936, p. 116).

Let us note at the same time that as the 20th century approaches, especially in the cities, the dotal house of the daughter, constructed by her parents, appears more often. The dotal house is thus cited in marriage contracts, contracts that were nonexistent in the villages. A document drawn up in 1786 in Bucarest informs us that the wife of a lord acknowledges "to madame Ilinca, so that it be known, having a daughter of required age, named Catina, and wanting her to marry, came to my house seeking help, according to my means. And since she is a former tenant of mine and since she has given the house as a dowry to her daughter, I have also gratuitously given the ground on which the house is built, because I was not able to do otherwise" (Potra, 1961, p. 546; also see p. 723; the same, 1975, p. 115).

The dotal house seems to become more frequent to the extent that the dotal system changes. Girls, who formerly did not receive any pieces of land, begin, as boys do, receiving them some. This evolution does not unfold everywhere at the same time, but in the 19th century, it had a tendency to be generalized. In the end, the endowment of lands of females with land becomes obligatory in most of the regions of Romania in the 20th century, as we see in the following passage concerning a village in the plain situated in southern Romania: "Peasants who marry their daughters to boys originating from the village itself, are under strict obligation to give them land" (Stăncescu, 1938, p. 345).

Whether it was the obligation of having a house passed on to the daughter, or to the son, the house was always the result of a collective effort. This was particularly true in the past, when each person built a house for himself without requiring master builders. Just as all women knew how to weave and sew in order to get married, each man knew how to handle an axe: "Each peasant was a master carpenter and needed no help cutting, thinning, assembling and even decorating..." affirms Nicolae Iorga (1906, p. 75). The Austrian traveler, Johann Friedel, describes a similar situation in Banat, in 1769 (Păunel, 1935, pp. 39 sq.), which is confirmed by Griselini (1926, p. 111).

This work was carried out by a group which varied in number. We see this in the production itself in the cases where a master builder was directing the work, surrounded by members of the family. The obligation of the future owner to assist the builder was outlined in the verbal understanding concluded between them, which specified the exact task of each person involved. Men and women worked together, with certain tasks reserved for each one. The more difficult jobs were reserved for the men. They cut the wood, thinned the beams and the boards, and did the assembling. Women covered the walls with a layer of plaster, whitewashed them and then decorated them at regular intervals.

In general, parents, brothers and sisters all worked along side the boy who was to be married. Even boys who have already left the paternal house were called on to help their younger brother, in the same manner that they had been helped. The framework of kinship was often extended to include neighbors who also participated. House construction was always considered an operation of mutual aid, a common custom among the group of peasants.

Toward the middle of the 19th century, Ion Ionescu de la Brad believes that this custom was better conserved in the regions located near the mountains: "These people helped each other in their work by performing hard labor, without monetary compensation in money" (Ionescu de la Brad, 1868, p. 201). Mihail Gaspar indicates the fact in Banat: "The beautiful solidarity which reigns among these people is noteworthy. As soon as someone wants to build a house, he only has to obtain the necessary materials. Once he has what he needs, his neighbors, within only a few days, during times when they are not at the factory, put up his house" (Gaspar, p. 20; also see Iordache, 1977, p. 28). Danielle Musset (1981, p. 23) points out that, in a contemporary Romanian village, even if other forms of mutual aid have disappeared, the effort concerning the construction of a house continues. The same custom existed in Moldavia and in Bessarabia; in Transylvania the administration of the State imposes precise rules which concern the neighborhood groups, rules which recall those of *Nachbarschaft* of the Saxons of Transylvania (Weber, 1968, part two). All these rules were recorded in a register which said among other things: "He who does not come at the agreed upon time for the foundation and construction of a neighbor's house, will pay a fine of 6 sous for each hour lost. And for the whole day, 24" (Manouilea, 1942, p. 524).

The participants in the construction project are usually fed by those who called on them for help. Sometimes a more sumptuous banquet followed the work, as is the case of the Romanians of Bessarabia (Arbure, 1898, p. 153). In the northern part of Moldavia, after having erected the walls, the floor of the house was formed with large stones and dirt; the host then calls in musicians and organizes a feast during which young girls and boys dance and pack down the dirt in the floor at the same time (Dan, 1897, p. 26). Valeriu Târziu (1939, p. 44) notes that "at the time of the construction of a house . . . the majority of the village participates with joy and good will. During these rare occasions, proverbs, parables, and jokes are told." The construction of the house and the participation of the relatives, or even of the entire village, also constitutes the opportunity for everyone to learn that a new household had been established, a household which will, in turn, demand its rights to equality along with the other households.

Despite its interest, the table is not clear; we do not know, for example, if the "purchased" houses were acquired from the master builders or from other village residents. However, several significant figures emerge: the proportion two times greater of inherited houses in the villages than in the cities; or, the proportion four times greater of houses purchased in the cities; or still, the proportion three times greater of houses constructed by those who are living in them, in the villages than in the cities. The table neither indicates if the newly-weds or their parents carried out the various transactions. The figures concerning Dobroudja differ greatly from the others, because it is a question for the most part of a new installation on lands abandoned by the Turks after the war of 1877-1878. The inherited houses represent only 11.5% while those newly constructed reach 66.6%. But in general, in spite of its imprecisions, the table confirms what social surveys have pointed out.

A census taken in 1912 (Colescu, 1920) gives the following (the figures represent percentages):

| Village houses | Inherited | Purchased | Dotal | Rec'd gift | Self Constr. | Other orig. | Non-spec. |
|---|---|---|---|---|---|---|---|
| Moldavia | 56.8 | 16.8 | 13.4 | 1.6 | 10.1 | 0.7 | 0.6 |
| Muntenia | 58.2 | 12.9 | 11.1 | 1.2 | 15.4 | 0.6 | 0.6 |
| Oltenia | 69.8 | 11.6 | 7.2 | 1.0 | 9.8 | 0.6 | 0.6 |
| Dobroudja | 11.5 | 17.3 | 1.2 | 2.0 | 66.6 | 0.6 | 0.8 |
| Rural Tot. | 58.4 | 13.9 | 10.6 | 1.3 | 14.6 | 0.6 | 0.6 |
| City Tot. | 24.0 | 53.7 | 12.8 | 1.3 | 5.8 | 0.5 | 1.9 |

\* \* \*

In the villages, the house is always placed in the middle of a court-yard; often there is also a garden, which becomes a vegetable garden and an orchard for the newly married couple. The grounds are enclosed, the house built, and the garden. planted. In regions where life was relatively peaceful it is customary to see this alternation of houses and gardens. The same is not true, however, for the plain regions in southern Romania, near fortified points, occupied by foreign troops, where frequent attacks and pillages originated. The villages enslaved by lords were established primarily in the plains, and those inhabited by free peasants, in the hills and near the mountains. Thus the alternation also appears as a characteristic which distinguishes these two other categories (Stahl, Stahl, 1968, Preface). Camille Allard describes the miserable aspect of the villages situated along the Danube in the middle of the 19th century (Allard, 1864, p. 110). See also the work of the doctors of the 19th century, for example the work of Gh. Crăiniceanu, 1895; N. Manolescu, 1895; or Charles H. Laugier, 1910).

The development house—courtyard—garden is found again in the cities, which appear to travelers as vast gardens. Stanislas Béranger describes in 1846 "Bucarest extending itself on all sides as far as the eye can see, submergered, flowing into an immense savannah of gardens" (1846, I. p. 23). This, then, is a characteristic aspect of the cities of all of this part of Europe, which, not being surrounded by fortifications, developed itself easily. In the fortified cities of Transylvania, especially those considered to be Saxon, and resembling western cities, gardens were rare and cramped. The data given below (Colescu, 1920) for 1912 gives the following situation (in percentages):

|  | House with garden | House without garden | Non-spec. |
|---|---|---|---|
| **Rural Milieu** | | | |
| Moldavia | 77.6 | 19.8 | 3.5 |
| Muntenia | 58.0 | 35.9 | 6.1 |
| Oltenia | 66.1 | 30.0 | 3.9 |
| Dobroudja | 54.5 | 38.1 | 7.4 |
| Rural Total | 65.0 | 29.4 | 4.9 |
| **Urban Milieu** | | | |
| Moldavia | 32.5 | 62.2 | 5.3 |
| Muntenia | 24.8 | 67.5 | 7.6 |
| Oltenia | 35.1 | 59.5 | 5.4 |
| Dobroudja | 23.0 | 58.7 | 8.3 |
| Urban Total | 28.0 | 65.3 | 6.7 |

Rural houses with a garden can therefore be estimated to be two-thirds of the total, while urban houses only number one-third.

### The domestic group: composition and hierarchy

The Romanian domestic group is composed primarily of two people: the couple made up of the husband and his wife. They form a new household at the time of the marriage, when they receive a house and are endowed with lands. Besides the parents, there are the children who live with the parents until marriage. At this time, the boys in turn establish themselves in new houses and the girls, when they marry, live in their husband's house. Research conducted in the village of Sanţ in 1936 outlines the composition of domestic groups and brings out the domination of the domestic group just described (Cressin, p. 56). Daniele Masson notes the persistence of the same structure in a contemporary village (1982, pp. 12 sq.).

"There is a custom in this country, that the youngest sons or daughters are not engaged before their elder siblings" notes Paul de Alep in the middle of the 17th century (1976, p. 208); this rule is still respected, even though it is in the process of losing its stringency. There is a correspondence between this practice and the same practice, as it appears in folk tales; here also the order of birth, considered the natural progression, is respected because it is normal to marry children in turn, as they reach marriageable age.

The last of the boys remains in the paternal house and lives with his parents where his wife joins him. In all these cases, a new house is not built since the youngest inherits his parent's house. A document dated 1775 states that "the old house of Ionaşcu Candre will fall to Simion Candre, he being the last born of the brothers, just as his father was the last born of the boys of Ionaşcu Candre." Another document, dated 1763 states: "This house I give to my son Andronic, being the last born; or still in another document of 1766 an inhabitant of Câmpulung is said to have "a small house with a surrounding courtyard and trees, received from father because I was the last born" (the three documents are taken from Stahl H. H., 1958, p. 117). The domestic group thus succeeds in comprising three generations; the grandparents, the parents, the children. Little by little, as age deprives them of their strength to work, the older couple relinquish their leadership role.

Thus the Romanian domestic group changes composition throughout its life, being formed either from a single couple, from a couple with children, or from two couples and children. This does not imply that the group changes nature, it is quite simply a matter of successive evolutionary phases of a single form of the domestic group.

When there are only girls in a household, a situation formerly considered unfortunate (Popovici-Raiski, 1939, p. 220), one of the girls remains with her parents and her husband comes to live in their house. The marriage becomes uxorilocal, an exceptional situation which has nothing to do with the matriarchy. The woman fulfills, in these cases, the social role of the man in order to prevent the disappearance of the household, and her marriage consequently puts her husand in a position of inferiority which carries over into familial relations, the relationship with regard to the property, and the name by which he will henceforth be known. It is considered a son-in-law marriage (called "ginerire pe curte" by the Romanians, literally "becoming groon of the court.")

Lastly, if the couple has no children, they adopt someone in order to assure the longevity of the household (Stahl P.H., 1981). Past documents confirm the custom of adoption, especially of a boy, a near relative, such as it is known from direct survey. Here is an example furnished by a document dated 1718: "I, Despa, who was the wife of the late priest Ghidu, of the district of the *Dintr'o zi* church, have given this letter to the hand of Mihai, our nephew, so that it be known that, when my husband was still living, and we had no children of our own, I took him into my house while still a child so that he would learn to read and to write and he was useful to us and helped us with everything, serving as the church scribe while my husband was still alive. And later, having reached a state of weakness and old age, my late husband, who, as mentioned above, was still living, made a decision about the house and decided to leave it to his nephew, Mihai, with the stipulation that as long as I am alive, I will live in it and rest there, and after my death, the house will go to Mihai." (Potra, 1961, p. 279). The gift of the house in this case, as in all the cases where the youngest children stay with their parents, is the customary manner of assuring old age for people in times past (see also Serres, 1814, IV, p. 217).

The woman without children "is not liked by God"; that is the reason she cannot have any children. The woman who is fertile, but who calls on various methods to prevent having them is considered to be a devil and she will pay for her transgressions in another world. There are many means of help to which people without children will resort in order to have them; expert women of the village, prolonged fasts, pilgrimages to monasteries and renowned relics, miraculous iconic invocations, magic objects carried on the body (Marian, 1892, pp. 1-2; Marian, 1893, p. 25; Golopenția Șt., 1944, pp. 39 sq.). Folk tales often refer to this: "Once upon a time there was an emperor and an empress. They loved each other dearly. But they were very sad because they had no children. And all the remedies that the empress had found at the enchanter's and the sorcerer's had been ineffective." (Ispirescu, 1882, p. 243). Adoption takes place as a last resort, and once a child is adopted, he will have the same rights and obligations as a natural child.

Servants were extremely rare in rural households. On the other hand, they were usually found in the households of lords or of rich inhabitants of the cities; it is not until later, when the rural mass begins to differentiate itself from an economic stand point do we find peasants having any servants.

Domestic groups comprising several married couples are rare in Romania. They are found among the Slovakian minorities of Transylvania, the Serbs of Banat, the Turks and the Tatars of Dobroudja, and even occasionally among the Romanians.

A person belongs to a paternal household as long as he lives there, and, it is only when he leaves the household in order to establish himself in his own house or in the husband's house (for girls) that he obtains the rights of an independent household. An ancient law code, published in Moldavia in 1646, outlines the situations where a father can punish his daughter; among other things, we find: "Whosoever separates from his daughter, giving to her dowry, as soon as she lives alone, he will no longer have the right to kill her if he finds her prostituting herself" (Carte, 1969, p. 96). The voievode Constantin Brâncoveanu, points out in a document dated 1698 that priests "with their house, their fortune and their sons who have not already left the paternal house" will have certain rights (Giurescu Dinu C., 1962, p. 391). It is clear, then, that sons living in the paternal household are considered members of that household and are subject to its regulations, thus forming a single group with their parents.

A strict hierarchy separates the sexes and ages. The husband is the head of the household and, as I have often noted, the other members of the family do not use the familiar form of "you" with him, but instead address him with a polite form, halfway between the French 'tu" and "vous" ("dumneata", "mata"); these situations seem more frequent in the southern part of the country. The husband directs the lives and the work of everyone in the household with authority, applying force when needed. And if it is necessary to beat his wife from time to time, he is not to beat her to excess, since weakness and cruelty are also condemned by public opinion. The right of a husband to beat his wife was recognized by the ancient law codes, which include, however, the banning of cruelty and the criterion defining it. Thus, if a husband breaks his wife's limbs or if he breaks the stick that he uses to flog her, that would be considered an act of cruelty. This distinction between the right to beat one's wife and cruelty is made today by peasants. For example, a woman too severely beaten is protected by his blood relatives with whom she can even take refuge in case of danger (Musset, 1981, pp. 157 sq.). Occasionally, actual non-written rules are cited by peasants which justify wife beating, for adultery, for example. These are rules that are even accepted by women (Masson, 1982, p. 103).

In public, a man avoids showing outward affection that he might have for his wife. This would be a sign of weakness, and is frowned upon by village opinion. Moreover, in areas where traditions are well conserved, men and women form two separate groups in public settings. Women were seen up until recent times walking on roads behind their husband, a custom which dates far back in history. Miron Costin cites the practice in the 17th century in the following words of an Italian bishop: "I do not need to read books in order to know how the inhabitants of Moldavia behave. I know them by their customs; they like banquets; their women avoid the look of strangers and do not like to be noticed; the wife does not pass in front of her husband, neither on the road nor on paths . . . and all of this behavior is identical to the Italians" (Kogălniceanu, 1872, I, p. 11). The priest, Gh. Verşescu (1942, p. 280), notes the respectful appelations used by the wife to address her husband: "Formerly the wife addressed her husband by calling him 'bădiţă' or 'dumneata' (. . . ) sometimes she kissed his hand (. . .) when they were walking together, they did not walk side by side, but rather the man in front and the woman behind, always as a sign of respect for the preeminence of her husband" (see also Herovanu, 1936, p. 69).

Having said this, it should be stated that the wife's situation was much better than it had been in certain Balkan Christian or Moslem societies.

This relatively privileged situation seems to have existed for some time. Tommasso Alberti crossed Moldavia in 1612 and 1613. He states that in the houses "women direct and do all that is required within the house itself; they converse without embarrassment and unceremoniously with people, in public or in private, since that is not forbidden. When they bring something to eat or to drink, they are the first to partake" (Călători, IV, p. 361). Robert Bargrave traveled through Moldavia in 1652. During his trip he was received in a village where he observed "the extraordinary liberty that women have everywhere, married or not, since they even slept in the same room as the men and near their beds" (Călători, V., p. 487). Paul de Alep observes women who came to the patriarch Macaire bringing him an offering: "All the women, even those considered young and even young girls, came toward him in a horse-drawn coach, their faces exposed" (Călători, VI, p. 121). Arrived from Liban he was impressed by the fact that women were able to present themselves to men with their faces uncovered.

Wives serve their husband at the table, even if there are guests: "The Romanian women do not sit beside their husband at the table, but rather eat their meals afterward, standing, during which time they take care of domestic chores," Griselini tells us in 1780 (1926, p. 163). At the beginning of the 19th century, Caronni affirms: "Young Romanian women serve the meals and eat afterwards, standing up and working in the kitchen. Except for the days immediately preceding, or the very day of, the birth of a child they are working at all times." (Caronni, 1812, p. 11)

Even if occasionally wives avoid talking to strangers, they are allowed to address men in a normal manner, but without exaggeration, since this would not be considered appropriate.

Since every couple longs for a son, the situation of the inferiority of the wife vis-a-vis her husband, in general, begins before her birth (Stahl P.H., 1981); the joy of having a child is much greater if the child is a boy. The marriage ceremony itself contains passages which are destined to assure the superiority of man (Marian, 1890, chapters XXXII and XXXIII). In front of the priest, it is the husband-to-be who is on the right; at the table he also takes the place of honor and is served first. According to peasant beliefs, the inferiority of women dates back to the beginnings of the world and seems to justify the former situation in society. (Voronca, 1903, I, p. 9; Pamfile, 1915, pp. 13 sq.).

### The domestic group and the composition of the house

The composition of peasant houses reflects the composition and the life of the domestic group. The pages which follow will attempt to bring to light that correspondence.

The simplest construction comprises a single room; the only room (the same name given to the entire construction —'Casă'), serves concurrently all the functions of a house. The second room which is added to the plan, serves most often as a passage to the central room and the house has a single hearth and a single occupied room; it is followed by the appearance of a third room, the storeroom. Here, as well, the house maintains a single entry, a single hearth, and one occupied room (where the hearth is situated). Lastly, the fourth room which is added to the plan is the dining room. Used only occasionally, it is rarely heated and contains the most beautiful furniture and fabrics (Stahl P.H., 1958). A similar evolution is observed among underground houses.

The rooms described, characteristic of old houses, are more and more often accompanied in the 20th century by a kitchen which is a part of the house and which is situated near the ends of the plan. The kitchen includes a hearth, which, at first sight, seems to contradict the principle of the single hearth. In fact, the kitchen is becoming, little by little, an inhabited room, at least during the warm months of the year. On the other hand, because the kitchen is less solidly constructed than the rest of the house, members of the household will often leave the kitchen in the winter, prefering the main room of the house which also has a hearth. Therefore, even with two hearths, the principle remains the same because they are not used simultaneously, but rather alternately. In other cases, a single fire serves for cooking purposes and for heating the adjoining room. The heat from the fire used for cooking food in the kitchen passes into the adjoining room where a false stove is located, circulates and comes out of the kitchen again in order to rise toward the attic. This is the solution for the old houses. In those constructed in the 20th century, the stove fire in the kitchen passes under a metallic plate (on which food is cooked) and then crosses another stove which forms the partition separating the kitchen from the adjoining room. Next, the heat rises directly into the attic through the chimney.

Light one fire at a time. That is the principle insistently conserved by the peasants. Thus one is able to identify the household, the house, and the "smoke." Such and such a village is cited as being composed of so many smokes; there was even a tax on smoke ('fumărit") which, in reality, corresponds to a tax on the household.

When the Austrians established colonists in Banat during the first half of the 18th century, they built houses for them whose principle of composition is the same: a household, a couple, a hearth. Much later, in 1894, a regulation of the Romanian state makes a provision that the peasant house must have "two rooms to live in, one on the right and the second on the left, with a room situated between them where the kitchen will be placed" (Cazacu, 1906, pp. 540-551). It goes without saying that the regulation would never be applied because the peasants were insistent upon preserving their way of life that they could not change at will, upon order of the State. Even in trying to impose houses with two inhabitable rooms, the regulation concerned domestic groups composed of a single married couple or of the parents and their children. A room was reserved for each generation, even though in winter they all lived in one room. Between the two world wars, the village of Dioşti, situated in Oltenia, burned almost entirely. In its place a "model village" was constructed, with houses with several rooms. But the peasants established themselves in one room only, or at the very most in two, leaving the other rooms empty and using only one hearth. More recent examples (the "bloukhous," for example, constructed in the upper valley of the Jiu, in a peasant, mining environment) bring to light a contradiction of the same nature contrasting the urban dwellers of the house and the peasants, based on a single domestic group, a single hearth, a certain function of the rooms.

The inhabited room includes one bed; the bed is slept in, but small benches situated along the walls are used also for sleeping. The beds placed in the dining room are only used by the newly-weds during the first days of their marriage, and later by guests. The children and the elderly can sleep on the furnace to stay warm in the winter. In cases where there are three generations (grand-parents, parents, children) they generally live in one room, especially in winter. The grand-parents sometimes occupy a small room of the house, the storeroom, for example, or even sleep on the massive furnace (where there is one).

Was the principal household-house-hearth also followed by peasant constructions of two levels, where the number of rooms in generally larger?

The two level house, which became widespread at the end of the 18th century, includes two or three rooms per floor. In the beginning, the main floor housed a cellar, and eventually a storeroom. The people packed themselves in one room on the first floor. The modern evolution of these houses favors the installation of a kitchen on the main floor which becomes the principal room of the house; it is placed, in the beginning, side by side with the cellar or the storeroom, which little by little disappears, replaced by a second inhabitable room (Stahl, Petrescu, 1966). The family members use the main floor during the summer months, but they must take refuge in winter on the first floor due to the cold.

The lords' houses are bigger and include more rooms. The plan must meet the needs of a single household, similar to the peasants' needs, but this time the conditions of habitation are different. A 1815 document speaks about a seigniorial house in Bucarest having "three rooms with a dining room and a storeroom, with two iron stoves, beds, doors, locks, windows, and below a kitchen with its small bedroom for the cook" (Potra, 1961, p. 658). A similar organization is noted in a monograph about Muntenia written at the beginning of the 19th century. The first floor included the rooms inhabited by the parents and guests, and the main floor the rooms for the children, tax collectors, servants (Samarian, 1937, p. 172). While respecting the principle of a single household, the house now has several hearths and several rooms inhabited on a permanent basis.

Several figures can help us clarify other aspects of this situation. In 1912, 91.3% of the existing buildings ('clădiri') in the villages were composed of a single apartment, 8% of two apartments, 0.5% of three and 0.2 of four (Colescu, 1920). In the same census published by Colescu, we find data on the number of rooms in rural houses; I have retained the totals by provinces. The figures on the following page represent percentages.

More precise is the data of P. Cazacu, although resulting from the analysis of a restricted number of cases. In 1906, out of 12.669 houses (from Moldavia, Muntenia, Oltenia and Dobroudja) there were:

    3.7%  with one inhabitable room
    34.7% with a single inhabitable room and a room which serves
          as a passage

50.3% with two inhabitable rooms and a room which serves as a
     passage
11.3% with more than two inhabitable rooms

\* \* \*

|           | 1 Room | 2 Rooms | 3 Rooms | 4 and 5 Rooms | 6 Rooms and up |
|-----------|--------|---------|---------|---------------|----------------|
| Moldavia  | 32.4   | 39.0    | 17.9    | 8.8           | 1.9            |
| Muntenia  | 17.1   | 43.0    | 22.1    | 13.6          | 3.3            |
| Oltenia   | 9.4    | 59.5    | 33.0    | 7.7           | 1.4            |
| Dobroudja | 15.3   | 38.8    | 26.6    | 15.3          | 4.0            |
| Total     | 20.2   | 45.5    | 21.0    | 10.9          | 2.5            |

\* \* \*

We learn that in 88.9% of the houses having two inhabitable rooms,
only one was used. Adding these latter ones to those composed of a
single room or of a room and a dining room, one notes that in 82.9%
of the cases, the peasants lived in one room. In fact, the proportion was
larger, because in houses which include several rooms, still only one of
them is used, as I have been able to state in my research. Others also note
this; thus, in a village of Muntenia, 269 houses had one room, 64 had two,
and only one had four. On average, there were 5.35 inhabitants ('*suflete*'—
souls) per house and 4.80 per room (Voinea, Stoian, Dumitrescu, 1905).

It can therefore be maintained that, in the past, the peasant household centered its life around a fire, around a pot and in one room, even
in the case where three generations cohabitated.

### The name and designation of the household

On various occasions, households have to be designated; thus when
the population is counted, the number of inhabitants is achieved by
noting the number of households. To estimate the importance of a lord's

property, one still indicates the number of households which make it up. Finally, and this is most frequently the case, taxes are determined per household.

The manner in which a household is named varies and the origin of its names dates far in history. The first means, which has just been cited, is one which speaks of "houses," the house being the obvious sign of the presence of a domestic group and all that accompanies it. The expression "his house was extinguished" (Cronici versificate, pp. 38, 89, 90) was common in the past. It signified that a household had disappeared, as did the life of the domestic group which composed it. One of the most dreaded curses was "may your house be extinguished," and it appeared in everyday language, as well as in judicial documents, written by individuals of a religious nature. The Pope's envoys counted their believers by houses, as did the missionary Andrei Bogoslavić (p. 5) in 1623, and numerous others followed. Foreign travellers, like Bartolomeo Locadello (pp. 35-36), who crossed Romania in 1641, did this as well. The Romanians also practiced this: prince Alexandru Voievod makes a donation in 1428 to a monastery in Bistriţa, in Moldavia, of "12 underground houses ('bordeie') of the Tatars" (Tiktin, 1903, p. 121). It is evident that in reality the prince interpretes the expression "underground houses" to include the Tatars who inhabit them. A 1711 document states that "Chiru's house and his agricultural products" must be exempt from taxes (Giurescu Dinu C., 1962, p. 430); another, dated 1740, exempts a lord from taxes by designating "him and his house" (Giurescu Dinu C. 1962. p. 430); another document of 1800 tells that the lord "takes a lamb per house" (Iorga, 1930, I, p. 241). The chronicler, Ion Neculce, constantly speaks of households refering to them by the name of "*casă*" (house).

The evaluation of the importance of cities or villages by houses remains constant throughout the centuries. Moise Colarov evaluates ethnic groups which existed in 1774 in the city of Arad by the number of homeowners (Colarov, 1928). In the 17th century, the oriental traveler, Evlija Celebi, did this systematically (Guboglu 1963 and 1967); the Russian general, Frederic Guillaume Baur, crossed the Romanian countries during the course of the 18th century and appreciated the importance of villages made up of houses (Baur, 1778); one of the last Romanian chroniclers, Zilot Românul, evaluated at the beginning of the 19th century the greatness of the city of Craiova by its houses (Haşdeu, 1884, p. 34).

The door is also an obvious sign of the existence of a household. Georg Werner (Călători Străini, II, p. 59) notes in the tax registers of 1552 that there are "more than two hundred carriage entrances" or "more than two hundred fifty." Petru Grigorovici the Armenian, writes in 1604 that a lot of taxes were levied: "sometimes 60, sometimes 100 florins on each carriage entrance" (Călători Străini, IV, p. 298). It seems logical to draw the conclusion that not only did the door signify a household, but that each domestic group had a door in fornt of its courtyard, consequently it appeared to be a region dominated by non-dispersed forms of housing.

A third element (after the house and the carriage entrance) is always of a material nature; we have already seen above that each house and each domestic group lived around a fire. The hearth, the fire, the smoke, have been, since remote times, the testimony of the life of a household. Thus, certain Romanian villages situated near mountains have double living conditions: one below and one above that is utilized during the warm months of the year. This is the case, for example, of villages situated along the southern Carpathians. In the upper living area, ther are jointly used sheep pens; one shed serves as shelter for several households which raise their sheep together. On the inside of the sheep pen itself are several hearths, one for each associated household, the hearth here again being the symbol of the presence of a household (see also Herseni, 1941; Dragomir, 1926, p. 197). The authorities of the State were also able to register the household as "hearths" or "fires": Jeronim Arsengo, Catholic missionary, visits the region in 1581 and estimates the importance of the localities by fires (Italian—"fochi") (Călători străini, V, p. 34). The practice was to be maintained until very late.

The human element also intervenes in the designation of households. In rare cases, when the man is absent, it will be the woman's name which will be used. An 1697 inscription includes among those who do not pay taxes "great lords, small lords, troup commanders, large monasteries, and poor women" (Giurescu Dinu C., 1962, p. 384). A document dated 1698 exempts from taxes "priests' widows who have to rear children" (Giurescu Dinu C., 1962, p. 392). The role of the woman must be appreciated in the same manner that the perpetuation of the life of a household is understood. When there are no boys, a girl remains in the house and inherits it. When there is no man to work and pay the taxes, it will fall on the woman to become the provisional head of the household and her name will be cited. But that is an exceptional case; in the majority of cases it is the man's name which appears, not the women's. Here also, the custom dates back far in history. Iacob Wuyek-Vangrovicius estimates in 1580 the composition of the villages by indicating the number of serfs, widows, and abandoned houses, the three names in reality signifying the same thing: the households. (Călători străini, II, pp. 482n 484).

The code of laws published by the voievode Vasile Lupu in 1646, lists the heads of household (*'căsarii'*) in order to designated households (Carte, 1961, p. 113). A 1740 document does this as well (*'căsasii'*). The two words are from the same origin as the word 'casa' — house — and therefore the owners of houses and households are one in the same. Yet, still in other cases, one clearly sees that the reference is to the 'head of the household' (Călători străini, V, p. 36).

Documents from the past also speak of *"holtei"* — bachelors. This word needs to be understood in relationship to the notion of the household. In fact, bachelors are men who by their age would be able to be heads of households but who are not yet married (for example, in Mihordea, Constatinescu, Istrati, 1966, II, p. 211). The administration imposed a marriage order upon the young men because they often would delay leaving the paternal house in order to avoid paying taxes. In order to avoid their taxation as long as possible, the young men would continue to wear a typical child's shirt; wearing pants signified being capable to oversee a household, therefore able to pay taxes (Griselini, 1926, p. 164). Statute labor also concerned each *'căsar'* and each bachelor (Mihordea, Constantinescu, Istrati, 1966, p. 178). Similar cases are found south of the Danube, in the regions administered by the Turks.

The financial arrangements of the voievode, Constantin Brâncoveanu, tells of the taxation of "each man" ('tot omul'), but in reality it is not a question of each person, but of each head of the household (Giurescu Dinu C., 1962, pp. 374, 375, 384). The same register requires each person to pay "his name" but only the heads of households were noted. It is always the households that are designated. In another document (p. 388) after indicating "each man," persons included under that appellation are listed; without exception masculine names make up the list.

In Transylvanian documents, a reference is made to serfs. The censuses taken by the Austro-Hungarian administration note the number of serfs which corresponds to the number of houses. It is evident that each house housed several persons who were completely enslaved and that, in reality, their head of the household was counted as a means of listing the households. Elena Sighiarteu studied the village of Agrieş and found, in 1713, 10 houses, with 7 serfs and three daily workers; in 1750, 24 houses and 29 serfs. In 1857, the custom of registering only the heads of household and the boys of legal marrying age dims and the census notes that the village had 113 houses and 657 inhabitants. (Sighiarteu, 1926, pp. 17-18).

In Transylvania, households are still designated by the word '*gazdă*', which means host. In a monograph devoted to the village of Galaţi (Aron, 1905, p. 51), the fires that ravaged the area are noted. Thus, in 1872, "175 hosts were burned," in 1887, "185 hosts were burned". The identity between the house and its head is so strong that the affirmation cited is that the hosts burned and not their houses, as if that were indeed the case. The author of the work, native of the region, used everyday language in his book. In a regulation edited toward the end of the 18th century, the arrangements concern the "hosts of the house" ('*gazdă a căsii*'), in reality refering to the households (Manciulea, 1942).

In notations taken in the 20th and even in the 19th century, even though the identity between the house and its head is still clear, new appellations appear. The heads of the family ('*capi de familie*') or the family itself ('*familii*') are cited. These notions, which are essential in censuses and modern statistics, also become customary in monographs. Dumitru Dogaru (1937), in studying the Romanians of Bessarabia, cites the heads of the family registered in the census of 1838; Florea Florescu still notes the heads of families (1937); Constantin Chiru (1925) registers in one village 242 families and 232 houses, a rather remarkable correspondence of the two figures. Nicolae Şuţu notes in a census taken in Moldavia in the 20th century, the families (the figure of the population being rendered by the number of families), families which must, in reality, represent households (Suţu, 1957); Pavel Vitănescu (1937) counts in a village 522 families, 420 households ('*gospodării*') and 428 houses (the three notions, more clearly perceived by researchers, correspond numerically to each other; the word "family" in this case must have signified couple). It also occurs that the typical Romanian word which designates household — '*gospodărie*' — is cited, as Dumitru Galian (1903, p. 20 has done.

Finally, to conclude this point, it needs to be made clear that there was a movement to name a social unit entirely after one person, the others persons being totally omitted, or being mentioned only as a group. This was true for the household, and also true for a lineage or for an entire village. The expression "so and so and his lineage" (*"cutare cu neamul lui"*) appears frequently in old documents, as well as in the prayers of the Church.

### The name and the signs of property

Each household is designated by the name of its head; the wife takes the name of her husband (X, the wife of so and so), in reality of her husband's household if it is a patronymic. Ancient tax registers, for example, mention names and often nicknames: "And they decided that there would be four quarters (there were sometimes five 'quarters') to pay each year, and that each man having his house (*'tot omul căsaş '*) would give 105 *'parale'* per quarter, and bachelors with parents (meaning those living with their parents) would give 55 *'parale'* per quarter: all were given specially printed papers, on which their face, name and nick-name were noted" (Kogălniceanu, 1872, II, p. 416).

The customary means formerly used to name people was to call them by the given name and the father's, for example, "John, son of Nicolas;" when the grandfather had a certain notoriety or if described items in documents necessitated the mentioning of the grandfather, the appelation was changed to: "John, son of Nicolas and grandson of George." In this manner, the household was named with its members (as shown above) and also the households from which it had descended. The expression even made clear "so and so with all his house," or "so and so with his children," or "so and so with his wife and his sons," rarely also mention-ing daughters. The wife was "Mary, daughter of so and so" until her marriage; at which point she was "Mary, wife of so and so" and if her husband was deceased, she was "Mary, widow of so and so." This last designation signified that the wife represented the household in the absence of her husband.

Once beyond the limits of the village, the name of the original village is added: "so and so, son of so and so, from such and such village." Often this is the formula used in proceedings which take place far from the village, in the presence of the prince.

To the extent that the necessities of the interior organization and of the property of the village render it necessary, a second name appears: the lineage of which the person is a member. Thus the household is able to carry the name of the lineage of the head of the household, and his first name. Each household, whose son founds a household, passes on his name to the new household.

Different necessities require that among lords the name of the family, that is of the family line, appear earlier. We thus observe the appearance family name first among lords and the inhabitants of the villages, and much later among the peasants. The names of the latter also follow different evolutions according to the particular regions. In the case where Austria administered the territory, the family name appears early in documents. For example, in Bucovina, tax records list everyone from the small city of Câmpulung with their first name and the family name. It is interesting to note that in the same table (with few exceptions), the lists are composed exclusively of men (Ştefamelii, 1915, pp. 205sq.).

When a boy establishes himself in the girl's household, it is easier to observe the predominant role that the household plays in the allocation of the name. The best described, and perhaps most typical situation comes from the village of Drăguş , studied during the nineteen thirties. (Henri H. Stahl, 1959, p. 128) describes the local onomastic system: "In this particular instance, when a man marries (*mărită*'), becomes a 'son-in-law' ('ginerire pe curte' — groom of a court), sharing in his wife's inheritance, thus leaving his own household for that of his wife's, he takes the name of the household of his wife, abandoning his own family name. This is symbolized by the name of the father-in-law in the case of the 'son-in-law' and by the wife's name when he shares in his wife's inheritance." In a table, he notes all the cases where the husband takes the name of the household in which he is established. Out of a total of 69 cases, 45 husbands clearly apply the rule which has just been described, and 8 apply it while also keeping their former name; in 7 cases the wife keeps her name as does the man (which represents, nonetheless, a bending of the rule); 10 cases constitute exceptions. In 6 cases, the husband had married a woman who bore the name of the household of her first husband; the second husband, once established in the widows's household, takes the name of the household of the first husband.

It is interesting to observe that in Rumanian there are two words which designate marriage: a man "*se 'însoară*" and a woman "*se 'mărită*". In the case where the man establishes himself in the woman's dwelling, it is said that he "*se 'mărită,*" therefore placing himself in a situation of inferiority, clearly perceived by village opinion (Stahl H.H., 1959, p. 128; Frâncu and Candrea, 1988, p. 115; Evaşcu, 1978, p. 75). These exceptional situations are justified in a majority of cases by the absence of boys in a household, the girl thus being the only person able to continue the tradition of the paternal line.

In the past, peasants calculated with the help of small cuts and notches; moreover, they used them for property marks which equaled signatures but which had no resemblance to alphabetical writing. Nor did these marks have any rapport with the name, since the name of the person who had placed it was not significant, rather his right to property over an object was read. This does not imply, however, that the other villagers did not know with precision the name of the owner of each property. This mark is not the graphic expression of a person but of a domestic group; the objects which bear these signs are therefore considered as belonging, not to a certain individual, but to a certain household.

There were also property signs belonging to a single individual, for example those inscribed by artisans on products they were selling. Popular in the Middle Ages, they are still being maintained by peasants in the 20th century (Bănăţeanu, 1954).

Just as for proper names, known within a determined social group, property abbreviations are known to each household of the group. (usually the village). There is therefore a social memory indispensable to the functioning of social life. A peasant will be able to tell you the names of all the persons in his village, as well as identifying to whom each parcel of land belongs.

The occasions where the property signs appear in everyday life are numerous. If someone chooses a tree in the forest and puts on it the property sign of a certain household with the help of an axe, no one can cut it down or remove it. Even standing, the tree belongs to the person who has marked it. Peasants, working in forestry development, continue in the 20th century to inscribe their mark on each cut tree in order to know which ones represent their rights to wages (Burada, 1880).

The women weave or embroider abbreviations on fabrics before giving them to the fuller's mill, where they will be mixed with fabrics worked by other women. In the past, the owners of the fuller's mills left the regions near the mountains where they had their installations, and travelled through the lower regions carrying the fabrics in their carts. They returned to their villages, worked the fabrics, and subsequently returned to the plains. The women easily recognized their fabrics from the property signs that they had sewn on them.

These types of signs of ownership are all the more necessary now that popular art produces objects which resemble each other, especially if they come from the same village or region. Cornel Irimie gives interesting details concerning this (1956, pp. 65-66) about a region in Transylvania: "In Gura Râului, where the center of the fuller's mills of the Mărginimea Sibiului region is located, thousands of pieces of fabrics, gathered from a wide territory, are worked on annually. The peasants of the neighboring villages carry their fabrics directly to the mill. Those situated farther leave them with a collector in certain villages, where the artisans come to collect them in their carts; sometimes it is the tailors who carry them to the mill (as for example those in Tilişca and Rod). Thus the tailors are filling the function of the caravaneer. The owners of the fuller's mills in Gura Râului have a fixed day, Mondays, when they go to the market in Sălişte and pick up the fabrics to be worked on and deliver them when ready ... Some groups of villages in Târnava Mică ... situated about 50-100 kilometers away, come here to the mills in Mărginimea Sibiului .... All these relationships are based on a lot of confidence between the artisans, the collectors, who agree to keep the fabrics, and the tailors. The system of property signs is practiced commonly, but in order to be able to recognize the piece of fabric than to indicate its dimensions. The mark is made by its owner, the woman, by weaving on the loom or by embroidering it on the piece. When clothes are first given to the collectors or to the tailors who keep them, a second mark of ownership, a common one, which belongs to the collector or the tailor is added. The memory of the owners of the mills is remarkable since many years later, they are able to distinguish the pieces that they have worked on from those done by other artisans. In a similar manner, they remember by heart hundreds of marks of ownership.

When large feasts are organized for religious holidays and where important crowds are assembled, each family brings its own pottery bearing its ownership mark. One must therefore order a dish from the potter bearing the ownership mark of the household because the decoration of the pots themselves is not sufficient to distinguish them from each other (Petrescu, Stahl, 1956).

Branding or cuts made in the ears of animals are frequent, also constituting marks belonging to households. An interesting case was pointed out to me by Valeriu Butură in the regions of the Apuseni mountains: the peasants put their signs of ownership on beams forming a public bridge. If one of the beams begins to rot, the mark of ownership inscribed on it signals who must replace it. In the same region (Valea Arieşului), I had the occasion to see these marks inscribed on the carriage entrances enabling them to be seen and known by everyone.

The transmission of the marks of ownership is accomplished according to the same rules as those involving a name. The wife takes on her husband's, unless the husband is established in her household, in which case the opposite situation occurs. It should be added that the mark of ownership of a newly founded household resembles that of the household from which is descended, whenever possible.

## PROPERTY AND ITS TRANSMISSION

The concern for equality dominates the use and the division of properties within the village structure as well as in each separate household. In an economy of subsistence, each household needs access to all categories of land. He must have access to water sources, to wood in the forests, to pastures. The household shares everything which constitutes its patrimony, including arable lands (old, or newly cleared in the forest). In addition, each household will have rights to the community sections of the village, sections which are not divided.

The farther one goes back in time, the more the utilization of agricultural lands seems to pose no problems. Land existed in relative abundance and each person cleared the land he needed in the forest. It is not until certain parts of the territory become 'individual' property (in reality, property by households), that they become the object of litigations, litigations that are most of the time avoided by the equal division between eligible parties. Even the cleared sections of the forest were usable, for the time being, by the members of a household, who abandoned them once they were no longer fertile. I was able to document the existence of such practices until 1948, primarily in villages which had not formerly been enslaved and which thus continued an ancestral practice. These particular villages were situated in northern Muntenia.

The obvious owner of the household land appears to be the father. Although he is the undisputed head of the family, he is not an owner in the modern sense of the word, but rather the administrator of the possessions of the household. He cannot give up land iwhtout the consent of his sons, something he would not do except in a situation where he would be forced to do so. He is also unable to disinherit one of his children except where he establishes serious grounds for the disinheritance based, for example, on the unacceptable behavior of the child. He cannot give unequal sections of land to his sons and cannot refuse to endow them with lands at the time of marriage. The father, "is thus not an individual owner, but simply the head of a family work-group, a team leader. The creator of private rights for the utilization of lands, as well as of products, is the family unit, the group, and thus it is the family which is considered the true master" (Stahl H.H. 1959, p. 112).

It has already been stated the foundation of a household accompanies the construction of a house and the endowment of the new couple with land. In the past, the endowment of lands pertained only to boys. The land must therefore be divided into as many parts as there are boys. "The division of the land among the children is done by the parents during their lifetime. Each son receives his share and among several boys, the father keeps the last born in his house. His parents will continue to live with him and they will eventually pass their estate on to him while still alive in exchange for agreeing to take care of them, to honor them, and after their death, to bury them according to Christian custom. Cases where the parents ask a judge to terminate the contract due to ingratitude are rare" (Jivan, 1937, p. 442).

Formerly, these practices were not accompanied by any written act. When the modern State begins imposing written acts, the old custom of the transmission of lands by endowment at the time of marriage continues. In the village of Belinţ, in Banat, children are only endowed with the right to work a portion of the lands. The property right is obtained toward the end of the parent's life, by inscription in the register or by testament, or sometimes by an endowment granted at the last moment. Thus, the father, or the grandfather, remains the owner: "We do not give land with inscription in the cadaster because if children see themselves as owners, they will no longer respect our commands." said an old man. Another justified this practice by affirming "I do not know how the young will act toward me; so I will leave my estate to the child who best proves he will take of me" (Radu, 1938, pp. 306-307).

Usually parcels of land are divided in such a way as to be equal quantitatively and qualitatively. Such parcels are obtained by dividing the plots in groups which run along the property. Henri H. Stahl gives an example (1959, p. 116) of the structure of this division in a family with four boys. The family plot is divided into four strips ('sfoară, 'funie' — string), and each has a perpendicular band near its borders which crosses the four stripes of the children's plots, and which belongs to the father. Termed the 'soul's part,' it will be divided up upon the death of the father by simply extending the lines which separate the properties from each other. But "once the father has divided his assets among his children, he nevertheless continues to consider himself the owner of the lands. Thus he finds himself jointly owning, with each one of his children, the plot of the latter. His children, however, are not considered joint owners in relationship to each other" (Costa-Foru, 1936, p. 117).

In everyday language, the equal division which doesn't put anyone at an unfair disadvantage, is called the 'fraternal division.' The expression appears often in ancient documents. For example, in a document dated 1791, we find the following entry: the wife of a lord having two daughters, gives to her two sons-in-law properties that they must "divide and own fraternally ('frăţeşte'), half and half" (Potra, 1961, pp. 559-560).

This, then, is a question of a particular form of transmission of real property which accompanies the birth of a new household and which prevents the disappearance of the former method. Inheritance plays, at least in the past, a minor role. The obligation to divide property during the father's lifetime was so strong that it was difficult to do otherwise.

As a result, the practice was continued up until the collectivization of lands, despite modern codes of law. The study made by Danielle Musset (1981) proves its persistence even today.

Once sons are established in their households, they will have the same obligations toward their own sons that their father had had toward them. In documents written in the past, each time that it is a question of the transmission of real property, the fathers name appears in the deeds accompanied by those of his sons. Their agreement was necessary so that the sale, for example, would be valid, since father and son were considered co-owners. The land thus belongs to the lineage, (deceased as well as living descendents). The transmission of lands is therefore not only a transmission from individual to individual, but from one household to another.

A text published at the beginning of the 19th century by Marcel de Serres is characteristic of this process. In a region where village life is framed by the regulations of border regiments ('Militärgrenze'), regiments that the administration of the Austrian Empire installed along its borders with the Ottoman Empire, the peasants continue to live according to their own custom: "The inhabitants enrolled in a session, or under the same number, are considered together, forming one family whose head bears the name of the father of the family. Following the spirit of the regulations, this head of the household must watch after the affairs of the family over which he exercises a patriarchal authority( . . . .). The members of the family are not permitted to abandon him due to inconveniences which would result from the military service. But if the family grows to the point of not having enough land to assure a comfortable existence, then the authorities divide it into several branches. However, even though the regulations are carried out in all matters concerning the division of the families, it is almost impossible to avoid several illegal divisions( . . . . ) . Although, following the spirit of the regulations, all men registered under the same number must live together in the same session, however each one lives, as he wishes, in a private house and cultivates, as he wishes, the portion of land which has been passed on to him as a result of the division of the families" (Serres, 1814, IV, pp. 208-211).

The custom of giving land only to boys is not practiced in the same manner in all places, nor in all eras. For example, we note that the custom was adhered to first by the peasants because, among lords, girls also received an endowment of real property at the time of marriage.

Among the peasants, property transmission to girls undergoes an obvious evolution according to the more or less traditional character of a region. By the 19th century, this was already widely practiced and the endowment of girls with lands at the time of marriage subsequently ends up being considered indispensable (Stănescu, 1938, Musset, 1981, Massion, 1982). Despite all of this, a disparity often remains: boys received more property than girls (Evaşcu, 1978, p. 74).

The most notable exceptions in the past are those where, in certain households, there were no boys, only girls. The manner in which the Romanian peasants settled the situation was widely known. At least one of the girls was obligated to fulfill he boy's social role. She stayed with her parents; her husband came to live in her house; and she inherited her parents' estate: "among the mountain dwellers (affirms Frâncu and Candrea, 1888, p. 115) the succession of the lineage is passed along even by women if the men of the group are extinct . . . in which case the inheritance belongs to the women."

If in the past, girls did not have the right to the paternal lands, they were nevertheless under strict obligation to have a dowry of fabrics and a chest in which to keep them. This is regularly mentioned in all studies and in numerous documents. And even when girls began to receive lands, they had an additional endowment of fabrics and a chest. These fabrics were worked on by the girl herself, with the help of her mother, over many years. She thus had not only what was needed to decorate her husband's newly constructed house, but her handiwork vouched for her household talents as well. The fabric dowry was carried to the 'girls' fairs' where, during which, in certain regions, marriages were formerly arranged. The dowry was displayed in order to be admired. The appearance and the quality of the fabrics were appreciated as connoisseurs by those who looked at them. The possessions of a family were also evaluated on the basis of the fabrics which decorated the dining room of the house, covering the bed, the walls, and sometimes even a part of the ceiling (Gâdei, 1904, p. 129; Patriciu, 1935, p. 71).

## THE ABSENCE OF WRITTEN DEEDS

The transmissions of property were not accompanied by written deeds among the peasants. Princes, monasteries, and lords, however, were still writing out the bills of sales, as well as endowments. As peasants began writing out bills of sales, documents continued to be transmitted orally. A marriage was a matter of concern for the entire village; villagers learned when a particular person would be married, and that he would receive a certain endowment, and that information was considered sufficient.

Even today, written deeds are not drawn up for smaller transactions. This was the general rule at the fairs where animals, tools, and pieces were bought or sold, and when transactions were made among lords, and among lords and peasants. For example, the principal builder who is hired to construct a house concludes a verbal agreement with the person having it built; the lord hires shepherds or daily workers in the same manner.

The conclusion of an agreement is sealed in the following manner: right hands are shaken, and, in order for the agreement to become final, the parties consume an alcoholic beverage. A deed dated 1581 (Documente, 1952, p. 16) states: "And Sârbu, with all of his sons sold, concluded the sale, and consumed two large 15 liter bottles." The consumption of such a large amount leads us to believe that the beverage was not only consumed by the sellers and the buyer, but also by the witnesses who were always present at important transactions. The obligation to pay for the drink fell to the buyer, but more often the seller (in order to honor his name) also offered drinks. Hand shakes were also exchanged in order to undo certain transactions. Thus, a husband and wife, in 1773, "being very angry at each other . . . shook hands in front of us (the witnesses), and confirmed that, henceforth, they would be separated . . . ." (Iorga, 1906, p. 88). Lastly, alcohol was consumed at the time of any important decision made between several people, for example, between peasants who jointly labored on a piece of ground (Iordache, 1977, p. 27), or upon any termination of a work contract. Shepherds, for example, were hired on Saint Demetre's Day for the entire year which followed. The salary, clothes to be given, the detailed jobs to be done for each period of time and each breeding operation were all memorized by heart and confirmed by the consumption of an alcoholic beverage by all participants. All this was quite normal for a society where alphabetic writing was known on a limited basis. The road to literacy among the peasant population has been a long one, finally achieving notable results in the 20th century.

It is evident that for the administration of the State, the existence of this type of situation has been the cause of numerous disputes which end up in court, a situation the administration would like to have improved by introducing written deeds. The efforts in this direction had already begun by the 18th century. In 1754, in Moldavia, the prince decides (in a rather difficult style to follow): "My lordship announces by this deed, to whom it may concern, having learned from the Very Holy Metropolitan of Kir Iacov country, our highly respected spiritual father, and from all the great boiars, that in this country there is a custom, among the laity and the people of the church, that the bargaining between people, the hiring of servants, temporary employees, shepherds by cash, or other questions of a similar nature, are settled without witnesses and without written deeds. And when the need for court proceedings arises, judges have nothing which can help clear up the matter, neither a letter, nor witnesses. It is for this reason that most of the judgements can only be based on word of honor, or on curses. This is why each day there are souls that are lost and church cemeteries full of scorned people, the former due to their poverty and the latter because they do not know that it means to sin against a word of honor, which is the renunciation of God. For that reason, whether a monk, a boiar, a shopkeeper, whomever; or whoever henceforth, each one who wants to make an agreement with another person, whether a monk, a boiard, a shopkeeper, whomever; or whoever wishes to lend money, will be required to write out bills of sale, agreements with employees and servants and with people who help them in their courtyard, or with shepherds, and must confirm the deeds by two or three witnesses, concerning both important and the most picayune of matters . . . . " (Codrescu, 1871, I, pp. 329-331).

Even though verbal agreements still largely dominate in the 20th century, there is an increase of deeds especially concerning important processes, like inheritances or endowments. But here also we are far from having a systematized practice with regard to the civil codes. Differences exist in this regard between the regions of Romania which are explained by their more or less traditional character or their openness to urban influences. In the village of Şanţ in Transylvania, the peasants seem to remain co-owners since they did not register property changes. In reality, the properties were regularly divided, according to custom (Jivan, 1938, p. 350). In the village of Năruja (Putna), situated in one of the most traditional regions, only one dotal deed had been executed between 1927 and 1938 (Stahl H.H., 1959, p. 115). On the other hand, in Ruşeţu, in the Danube plain, there exists a situation of transition between custom, with some divisions being carried out without written deeds, and others requiring them (Stahl, H.H., 1937). The survey takes into account, among other things, sons who no longer fulfill their moral obligation to take care of their parents, and parents who do not endow their sons with land at the time of their marriage, thus taking advantage of rights of the modern civil code.

### The Distribution of Work

Daniele Masson (1982) notes from a recent survey in a village of Maramureş that the women's habitual territory is the house and the court-yard, while the man's domain is the out of doors. This distinction is the typical, historical distinction and remains true even at present for the peasant population. The man and the woman work equally, and the quality of the woman's conscientiousness is an important consideration when choosing a bride. The marriage ceremony includes nuptial songs which make this clear to us. For example, in Transylvania (Vancu, 1905, p. 75), the following verses are sung while the bride is being brought into the house of her in-laws:

> (the husband)
> Mother, open the door,
> My wife I bring to you;
> The pots she will wash,
> The house she will sweep,
> The fields she will weed,
> And she will help you.

> (the guests)
> Hello to you good mother,
> Your daughter-in-law is here,
> She will help you.
> A helper we bring you,
> Your life we ease.

(the mother-in-law)
Thanks be to God
Who fulfills my wish
What I have wanted
I have obtained
I have yet another
To help me if need be.

I have often noted that the criteria for appreciating a women's beauty are linked to her abilities to work hard: "She is beautiful because she is strong," constitutes a common assumption. The woman must work. From childhood on, a woman works, waking up earlier than her husband and being the last to retire in the evenings. She serves everyone and remains standing while the others eat or rest.

Her chores are those pertaining to the house and the courtyard. Once constructed, the house remains the responsibility of the woman who must paint it, periodically replaster, sweep, wash, build the fire, cook, weave and sew. The chickens and other birds are also her responsibility, as is the feeding of the animals, on occasion. She will even go beyond the limits of her domain for two important activities. Once the field has been plowed by her husband, it is the woman who will take care of the raising of hemp and flax, a chore directly linked to her work as a weaver. She will also go into the forest to gather wood. Her husband will also gather wood, but he will carry the large tree trunks that he has cut and transport them to the house. She, on the other hand, will merely pick up the twigs that have fallen to the ground, putting them on her shoulder and carrying them to the courtyard to be used as wood for the kitchen fire.

The man is in charge of the major chores associated with areas beyond the courtyard: plowing, harvesting, and transporting of the crops and wood. In the house, it is the husband who cuts the large pieces of wood for the fire and who often, in winter, feeds the animals. He always takes care of the sheep since the women are excluded from this job for the same reason that they are excluded from it by other populations of the region. Sheep are considered pure animals, while a woman is often seen as unpure. Therefore, it is usually only the man who can come near the sheep.

Curiously, since this is an obvious contradiction to the dominant role of the man in a household, it is the woman who takes care of the money of the house. She hides it or hangs it in a purse placed on the main beam of the bedroom. Sometimes the money is buried after having been entrusted to the woman (Griselini, 1926, p. 172; Caronni, 1812, p. 26). "As far as finances are concerned (affirms Comănescu, 1885, p. 22), the rule is that the woman is the cashier, and, one might even go so far as to say that she, in doing so, assumes a quasi-management role."

Children begin helping their parents at an early age. Most often they are sent to tend the animals near the village, sometimes even those in the forest. Rarely are they sent far away from home where they would be required to remain isolated for long weeks at a time (Petrescu I, 1869, p. 37).

## THE VILLAGE ('Satul')

### Property and Work

The needs of each household were complex. Each one needed lands to plow, pastures, woods, water and consequently the rights of each one focused on all the economic categories of the village territory. In the past, the forest played an essential role for the Romanians as it had, for that matter, for other European populations. It was the forest which provided materials for construction, clearing, game, and also aided in animal breeding and originally furnished fields for plowing.

Vegetation maps of Romania allow us to follow the evolution of the forest, where we note a continual expansion of arable lands, cleared of trees, at the expense of the forest. The villages advance in their conquest of arable lands along the rivers, or even in the interior of the forest. The best lands are sought, for their quality or their closeness to the family dwelling. This process continued up until the 20th century, in spite of various laws which tried to prevent it. Toward the middle of the 20th century, the forests became rare, even endangered. And as early as the 18th century, the forests were already becoming rare, as noted in this testimony taken from a complaint lodged by the superior of a monastery in 1735: "the Costeşti village, where there are 150 households, did not work this summer, not even for 20 tellers, and the Furnigariul village, with 50 households, did not work at all (for the monastery), eating off the lands along with the animals and cutting the forest and transforming it into arable fields, borne out by the fact that all the houses which make up Ocna and Râmnic (nearby cities) are made of this wood" (Mihordea, Papacostea, Constantiniu, 1967, p. 347).

A part of the forest was allowed to be cleared for temporary use, and then was later abandoned when it lost its effectiveness. The forest thus regained its rights and the area was reforested. Clearing techniques were widely known and practiced since they actually played a role in animal breeding and agriculture. The bark of the tree was removed from the tree which was then dried and cut, or, the tree was simply cut and left to dry and rot. A fire was built and as many of the roots as possible were cleaned off. Fertilized by the ashes, like the layers of leaves which had been deposited over many, long years, the ground then yielded good crops. The peasants made a distinction between the crop yield during the four year period which followed the clearing by using four different names *('ţelină', 'prosie', 'răsprosie', 'samulastră'),* the fourth crop naturally being the weakest and resulting from fallen grains at the time of the harvest from the preceding year. Groups of kin cleared the land and the actual plowing land was carried with primitive tools (the spade or the swing plow). Even when the modern plow was introduced, these more primitive techniques were relied upon during difficult periods. The chronicler Nicolai Costin affirms that in 1692, "the poor inhabitants of the country had grown accustomed to plowing the fields with the space, in the forests, in the land left lying fallow, or in the shade of the forests. They planted corn in order to feed themselves and no one wanted to use the plow" (Kogălniceanu, 1872, II, p. 40).

The land obtained from the 'green forest' is often mentioned in historical documents, especially during the era when this practice was widely used. Having cleared a certain piece of land in the community forest of the village, a peasant became the owner of this land if he so desired, but more often he was considered a temporary owner who abandoned the area once the land no longer yielded (temporary property that H.H. Stahl calls *'stăpânire locurească').* But, in this case, the peasant was required to fence the cleared space in order to protect it from animals. Even the verb itself which designated the occupation of land was the verb 'to enclose' *('împresurare').*

The peasants' familiarity with the forest has remained strong up to the present. The long tradition which held that the forest belonged to everyone made the passage toward a rational forestry development difficult with the silvicultural offenses multiplying to the extent that the regulations become more harsh. "God has sown the forest for all men; no one has worked the land in order to sow the forest and therefore claim a special right to it" said the peasants of a village in Transylvania in 1934 (Prie, 1934, p. 43). This manner of perceiving things has greatly contributed to the rapid disappearance of the forests (Pittard, 1917, p. 44).

The social group which made up a village had a clear idea of its rights to the territory as a whole. This was normal considering the particular historical conditions where cleared lands, which were only temporarily used which gave rise to temporary property based on an intinerant agriculture, were of little importance. The community property was largely dominant and included forests, waters, pastures and high mountain pastures.

At the time of its founding, each household needed arable land. A piece of land covered by the forest was cleared and then prepared. The size of this area depended on the efforts of those doing the work and, consequently, the properties were unequal. But a boy was also able to inherit land that had been cleared by his parents. A long evolutionary process leads, little by little, toward the enlargement of regularly cultivated lands which join together to form the village's permanent land slated for cultivation.

These plowed lands undergo a regime of development which now depends on the entire village community. Henri H. Stahl (1959, 3rd part; 1969 a) distinguishes two forms of village property among the plowed lands: the equal, where each household receives a share equal to all others, and the unequal, where originally equal properties become unequal due to the unequal number of births, beginning with the second generation. In fact, the household where there was only one boy did not share its property. On the other hand, the household with several divided the property into as many parts as there were boys.

As soon as a property is well defined and passed on to its descendants, it becomes necessary for the village to determine, without question, the male ancestors of each one in order to assess their rights to the land. The eponymic legend based on the ancestors of the village takes on a concrete form with regard to the land. The lands are divided into as many parts as there were founding ancestors (*'moşi', bătrăni'*). The land itself bears the name of a particular ancestor; his real or ficticious descendants receive their land based on it having belonged to an ancestor of their lineage. Within each section of land to be reserved for crop rotation, the lands were divided equally among the households and, in turn, each household divided its share into as many parts as there were boys.

This system also applied to towns where the number of sections of land to be used for rotation corresponding to the number of ancestors, changed. Thus, in order to satisfy the needs of newcomers, the name of a common ancestor, kin to preexisting ancestors, was invented for them. This was the case of Câmpulung (Stahl H. H., 1936, p. 464). Different cases have also be studied, beyond the complete study credited to Henry H. Stahl (1958, 1959, 1965), several of which merit mention, including the village of Negoeşti, located in the north of Oltenia (Filip, 1966) where there were four 'great ancestors' (*'moşi mici'*). Xenia Costaforu (1936, p. 113) describes them in Cornova in Bessarabia and in Runcu in Oltenia. C. C. Giurescu also describes them in a small locality renown for its vineyards and publishes a deed of great interest which describes the division carried out at the beginning of the 19th century. The document begins with the quotation of the original ancestors and, by successive divisions, cites the rights which will fall to each existing household at the moment of the division (Giurescu, C. C., 1969, pp. 53-64).

Once these lands, which were initially equal, enter into the property of the household, they become unequal beginning with the second generation. The more the generations succeed themselves the more necessary it becomes to know the position of each person within the different lineages in the village in order to establish individual rights. A tendency to apply this division to the lands slated to remain communal emerges with the rights of each person being proportional to his place in a particular lineage.

Showing solidarity, the descendants of a common ancestor were able to decide to sell their "ancestor," in other words their arable lands, and their rights to the yet undivided section of communal land, while at the same time selling themselves, becoming servants of a lord, of a prince, or of a monastery. Some partially free and partially enslaved villages are thus

mentioned in historical documents. The lineage (*'neam'*) therefore appears
as an intermediary unit between the household (because it includes several
lineages). The lineage was also able to separate and form a new hamlet, or
to leave the community, with its rights being calculated on its place in
the genealogy of the village. Lineages continued to be present in village
life and in the mentality of the people, who, according to custom, re-
united the dead and the living belonging to a single lineage (Musset, 1981,
p. 23; Masson, 1982, p. 8). Their importance decreases as property rights
no longer have a rapport with the membership of a lineage.

In our day, there are no more lands acquired from the forest and therefore, the difference between inherited lands and newly acquired lands, no
longer exists. In the past, this difference was also apparent in each person's
right to sell cleared lands on his own, and the inherited lands which were
required to be passed on to this sons.

The two forms of property, village and household, seem to have coexist-
ed for a long time. The second develops continually at the expense of the
first, so that as arable lands increase, communal properties disappear. A
new form of property, individual, documented in deeds, develops notably
in the 19th and 20th centuries under the influence of modern laws imposed by the State. The forests and the high mountain pastures are the
areas which remain for the longest period of time under the category of
community property.

The right to common grazing ground, widely used up until the collectivization of villages, is a hold over from the former right of peasants to
access to the entire territory, but it is also the result of real necessities.
Once the harvest is finished and the crops transported into lofts, the fencing surrounding the parcels of land set aside for rotation or separate household lands is destroyed or opened. The animals, without distinction of
the property, enter these areas reserved for cultivation and graze everywhere (Stahl H. H., 1958, pp. 307 sq.; 1969 a, pp. 69 sq.; Donca, 1940,
p. 32). Occasionally, this right to common grazing ground goes beyond the
limits of a single village, and in some regions also implies a right of passage.
The transhumant shepherds, for example, were required to cross the territories of numerous villages in order to arrive at their destination: the
Danube (in the Fall) or the mountains (in the Spring). The inhabitants
of the town of Câmpulung in Moldavia, had these rights confirmed by an
act of 1747: "concerning the tending of the sheep that they send, according

to their custom, to the lower parts of the country, they will have the right to graze on anyone's property without being disturbed or hindered by anyone, even in the banned forests or elsewhere" (Ştefanelli, 1915, p. 44). Several years later, in 1767, another document gives supplementary details: "the sheep they send to the plains to graze beginning with Saint Demetre's Day until Saint Georges' Day, will have the right to go on to any property without being stopped by anyone; but they are not to destroy the hay harvested by the owners on the lands that they cross. . . and they will make arrangements with the owners concerning the stripping of the leaves from trees intended for the sheep" (Ştefanelli, 1915, p. 90).

If the work on the isolated, cleared parcels of land in the forest was allowed to take place according to the will of the individual, work done on neighboring properties follows a collective rhythm. The obligatory rhythm is also observed in other activities; there were deadlines for the spinning or weaving work carried out by the women. The two holidays of Saint Demetre and Saint George, divided the year in two and bring rhythm to the shepherds' activities (especially to their frequent relocations).

As far as agricultural work is concerned, it is apparent that once the gates of the fences surrounding the crops are open allowing the animals to enter, everyone's crops have already been transported to the village. Late-comers risked losing their crops which would be devoured by the animals.

The labor of the land was begun on a particular day, marked by a festival. A procession led by the priest who went to all of the fields, was organized. A time was chosen for sowing and for the harvest, the end of which was celebrated by community rituals.

Having a single parcel of land signifies cultivating it year after year, thus impoverishing it to a point where it will not yield (Ion Ionescu de la Brad, 1866, p. 135). It must therefore be allowed to lie fallow. But the peasants need crops each year; the village thus divides the lands to be worked into two parcels that will be rotated. Each household must have one parcel in each one of the two sections to be rotated in order to follow the collective rhythm of the village which presumes the alternate growing of these sections. Such an organization of fields has maintained itself up to the 20th century in numerous villages in Transylvania and also in other Romanian regions (Cothişel, 1904, p. 15 and 22; Frâncu and Candrea, 1888, p. 24; Pamfile, 1913, p. 27).

When the Austrians imposed the triennial rotation of crops on parts of the village, each peasant was required to have a parcel of land in each one of the three sections reserved for rotation (Cărpinișan, 1897; Prie, 1934, p. 32). This time the systematic alternation of crops was followed still more rigorously by everyone. Thus, each section to be rotated lies fallow one year out of three. Animals roamed their areas, fertilizing them with their dung. We thus see techniques for cultivation which use the manure of animals gathered from the stables for fertilizer. The village shepherds walked their herds on the lands and installed their enclosures on a temporary basis, continuously changing locations and fertilizing the soil in the process.

In the meadows, the people used to cut the hay together; any other practice would have resulted in some form of trespassing. Occasionally there was a day set aside for everyone when the fruits that grew wild in the forest were picked. I had the opportunity to observe this after World War II, in the village of Arpașul, in southern Transylvania, where wild apples picked in the forest were being made into brandy. In some villages located in southern Oltenia, the villagers went fishing together on a particular chosen day in the Fall. I saw them wading out into a shallow pond and catching fish by hand. In many areas situated near the mountains, associations of several peasants would work together to build their sheep pens. Sometimes a village feast would bring them all together, during which time they would leave their sheep in the care of one shepherd, hired by all.

## The Village Community and Assembly

In order for the village system to function, with its strictly defined and defended territory and its lineages closely linked to the property, it was necessary to have regulation of the human aspect of life as well. This regulation deals with two aspects: 1) who has the right to be a member of the local community (Stahl H. H., 1930, pp. 201 sq.) and how the local community functions, and 2) the relationships with outsiders, isolated individuals or groups. The village kept a watchful eye over its prerogatives and the struggle among those who were trying to undermine them took on various forms.

Being born in a village, being a member of one of its groups, and having a house plot within the settlement were obvious signs of community membership. All the peasants banned together to prevent outsiders from entering the interior of the village. In this respect, the study of preemptive right is exemplary because it clearly focuses on one series of rules. Even though the rights were found in written form in the former Roman law codes (*Pravilniceasca condică* of 1790, *Sobornicescul hrisov* of 1785, 1835, and 1839, *Manualul juridic al lui Andronachi Donici* published in Bucharest in 1959, or *Codul Calimachi,* published in Bucharest in 1958), the peasants still followed their traditions which were passed down orally. Preemptive right states that every part of the village territory that became the property of a household, be sold to related households. First the closest relatives, then the distant relatives, neighbors, and finally the other members of the village have, in that order, rights to buy an available piece of land. It is only after these groups of people have been warned and asked their advice concerning the sale that land can be sold to a non-member of the community. This was also true for any sale dealing with land (vineyard, orchard, meadows, house and courtyard). And if something is sold to an outsider without consulting the eligible parties, the sale can be voided by reimbursing the buyer. The mention of this preemptive right appears with great frequency in recorded bills of sale. This right becomes less prominent and disappears, first in the written codes, beginning in the 19th century (Georgescu Val. Al. 1965; also Emanuela Popescu, 1970). The peasants continue to apply the right as confirmed by responses to the legal questionnaire conducted by Haşdeu in 1878 (Georgescu Val. A., 1965, p. 372).

The second means of defending the village community and preventing the penetration of outsiders is the system of marriage and the manner in which property was involved in this event. The general tendency of the village is toward local endogamy where each person is forced to find a wife or a husband within the village itself. This represents a desire which responds at the same time to a profoundly human sentiment to neither be separated from relatives nor friends (Marian, 1890, pp. 45 sq.). Endogamy then applies itself to village groups which consider themselves related; in this case one avoids leaving his own village group for reasons of marriage.

The girls' fair which took place on Găina mountain in Transylvania (Frâncu, Candrea, 1888, pp. 43-45), was divided into two groups because the two village Romanian groups, the Moţi and the Crişani, were each participating. Each person chose a wife from among those belonging to his particular group. In describing the Vidra fair, which attracted villages from southern Moldavia, Petre Stănculescu and Gh. Serafim (1943) note the origin of the participants and they point out that they are grouped by villages. A particularly significant part of these fairs centered around the dance which was always organized by grouping the young people by village. Thus the dance constitutes a privileged moment during which the young people can solidify their acquaintance. The dance precedes marriage, the girl or the boy who begins to participate in the dance is, from that moment on, considered a candidate for marriage. By grouping the dancers by village, the tendency toward endogamy of each separate village is being expressed.

Observations made about a village situated in Little Wallachia, but one which is inhabited by Romanians from Transylvania ('Ungureni'), allows verification of the same findings (Ionescu C. M., 1937): "If today one occasionally sees girls who marrying into neighboring villages, they are usually the poorer ones, those who declare that they will not be able to find a native boy from their own village. The cases where a rich girl marries into a neighboring village are rare. When girls do marry into another village, they do so willingly if it is a matter of a village having the same origin as theirs, in other words, inhabited by people from Transylvania. . . . There are also cases where boys also marry native girls from another village, but these cases are even more rare and are confined to the Novaci, Băbeni, and Mihăeşti girls, or to those having the same origin since any other arrangement would result in humiliation. As it has already been stated, these cases involve the poorest girls who leave their village in order to establish themselves in neighboring or distant villages; boys do this much less frequently and, if they leave their villages, it is to obtain a better material situation. . . . Moreover, these are isolated, rare cases wich do not at all change the village mentality which continues to prefer the little that they have in their own village, rather than exile."

If for one reason or another a girl leaves her native village and settles elsewhere, the disorganization of the division system of property is avoided by the fact that the girls' dowries do not include land. We have seen above that household property was passed on to boys, and that a girl had rights to property only when there are no boys in the household. We have also seen that her dowry consisted of fabrics, furniture, silver, and livestock. This situation is easily explained if one remembers that, in former

times, the possession of a piece of property somewhere in the village territory (sometimes even a more house plot), gave its owner access to all of
the community property. Marriage would therefore constitute a means of
infiltration into the community and it could then be an undesirable situation for the other members. The increase of the endowments of lands for
peasant girls multiples during the course of the 19th and 20th centuries
and goes hand in hand with the penetration of foreigners and the loss of
authority by the village community.

Even if an outsider succeeds in penetrating a certain community, all
kinds of barriers are put in his way. For example, he would only be accorded a portion of the normal rights of natives. In addition, a long fight
follows which sometimes ends in the recognition of the rights of the newcomers. The latter are generally integrated by granting them a fictitious
relative in common with the rest of the village since they are considered
descendants of one of the ancestors of the village. Any future divisions
would be calculated with regard to this kinship.

In order for the endogamous system to function well, the marriage
must also be virilocal, which is truly the case in the vast majority of marriages. It is rare to see a man take up residence with a woman and in a
foreign village. His departure, which detaches him from his lineage, causes
changes within the interior structure of the village; in fact, he can leave
and still claim his rights to the property of his native community which
subsequently will be passed along to the inhabitants of the village where
he has recently settled.

The situation of the outsider coming to live and to marry into a community other than his native one is hard and will remain so for the rest of
his life due to his inferior social position in relation to the other peasants.
This is also explained by the fact that "men having left their village can
only be considered runaways, chased by poverty, by enslavement, or who
knows by what other situation or infamous cause. In the village they enter
as servants in the native families and can only marry women who can not
find a better husband: old widows, unmarried mothers, or those considered the most inferior of the village, in other words, those who are ugly or
stupid" (Stahl H. H., 1959, p. 246).

The situation of the inferiority of the outsider accepted by the marriage
in a village is clearly described in a document dated 1788 (Ştefanelli, 1915,
p. 175): "I, Pavăl, settled here in Câmpulung with Simion Ciuparcă for

eight years, give this authentic letter to Solomon Floce and to his nephews so that it be known, as I have stated above, that being settled here as an outsider in Câmpulung for several years, I have lived wisely, with Simion Ciuparcă, while working, and I have done no harm to anyone, nor been involved in anything, no scandals, no thefts, nothing. Now by the will of God, the moment of marriage has arrived, because God says that man can not live long on air; and perhaps fate wanted me to live here, having sheltered me here with the lineage known as Solomon since I am marrying his brother's neice. Therefore, I confirm by this authentic letter that I give to them that henceforth I will live with respect and peace in this family where I have established myself, and that I will be humble toward them as God would want it, because I am an outsider; and I will always given them the esteem that is due them and I will avoid scandals, brawls, and other forbidden things and I will not harm anyone. And I will own only what God gives them and that they in turn give me and I will only have that, without having to elaborate . . . signed, Pavăl, the outsider."

Community rights over the interior regulation of the village were substantial. Even if in principle all the men of a village had the chance to offer advice on a question, and on occasion the women as well, there was a group whose weight was decisive. Historic documents tirelessly repeat the formula 'old people worthy of confidence' (*'oameni bătrâni şi buni'*) in order to designate legitimate testimonies. The elderly effectively have a significant authority within the village assemblies; they are more acquainted with the custom and the territorial limits; they know the decisions that have been made in the past; they are sent to represent the village before authorities or during trials; they are listened to with respect when they speak; they are greeted with the term "uncle" (*'unchiule'*) even if the greeter shares no kin relationship with them, and they are greeted if they are met on the road even if the greeter does not know them personally.

Village inhabitants assemble when it is deemed necessary; they judge and decide issues of conflict between differing parties, they divide lands, set the dates when specific operations whould be carried out, demolish fences and forbid the placement of individual tenures in certain areas. They hire a fence keeper where fences are needed to surround an entire village or whole areas reserved for crop rotation; this keeper sometimes has a hut where he stays while guarding the village gate, in order to prevent the animals from roaming. They hire shepherds to lead the collective herds (in which each household places its own animals), they choose the village representatives for trials, and they decide the distribution of taxes owned to the State.

Although in the western European context these meetings take place on an obligatory basis, on certain pre-arranged dates, which are the same from one year to the next, this is not the case for the Romanians. They assemble when there is something to resolve, and they meet in various locations: in the street, in a square, under the shade of a tree. This tree can even have a special name, 'the judgement oak' (*'ştejarul judecăţii'*), when judgements are being made. The elderly members are primarily in charge of making judgements, a practice clearly outlined in historic documents: "the 21st, 1841, we, the elderly judged Iaon Toflea . . . and we have imposed a 5 florin fine on him, and he is happy with that decision," as stated in a Transylvanian document (Iorga, 1906, p. 216; see also Olinescu, 1944, p. 94; Antonovici, 1906, pp. xlvii-xlviii). The most common meeting place for these assemblies was the balcony or the church courtyard, every Sunday. After a religious service, discussions are held and judgements passed. Certain churches of Bihor (as indicated to me by Ion Godea) had an outside compartment where the guilty could be detained and punished.

One of the most important questions debated by the village assemblies is the fixing of taxes and, in general, the duties owed the State. The State sets the taxes by village which are then allocated by households by the peasants themselves. And even if the State sets taxes by household, the assembly totals these taxes and conducts a new distribution of charges taking into account the real possibilities of each person, possibilities that they know better than anyone else. A civil servant who had the responsibility of collecting the taxes was appointed and who often is mentioned in historic documents or remembered by the peasants themselves. This employee was chosen from among the most renown peasants (Thomescu Baciu, 1943, p. 39; Rădulescu and Răuţescu, 1923, p. 190; Griselini, 1926, p. 171); he even bore a special name (*'răbojar'*—Thomescu Baciu, 1943, p. 39) and took note of the amounts received on a piece of wood with the help of notches (Griselini, 1926, p. 171; Rădulescu-Rudari, 1926, pp. 362 sq.; Caramelea, 1946, pp. 75 sq.; Davidoiu, 1944, p. 83). Josifu Comanescu, who also points out this practice (1885, p. 28) notes that in the village of Codlea, in Transylvania, the notches are replaced in 1708 by documents written on paper. Moreover, the use of cuts in wood or notches still continued for a long time (Stahl H. H., 1960); and if the practice disappears with respect to the collection of taxes, it remains in use on other occasions, for example in the measuring of the amount of milk in the dairies and, on occasion, for noting crops and lending.

In the more important villages by virtue of their population, this employee was able to have even larger allocations; aided by other civil servants, he was named during a special ceremony where the religious rituals and the formulas of the civil ritual were combined (Stoianovici, 1942). He was recognized by the stick that he carried, symbol of his office, a stick with which he could even hit the more recalcitrant and which was given to him by the village community along with the following charge: "Honor it, otherwise it will be given to another. Be wise and of good health."

## THE "COUNTRY ('TARA'), VILLAGE CONFEDERATION

If one observed the intervillage lines on a map, it would be easy to distinguish territorial complexes whose lines must have been established at the same time and by someone who knew the full extent of all the region. The study of the Country of Olt (*'Ţara Oltului'*) located in southern Transylvania enables us to see that the villages divided territory in a rational manner in order to assure each person's access to each of the economic categories of lands (fields, forest, pastures, high mountain pastures). There is one row of villages located near the mountain; a second, situated lower, has access to the mountain along the corridors reserved for this purpose and has some properties in the high mountain pasture and forest zones. Occasionally two villages will have the same name; one located near the mountain and the other farther away, in addition, they have the indication "down below" and "up above" attached to their names. It is obvious that an organization so complex is not the result of chance, but of a supravillage authority (Stahl H. H., 1958). Similar territorial complexes can also be found elsewhere.

These groupings often bear the name "country" (*'ţară*–from the latin 'terra'), a country which at times corresponds easily to outlined geographical units, as for example, the intercarpathian depressions. The chronicler Simion Dascălul, speaking about Transylvania, states: ". . . near its borders there are small countries which are a part of it and are under its allegiance; first the Maramureş, near Poland, the country of the Sicules (from the Hungarian expression) near Moldavia, and the country of Olt near Muntenia, and the country of Bârsa, and the country of Haţeg, and the country of Oaş. . . ." (Kogălniceanu, 1872, I, p. 412). Ion Ionică tries to establish several of the local organizational elements of one of these countries, Ţara Bârsei (Ionică, 1943).

Other times these territorial complexes coincide with the ancient ad-ministrative divisions of the State, which probably took into account, in the beginning the social realities which preceded them. Thus, one finds correspondences between departments and what are called ethnographic zones. These zones constitute ideal frameworks for the study of customs, architecture, of other aspects of past life, and admirably aid the compre-hension and classification of traditional life in general (Iorga, 1940).

When other elements are absent, the name that a certain group of vil-lages gives itself indicates whether or not it is part of an anciet supravil-lage unit. In all these cases it would be interesting to go back into the past and look for ancient tribal life, but the historical information is insufficient since tribes seem to have disappeared in Romania since antiquity.

The interest that these social and territorial supravillage units present is that much greater when they maintain some concrete elements of a pre-state organization, coexisting with a centralized State. The oldest descrip-tion of these organizations dates back to the beginning of the 18th cen-tury and is credited to the prince and illustrious Romanian scholar, Dimitrie Cantemir, who reigned during this period in Moldavia. In a descriptive work about Moldavia, he cites three peasant "republics." The inhabitants of these republics still conserved, under his reign, a part of their prero-gatives, which distinguished them from other peasants, especially from en-slaved peasants. They themselves managed the territory, thus preventing the lords from being able to monopolize their lands.

The least known of these is Tigheci, located in Bessarabia, which boast-ed a renown warrior. Here is Cantemir's description: "Tigheci is located in the Fălciu region, a neighboring forest to the Tatars of Budjak and which constitutes the most powerful Moldavian rampart situated between the Prut river and Bessarabia. The inhabitants pay a small tax each year to the Prince; they are all knights. They were formerly eight thousand (men) but today they can scarcely assemble two thousand; they surpass all the inhabitants of Moldavia in bravery, as a well known proverb affirms: "five Tatars from Crimea make ten times more than ten from Budjak, five inhabitants from Moldavia surpass ten Tatars from Crimea, but five 'Codreni' (Romanians living in the forest), the name given in Moldavia to the inhabitants of Tigheci, will know how to defeat ten inhabitants from Moldavia'" (Cantemir, 1973, p. 302).

The two other republics described by Cantemir are better known through documents which have been preserved. Câmpulung, which was mentioned on several occasions, had kept its freedom almost until the middle of the 18th century, when a prince handed them over to one of his relatives. In the second half of the 18th century, the region is divided into two parts, with Austria occupying the northern half. Thus any evidence disappears of this ancient supravillage unit (Stahl H. H., 1958). Here again is Cantemir's description: the inhabitants "are not noble, and moreover are not bound to any lord thus constituting a sort of republic. . . . Câmpulung, in the Suceava region, is surrounded by a very high chain of mountains. It includes fifteen villages which all have their law and their judge. Occasionally, they receive two messengers from the Prince; but if they offend them, they are always chased away, relying on their natural defences provided for by nature. They do not know how to work the land, which, for that matter, is non-existent in their mountains, and the focus of their work consists of raising sheep. They pay an annual tax whose total is not set by the Prince, but rather by themselves; they renew this agreement through their emissaries each time that Moldavia has a new Prince. If the Prince conducts himself harshly with them and imposes additional duties, they do not hesitate to retreat into their mountains and refuse to pay any tax; that is why the Princes never ask more than they should. Occasionally incited by agitators, they do not ask anything of the Prince and receive protection from Poland" (Cantemir, 1973, p. 300).

The most interesting of the three village confederations is the country of Vrancea: ". . . smaller, Vrancea is located in the Putna region, near the Muntenia border, surrounded by rugged mountains. It has twelve villages, includes two thousand households, and, similar to the Câmpulung republic, contents itself with raising sheep, not yet familiar with a plow. The inhabitants pay a tax each year to the Prince, but otherwise they conduct themselves according to their laws and receive neither orders nor judgements from the Prince" (Cantemir, 1973, p. 302). The confederation is well known through documents (Sava, 1929; C. Constantinescu-Mirceşti and Stahl H. H., 1929) and direct research gathered in these villages between the two world wars (Stahl, H. H., 1929, 1939, 1958, 1969), which have permitted the piecing together of essential traits of the operation of this "country."

The same principle of equality which applies to the division of lands among sons, or of village lands between households, governs the distribution of lands between villages making up this village confederation. Each village must have access to the arable lands, to the forests, and to the high mountain pastures. The first of these categories to become definitive property of the villages are the fields, while the forests and the mountain pastures continue to be considered community property by all of the villages. The successive divisions of community holdings allows us to observe how a particular category leaves the community system in order to become village property. The division of the mountains, for example, is done in proportion to the taxes paid by each village.

The tradition which held that a village is descended from a common ancestor is also found at this level. The protector of the region is considered to be Stefan cel Mare, illustrious prince of Moldavia; the ancestor is a wife who gave birth to seven male heirs. Common matters of each village were handled by the village assembly; the villages located in a valley formed a valley assembly ('ceată de vale') and the country of Vrancea had its own assembly ('ceată de ocol') (Stahl H. H., 1936, pp. 586 sq.). The assembly for the entire country did not bring together all the peasants, only those representatives from each village; the primitive democracy which was still direct at the village level, becomes representative at the level of the country. The powers of this assembly were varied; it decided the division of community shares or of revenues resulting from the working of a particular part of the country. It governed the differences between opposing villages, or between the country and the State by dispatching emissaries to the Prince. It oversaw and managed the local life of the monastery; it mined salt, which elsewhere in Moldavia was a privilege of the State; it awarded one merchant the right to trade with the country. In summary, it is therefore a truly pre-state organization which has at its origin an ancient tribe. In contrast with the tribes located in the Balkan peninsula, where leaders are found at each level, here the entire country seemed equal, at least during the last two centuries.

# CHAPTER II

## THE SOUTHERN SLAVS

### THE HOUSEHOLD

Among the Balkan populations, the Slavs are among the best studied in terms of their former social organization. Numerous publications have been devoted to them as far back as the 19th century. They are also the only population to have been the subject of a survey of customary law sufficiently covering the territory that they inhabit (Bogišić, 1874; Stahl, Guidetti, 1979, pp. 59-74). The concept of the household is particularly well known, and subsequent studies concerning the idea have grown in number (Gavazzi, 1976).

The household of the southern Slavs is known in specialized literature under the name *"zadruga,"* a name which their own peasants do not use. Christo Vacarelski (1969, p. 253) writes that among the Bulgarians it is termed *"družina," "kupčina," goljama k'šta";* other names were also used. Bogišič (1884) is the first to note the true names of the typical households of the past among the Yugoslavs of which *"kuča zadružna"* seemed to dominate. By utilizing the data collected by Bogišić, Fedor Demelić (1876, pp. 30-31) signals the utilization of other names, for example *"skupčina"* (also see Pavković, 1961; Vukmanović, 1963).

The domestic group of each household had a patronymic linked to the name of the founder of the group, to which could have been added the

51

name of the living leader of the group. Here, in progressive steps, is how Friedrich Krauss describes the naming process for an individual (1885, chap. III, p. 45): "1) the given name: Jovo. 2) the father's name used as an adjective: Jovo Petrov (Jovo son of Petro). 3) If in the same house there are several persons who are named Jovo Petrov, the name of the grand-father is added used as an adjective: Jovo Petra Markova (Jovo son of son of Petro, son of Marco, of the Janković house). 5) Finally, to this the Jankovič, thus Jovo's name becomes: Jovo Petra Markova Janoviča (Jovo fils de Petro, son of Marco, of the Jankovič house). 5) Finally, to this the name is added the name of the phratry: Jovo Petra Markoviča Jankoviča Kovačeviča (Jovo, son of Petro, son of Marko, of the Janković house, of the Kovačević phratry)." A part of the given name which is personal, all the other names are classificatory. Nikola Pavković (1973) mentions the case of groups of different origin who decide to unite in order to form a single group. The smaller of the groups takes the patronymic of the larger, while at the same time adopting the feast day of its patron saint, tied to the patronymic.

The great Ottoman and Austrian empires, which for a long time domin-ated the regions inhabited by the southern Slavs, experienced conflicts with the tribes whose influence they wanted to diminish; on the other hand, they favored the existence of the zadruga because they were better able to handle numerous domestic groups for which one person, the leader, was responsible and paid the taxes (Demelić, 1876, p. 25). In cert-ain regions, where they had installed their "military border" (Militär-grenze), the Austrians went so far as to prevent the separation of the do-mestic groups, even in the regions where the zadruga was not common, in Romania, for example (Utiešenović, 1859; Milutinović, 1958). In addi-tion to the reasons listed above, the zadruga provided administrative op-portunities for the empire from a military standpoint.

Similar households to the zadruga were widely known throughout the past in Europe, from the eastern borders to the west. In the Balkans, this was characterized by the Slavic and Albanian populations. The diffusion of the zadruga, characterized by the presence of several married couples in the same house, is known through the Bogišić survey (1874), but also through other studies (Sicard, 1943; Mosely, 1953). Covering a wide terri-tory, the household does not always present itself in the same forms. Two forms, which will be treated below, are primarily distinguished.

*The domestic group. Work.*

The factor which distinguishes the household of the southern Slavs from that of the Romanians is, in the first place, the composition of the domestic group. In effect, among the Romanians the domestic group is based upon the existence of a single married couple with its non-married children (with the exception of the youngest who remains in the parents' house). In the zadruga there are always several married couples (except, for example, following an epidemic or a war which leaves very few people alive).

Two forms seem to dominate: a) the first joins the father and his married sons, sons who will leave at the time of the father's death. b) The second, brings together, not only the couples composed of the father and of his sons, but also other persons; uncles, first or second cousins, also more distant relatives, but who are all descended from the same ancestor. The kinship community is always present in the consciousness of the members of the zadruga, providing a source of an explanation for the common life and the rights to property. In the first form, the death of the father can lead to the separation of the domestic group; in the second it has no consequence; at most, if the father is the leader of the group, he is replaced by someone else.

If the zadruga is the dominant form of the Southern Slavs, it is not manifested everywhere with the same intensity; its disappearance, for example, follows different rhythms depending on the regions. Other elements can also intervene; for example, in the northeastern regions of Serbia, where the minority group of Romanian origin is important, the organization of the domestic group seems to be the customary one for the Romanians. The close living arrangement of groups of different origins and the mixed marriages which unite them, can bring about some modifications to this concept (Draškić, 1973).

The zadruga was not only the privilege of the peasants; in the past, lords were organized in the same manner. The organization is found in the city among professions which have nothing to do with agriculture: artisans, merchants, sailors, lived and worked together in households organized under the principles of the zadruga. The discussion is open as to the existence or the non-existence of the form in Slovenia, at least for the last several centuries (Winner, 1971, pp. 59 sq.).

Studies focusing on the number of people who make up the domestic group are numerous, the most recent utilizing as much as possible recent numerical data taken from past centuries. One must again begin with Bogišić (1874) whose answers to this question are commented on by Demelić (1876, p. 31); in addition, the following names should be mentioned: Gešov (1887), Meitzen (1895, vol. III, pp. 341-350); Rovinski (1897, pp. 191-195); Novakovitch (1905, p. 88), Strohal (1905), Lodge (1941, pp. 108-109); Halpern and Anderson (1970), Halpern (1972), Halpern, Kerewski (1972, chap. 2), Hamel (1972 and 1976), Stahl and Guidetti (1979, pp. 59-73), Stojancević (1980).

The father is the natural leader of the Romanian domestic group; he can also be the leader of the zadruga based on the association of the father and his married sons, but this is no longer the case in a situation where the domestic group is composed of several groups of people and numerous married couples, couples also referred to as "beds" (Novakovitch, 1905, p. 54). An obvious hierarchy establishes itself within the group, a hierarchy which is not based on kinship. Here, I am merely summarizing the situation since it has been descrbed so often elsewhere.

Both a man and a woman serve as leaders for the group. The male leader is normally referred to as the *"domakin"* by the Bulgarians and his female helper is called the *"domakina"* (Vacarelski, 1969, pp. 254-255). Among the Yugoslavs, the names *"starešina,"* *"domačin,"* and *"gospodar,"* are primarily used and are mentioned in the order of their probable frequency. The woman leader is called *"domačica."*

The leader is the administrator and manager for the entire group: "He is named for life, but sometimes, he is only elected for a certain period of time. Most often, the leader is the eldest member who, in turn, relinquishes his position, by order of age, to a brother or to a son. The *domačin* manages all interests pertaining to the life of the zadruga: account books, taxes, money, business papers, etc. He is the first to get up and then he organizes the day's work. He gives the housekeeper, the *'reduša,'* what is needed for the workers' food, goes to the fields to see how the work is progressing there. He is in charge of repairing and purchasing tools, selling the animals, having the raki distilled, preparing the wine, etc. . . . The progress and the well being of the his family depends on his wisdom and his sense of order. A good leader is one who is fair and one whom everyone respects, incuding family members, as well as neighbors, friends and other relatives. If a zadruga collapses, the leader is held responsible and there is an immediate separation and dislocation of the community. A leader can rebuke the elderly and he can administer physical punishment to the younger members without anyone interfering. To be a leader of a zadruga is considered a great honor, not only vis-a-vis the family, but in everyone's estimation. When the leader of a zadruga is in the house, only his voice is heard, everyone else must speak in a low voice and keep quiet" (Vekovitch, 1928, pp. 9-10; see also Janjić, 1967).

The leader can be elected whereupon the best person is chosen. At the time of his death, or when age prevents him from continuing the job, another leader must be selected. There are also cases where the leader is designated in advance; either the brother or the eldest son of the former leader. A leader can also be replaced if he does not fulfill his responsibility. His nomination occasionally takes on a ceremonial appearance since the Church is called upon to consecrate him during a ceremony which normally takes place on a Christmas day (Yriarte, p. 430).

"The domačica, wife of the domačin, retains her status even after the death of her husband and enjoys a great deal of respect in her home; she oversees the housework and gathers the dairy and poultry products from which she sets aside a separate portion for the domačin; she allocates the work, assigning a task and an amount to each person. She educates the children, teaches them their prayers, guides them in matters concerning work and duty, assembles them on winter evenings, sharing with them the tradition of the wonderful stories she learned from her mother, including popular tales, national songs, and the history, in verse, of the Montenegrin people where each leader was a bard, each prince a rhapsodist, adding to the national feeling of the Pesmas. The domačica's duties also extend to matters concerning death; every Sunday, she goes to the cemetery or to mass for the deceased. She is charged with praying for the dead, which we had the occasion to observe and which was one of the most dramatic scenes that we witnessed during our various stays among the southern Slavs" (Yriarte, p. 431; see also Jasna Andrić, 1972; Rihtman-Augustin, 1982; Culinović-Konstantinović, 1982). It should also be added that the domačica was normally the wife of the leader, however, it was also possible for that position to be filled by another woman of the group, someone more capable than the leader's wife. Dušan Drljača and Dragoslava Slavković (1973) note a rare situation in which there are two women leaders, the *"bačica,"* who takes care of the preparation of dairy products, and the *"mesajica,"* who prepares the food and looks after the children.

There does not appear to be a lot of distinction among the other members of the group, but this is not always the case. The larger the group and the more important its property, the more specializations appear. For example, if animals are sent away from the village to graze, one of the members of the zadruga leads them, accompanied or not by his wife; upon assuming this responsibility, there are referred to as the *"bača"* and the *"bačica"* (Vekovitch, p. 11), names which are taken from the shepherds' language of Romantic origin, the Armân (Vlachs). One or several of the members of the group can specialize in a profession, for example, in pottery, and work for the group or for outsiders. There are also the well known cases of the *"pečalbari,"* who go off to work, but who continue to belong to their domestic group with which they share their profits; once they have returned, they are received with full rights. The zadruga of the Metohija region, studied by Milisav Lutovac (1935, p. 38) presents a specialization taken to the extreme: "Each job is assigned to a specialist: farmer, laborer, shepherds (there is one person for the larger animals, one for the sheep, one for the goats), mountain dweller, tradesman, housewife, etc., everyone has his place. This way, jobs are carried out rapidly and within the desired time limit" (see also Gruev, 1973).

Men and women have markedly different situations within the group. The men are born in their zadruga, live and die there, while girls leave their native zadruga when they marry, the group being strictly exogamous (Demelić, p. 62). Women are, therefore, outsiders who have entered into the framework of the group by marriage. The situation of the female outsider is particularly obvious in the case of the young bride; she does the hardest work, she can not address her husband in public, nor call him by his name (Trojanovitch, p. 176), nor can she show her affection for him, providing that she has any (Vekovitch, p. 13). She is the first to rise in the morning and the last to retire (Edith Kerecszeny, 1982). Only two factors can ameliorate her condition: the arrival of a new young bride to the house, and more importantly, the birth of a child, especially a son (see also Saint Rene Taillandier, p. 45; Stahl, P. H., 1979, pp. 110 sq.).

Lastly, the members of the zadruga are distinguished by age; the older members gradually work less and less and eventually do not work at all, yet they still remain quite respected and are cared for by the other members of the group.

All the members of the domestic group are equally fed, clothed, and cared for; they eat together and, on occasion, sleep in the same building.

## The House

The house often expresses the composition of the domestic group, but not always in the same manner. The fact that people live in the same house is already an indication that the individuals in question form a united group. "We are from the same house" (ot s'stata k'šta"), or "we are from a single house" ("ot edna k'šta") are Bulgarian expressions both meaning "we form a single group"; these expressions are recorded by Vaclav Frolec in western Bulgaria (1967, p. 75; also, 1966). Below, I have chosen several of the most typical of the available texts to illustrate the principal forms that the house in the zadruga may assume:

a) Archaic forms are maintained into the 19th century, in conjunction with difficult living conditions and poverty. Here, the house is composed of a single room inhabited by the entire group and, on occasion, the animals. Xavier Marmier (1884, p. 328) observes uniformly built houses in a village in Montenegro: "some walls of rough stone, a straw roof; between these walls, a single room without paneling or tiles, no fireplace, barely one or two small windows, and that is what they consist of, at least for the most part. One has a main floor topped by one story." An identical description, still of Montenegro, is made by Dora d'Istria (1859, p. 262): "Some stone houses covered in thatch, which do not have a single apartment, a door which is almost always open, takes the place of a window, a fireplace without a chimney, placed in the middle of the dwelling." Yriarte (1878, p. 370) describes a leader's house in Njeguš, in Montenegro: ". . . we climb several steps and find ourselves in a wide room, with low ceilings, whitewashed walls, exposed framework, a flagstone floor, lit by two small, grilled openings the size of a man. This is the only room in the house." Montenegro did not have the privileges of such constructions; in Croatia (Nouvelle Encyclopedie Théologique, 1853, p. 664) "these are merely cabins, divided into two compartments, one for the mens' living quarters, and the other for the domestic animals . . . there is no floor, no window, no chimney; the kitchen is set up in the living area in a hole opened up in the middle, around which they warm themselves during winter . . . they normally have no other bed except the hard ground; only the leader of the family and the richest peasants have raised beds, forming a sort of plank type cot covered with straw and several sheep skins." Many more such accounts can be found for Yugoslavia as well as for Bulgaria.

It is interesting to note that a similar house form was also common among those with a higher social status, the difference being the materials utilized, the presence of windows and, eventually, the presence of a floor and a stove. In central Dobroudja, I found several rare examples of houses having formerly belonged to Bulgarians; a main room of small dimensions served as the kitchen; a second, larger room, surrounded by a very long bed located along three of the four walls of the room which is heated by a blind stove (fed by combustion through an opening located in the adjoining room), served as the only sleeping room for the entire group (Petrescu, Stahl, 1957). But the houses just described can also be inhabited by the domestic group of a zadruga, or by the Romanian domestic group, based on the presence of a single married couple. Other house plans more adequately reflect the composition of the domestic group of a zadruga.

b) "The zadruga house is higher and much larger than that of isolated families. On the exterior, facing the road, there are eight windows, but no door. After stepping through the gate of the courtyard, there is a covered veranda on the front side of the house where the entrance is located. We are greeted in a large room where meals are eaten together. The furniture consists of a table, chairs, benches, and a cupboard made of natural wood. On the walls, always perfectly whitewashed, are colored prints depicting subjects of piety. To the left, we enter a large room which is almost completely empty. It is here that everyone making up the patriarchal family sleeps in winter in order to take advantage of the heat from the stove placed in the wall separating the two rooms, which are also heated at the same time. In summer, each couple occupies a small separate room" (Laveleye, 1886, I, pp. 126-127).

Therefore, there is always a single structure, but one which is composed of several rooms and is utilized different ways during the summer and winter. The structure can be made larger according to needs: ". . . each family forms a tribe and this tribe has only one dwelling. As the number of inhabitants increases, the house is enlarged. . . . When the children become adults, when one of the sons marries, a new room is constructed. The house grows longer and longer; some can be seen which form a complete street" (Saint Rene Taillandier, 1872, p. 43). Frolec

(1967, p. 64) also describes this form and considers it to be a form which characterizes a period of decadence for the zadruga (1967, p. 73). I have studied numerous long houses of the Dobroudja, houses belonging to the Tatars. Occasionally a single plan was repeated, under the same roof, with respect to the number of couples who lived there; in other instances, small differences appear (Petrescu, Stahl, 1957; Stănculescu, Gheorghiu, Stahl, Petrescu, 1957, p. 33). In the Polog plain, in Macedonia, I saw house plans, which in reality were composed of several identical units, located under the same roof and belonging to several brothers (Stahl, 1979, fig. 2).

The structure can take on characteristic aspects which will vary from region to region. Thus, in the Rhodopes, Rachel Angelova (Izvestija, vol. XIX) describes long houses which take up three or four sides of a rectangle, confining an open space in the middle; similar adjoining rooms open on to a common, open veranda. Georgi Kozukarov (Izvestija, vol. XIX) notes similar construction in the Rhodopes and observes houses which he calls "fraternal" ("bratski"), twin houses, those belonging to brothers. I found these twin houses in Romania, in regions where the Austrians had installed their "military borders" preventing families from separating from one another (Stahl, 1958); Gheorghe Focşa indicates their existence in Romania among the underground houses in southern Romania (1955), but they involve only two brothers.

The adjacent rooms with an opening on to a veranda have an appearance which is easy to detect; Saint Clair (1869, pp. 4-5) describes them for us: "The houses of the Rayahs (Christian subjects in the Ottoman empire) resemble one another... their size naturally varies in accordance with the means of the owners, a family of six or eight individuals often living and sleeping together in one small room not above eight feet square and six high; but hardly any houses have more than three rooms, even amongst the wealthiest peasants. There is generally a verandah in front of the cottage, upon which each apartment opens separately, instead of communicating with the others. The principal apartment is used as kitchen, parlour, and bedroom for the heads of the family . . . . " (see also Dora d'Istria, 1859, I, p. 224).

c) The principal room, the one where the food is prepared, where everyone gathers, can be separated from the rooms reserved for the different couples. I am using the description given by Laveleye (1886, I, p. 129) to illustrate this case: "Behind the large, common house and at right angle, is located a lower, long building which is also fronted by a veranda with a floored surface. As many apartments as there are couples and widows open on to this gallery; if a marriage creates a new couple within the larger family, the building is lengthened by one apartment. Frolec (1967, p. 63) and Zlatev (1955, p. 10) point out this type of construction in Bulgaria; Milisav Lutovac (1935, p. 38 and the map on page 55) describe it in Methohija and add characteristic details: "The principal building is located in the middle. The upper floor is occupied by a vast bedroom reserved for visiting guests, and the lower section serves as a stable and shed for agricultural tools. Around the principal building the outbuildings for the workforce and the beasts of burden. The importance of a single story house is brought to light here. It is divided into 25 apartments, which correspond exactly to the number of married members of the zadruga. For those who will marry, new apartments will be added. Each married member has his personal possessions in his apartment: clothing, beds, weaving loom, etc. . . . ."

There is frequent mention of the absence of a heating system in these bedrooms inhabited by the couples. The only fire is in the main room where food is prepared, where the heads of the group, and eventually the older people and younger aged children, sleep. One curious use of the cellar is pointed out by Nikola Pavković (1962); the newly weds settle in the cellar during the first months of their marriage in order to be isolated from the rest of the group. Another curious aspect is described by Friley and Wlahovitj (1876, pp. 188-189); "If the dwelling is large enough to allow the couple to live together, one or two rooms are allocated for the newly weds; but often the rooms do not meet similar conveniences and the couple settles in whatever place they can find. In other instances, several adjacent houses are occupied by the children of one family or by close relatives, and in order to reestablish a sort of community for everyone, care is taken to make an opening in the wall from one house to another to permit numerous services and to permit the exercising of a true and mutual policing of the women when their husbands are away from the house. . . ." The tendency to put young couples in separate rooms is widely practiced (see also Milić-Krivodoljanin, 1958), even though differences brought on by seasonal changes are mentioned (Frolec, 1967, p. 64).

d) The main house is, in this category, surrounded, not by adjacent rooms located under one roof and separated from the main house, but by small, isolated houses. "Around the leader's (*starešina*) better constructed and better covered house, are grouped the cottages of the sons and sons-in-law. . . " (Kanitz, 1882, p. 35). ". . . the small houses where the newly married couples settle. . . are built near the main house for all the members of the family. They consist, in accordance with general use, of a main floor raised over a cellar where supplies of wine, oil, lard, etc. are kept. . . . This is reached by a stairway leading up to the veranda. It includes two bedrooms separated by a fireplace; one of them serves as a parlor and lodging for guests" (Kanitz, 1882, p. 164). The same organization is described by Novaković (1905, p. 68) in Yugoslavia, which adds that the small houses do not have a stove. These maisonettes are called "*vajat*" or "*tchardak*" in Serbia (Vekovitch, 1928, p. 12) and "*tronjevi*" in Montenegro (Barjaktarović, 1976, p. 111).

e) In Macedonia, I was also able to observe houses belonging to several brothers, isolated from each other, but which had identical plans and were located in the same courtyard. The food was prepared in a small hut for everyone's use and the children were also brought up together. But it is clear that the more apparent the tendency to settle in separate dwellings becomes, the closer the community comes to dissolving itself.

What happens to the house in the case of the dissolution of the group? Vaclav Frolec (1967, p. 76) continues the observations made by D. Marinov at the beginning of the century: in a normal situation where the zadruga dissolves itself peacefully in order to give birth to two or several other zadrugas having better relations amongst themselves: "The stareshina prepared the joint family in advance for division. If he decided that the zadruga would divide, he determined the places where the new houses would be built." On occasion, the youngest member remains in the house and his brothers leave. But disputes can occur and instead of a division, there is pure and simple dissolution; in this case, the solution is difficult to find and expresses the hostility which exists between former associates.

## Property

The genetic inheritance of the family (designated by the term "*baština*") as well as its rights to the community sections of the territory, cannot be be sold except in a case of extreme necessity. The head of the family does not have any special rights in this regard and would not be able to sell the land without the entire group's consent. Moreover, even if he is in charge, he regularly calls the members of the group together for the purpose of making decisions. The fact that everyone normally takes their meals together in the evening facilitates these meetings. In addition, the lighting of a second fire symbolizes the desire on the part of certain members to separate from the group in order to form a new household.

The genetic inheritance, considered inalienable, is made up of arable lands, a house, a courtyard, and forms the *"baština,"* which is passed on from one generation to another. Boys must dispose of this property since girls do not receive land as an endowment (Andreev, 1974). Women that the men marry, and who come from the outside will, in reality, be the ones to profit from their husbands' property, forming a strong unit which demonstrates solidarity with the whole group. It is interesting in this respect to mention Nikola Pavković's (1973) observation which justifies the exogamy of the zadruga, not only by the ritual kinship ensuing from the celebration of a single patronal feast day, but (as reported to him by the peasants) also by the friendship and the friendly relations which are woven together among members of the domestic group. It should be added that this is a recent justification which may not have been the case in the past.

The periodic sharing of arable lands, rare in the Balkans during the last two centuries (the period of time which constitutes the essential focus of my study), also existed just the same in the Rhopodes, but seems, in this case to be more the result of a recent collective acquisition of certain properties (Markova, 1965). The group also has rights to community properties *(Komunica)* belonging to lineages, phratries, villages, and tribes. Community properties, here as well as in Europe, are essentially made up of forests, pastures, high mountain pastures, and water sources. The best and the most detailed analysis of this type of property among the southern Slavs is still credited to Sicard (1943).

At the time of the division of a zadruga, the division takes place in an equal manner between brothers; each one receives the same share, and so on. Rights are proportional to each person's position within the lineage: for example, if between two married brothers, one had only one son and the other five, the son of the former would have the half of the patrimony of the grandfather, and the sons of the second would each receive a fifth of the patrimony of their grandfather. Food products, the result of collective labor, are divided equally among individuals. Any eventual variations are determined with respect to age, children, for example, receive less than adults (Barjaktarović, 1976, p. 111; Sicard, 1943, pp. 209 sq.). If the group had communities belonging to it exclusively, members were able to decide whether or not they would keep that community property. In the past, since divisions were the result of a mutual consent, people were able to separate from the group and still continue to share certain group activities, such as religious celebrations, for example (Barjaktarović, 1976, p. 112).

If there were several brothers in one community, each one having his sons and grandsons, they each formed what is called a *"stup,"* found at the beginning of a new zadruga (Pavković, 1962, p. 138; Barjaktarović, 1976, p. 110).

Related by blood and demonstrating solidarity in all the affairs of the group, the members of a zadruga are collectively responsible for each member. Thus, the head of the group pays for damages caused by any member of his group. Legally, it is only through the division of a zadruga, or the separation of an individual from the group, that this common responsibility disappears (Novakovitch, pp. 54-55). It is significant to the nature of community property to note that in past legal deeds, property owners are mentioned in the same manner as we have seen among the Romanians: "so and so, with his sons, and his grandsons," eventually his brothers or other male relatives. The property of the zadruga, therefore, appears to belong to the lineage and not to individuals. This lineage is made up of ancestors, its living members, and members of the generations to come.

## Women and the Hierarchy of the Group

The fact that the *domakin* and the *domakina* enjoy a leadership role, assures them of a superior hierarchical position. Other elements intervene in order to structure the group as well. For example, men have a superior position to women, because they are men, because they are born in the house, because they are the owners of the land, and because in past society, men have always had a dominating role. It was the men who gave the group its name, a name adopted by the women at the time of marriage.

Additonal elements with regard to beliefs and the idea of the impurity of a woman in general are also taken into account (Leschenko, 1978-1979).

A complete series of dictates is respected with regard to the elderly, the leaders, on holidays, during ceremonies and special visits, at the table, or even while sleeping. Vera Erlich (1966) makes a striking presentation of the relationships within the domestic group in Yugoslavia where, as she points out, some regional differences appear. You kiss the hand of an elderly person and the necessity of knowing who must kiss the hand of whom, encourages the establishment of an entire social hierarchy which goes well beyond the framework of the family, extending even to the class of lords, of princes, and also touching the clergy and its hierarchy. Children kiss the hand of their elders, just as women would do for men and for guests who enter their home (Trojanovitch, 1909, p. 170). In Montenegro, ". . . when, in route to a destination, if the Montenegrin women meet a man whom they know, they would not dare greet him familiarily, but rather, with respect, they would bow before him as if before a lord and kiss his hand" (Marmier, 1884, p. 317). "Not only does the Montenegrin woman kiss her husband's hand, as is done in the east, but also the hand o strangers. A traveller, as he passes through the country, is surprised to receive this strange token of welcome, at the house where he lodges, and even on the road" (Wilkinson, 1848, I, p. 421). Vera Erlich (1966) includes additional details in her survey (pp. 68 and 230); the quotations taken from the responses of the people surveyed, underscore the importance of these practices throughout the past.

The hierarchy of the group manifests itself at the table: "Not all of the members of the group eat together; they are separated according to age and sex. Men over 17 years old eat at one table; children of both sexes, at another; young women have a table, as do the elderly women" (Lutovac, 1935, p. 39). There are other cases where members eat at the same table, but separately; in Montenegro, men were on one side of the table, and women on the other (Nouvelle Encyclopedie Théologique, p. 1335). Everyone can be seated at a single table except the "reduša," the woman who is serving (Kanitz, p. 81). The leader of the group is seated at the head of the table, followed by the elderly men, the younger men, the adolescents, elderly women, younger women, and finally the children. Divna Vekovitch (1928, p. 12) describes the meals in the following manner: "All the men of a zadruga eat at the same time and eat the same type of food. The children take their meals before or after the adults. The women serving makes sure everything is in order. The adults are seated first, followed, in order, to the smallest. The younger members of the group thus learn from a young age to respect those larger and older than they. At the men's table, the leader always occupies the place of honor, then, according to age, all the oter workers are seated. Occasionally, the mistress of the house is with the men and she is seated near the head of the family."

In all these cases, the position of the inferiority of a woman is apparent. I will try to clarify this question by examining the women's role in three situations: a) the position she assumes with respect to work and the subsequent manner in which she is viewed by society; b) the sterile woman and the woman who only gives birth to girls; and finally, c) the pseudo-matriarchal Slav in certain cases where the woman seems to ameliorate her position of inferiority.

a) The situation of the women in the southern Slav world has been mentioned often. With a situation inferior to that of men, a woman's role is not always the same in all cases. "The woman is apparently in a state of perpetual minority in all of the East. Whether Christian or Moslem, she seems to be a man's prey rather than his companion. She is never called by her name, neither among the Turks nor among the Christians" (Blanqui, 1845, p. 280). She may sometimes be called by her original lineage name ("rod") (Pavković, 1962, p. 137). "It is improper to ask a husband news about his wife; she must be considered as non-existent in the eyes of strangers, and figures as an abstraction rather than a real personality. The Serbs and the Bulgarians use the word 'she' when speaking about their wife, while the Serbs, will even, on occasion, use an even less flattering expression to describe their spouse: 'my wife, without your respect'" (Blanqui, 1845, pp. 280-281; a similar testimony is found in Vekovitch, p. 13). Blanqui also cites a Turkish government edict concerning the women of Constantinople, capital of the empire: "The women go out too much, returning too late, sometimes even after sunset; those who ride in carriages have young couchmen, Christian ones at that, in clothing much too elegant for the state. They have the audacity to enter small shops, especially apothecaries; they remain there beyond an appropriate amount of time talking and they have neglected modesty to the point of even going to refresh themselves with ice cream in the cafes of Galata and Era, the Franks' quarter" (1845 p. 267).

Among the Bulgarians, a woman's situation seems better, and resembles that of the Romanian women. Among the southern Slavic populations, in

Montenegro, the woman's situation seems the hardest. Descriptions for the 19th century abound from which I have chosen several of the most characteristic lines to illustrate this point. Gopčević sums up the situation in one sentence: "Das Weib ist die Sklavin des Mannes" (woman is man's slave) (1877, p. 75). The expression mentioned by Blanqui and also mention by other authors is the following: "Pardon me, this is my wife" (Gopčević, 1877, p. 76). "Begging your pardon, my wife" recounts Wilkinson (1848, I, p. 422). "Our woman and our mules," is the reference quoted by Dora d'Istria (1859, I, p. 256). She goes on to note that the women were seen "either cultivating the land, or laden with enormous burdens, slowing moving toward the brink of despair." "A woman is the working beast of burden, and his substitute in all labor related tasks" (Wilkinson, 1848, I, p. 421). Friley and Wlahovitj offer yet another revealing description: "The wife would neither know how to interefere in her husband's affairs, nor worry about them; whether he leaves or returns, she doesn't dare ask him where he is going, where he has been, nor does she become irritated over the longest and most irregular of absences. . . . A wife does not call her husband by his name; and the same applies to the man when addressing his wife. She will say 'That one . . . oh! you (formal form.' The man will use: "That one . . . oh! you (informal form).' Ask a woman her husband's name, and she answers laughing: 'I do not know, the devil carries him.' Should the husband, for his part, be put on formal demand for betraying the secrecy of his wife, he will answer with embarrassment: 'Begging your pardon, my wife,' as if his masculine decorum had been offended by this confession. Moreover, the Montenegrin woman never accompanies her husband on errands, be it to the capital or elsewhere; she can, nevertheless, go to the bazaar with friends from the house of her paranymphes. Should she meet her husband in route, or catch up with him, she keeps a distance or passes rapidly by him; on occasion, she may even take another road. . . . Even if she gives him no reason for becoming irritated, he may provoke a situation in which he could justifiably exercise his right to correct her, often in the most brutal of manners. . . . "

Testimonies affirm that womens' work is more difficult than that of men. Yryarte observes women on the roads of Montenegro: "the poor creatures, doubled up, talk while walking, knit stockings while spinning the distaff; although doubled up from the burden of bundles of sticks of firewood, from time to time, weak sounds of laughter burst forth from these faces stamped with an impression of sadness. . . ." (Yryarte, 1878, p. 369.) "The woman must tend to the livestock, cultivate the fields, harvest the hay and beat the hay. If her husband sets out for the market with his wife to sell a heifer or a sack of vegetables, the proud *sultan* (the husband) will freely walk in front, the humble wife will follow him, pulling the beast by the halter, or with her head sagging beneath the weight of the load" (Marmier, 1884, p. 295). ". . . the mountain dweller of Tsernagora, like the Dalmatian sailor, often leaves his mate with the burden of cultivating the fields, and gathering the harvest. She is also responsible for grinding the grain, knitting the stockings, weaving the heavy material from goat hair, cooking, and maintaining a certain order in her humble household" (Dora d'Istria, 1859, p. 261).

At the other end of the Balkan Peninsula, in Bulgaria, Kanitz affirms: "As much as the young Bulgarian girl is celebrated in love songs, her role as a spouse is equally painful and difficult. Overworked, she does not have one minute of leisure. If she is not in the fields, she is attending to the needs of the household, nursing the infant even while walking the older ones. She washes, bleaches and stains, prepares the family meals; she spins, embroiders, weaves, mends and sews; she looks after the stable, takes care of livestock, goats, and ewes. She is in charge of filling up the cracks in the house with clay, whitewashing its front, using sheep skin as a brush, and twisting the twigs of the *kolibis* (huts); she is also responsible for the garden where flowers are never lacking. . . ." (Kanitz, 1882, p. 32). It should be noted that if a woman does participate in some type of agricultural work, the men are still responsible for the heavier work; she tends to certain crops, primarily, vegetable gardens, vineyards, flax, and hemp. Moreover, in Montenegro, if women are in charge of any agriculture, it must be remembered that the agriculture carried out is on a smaller scale than that in Bulgaria. The amount of freedom and consideration accorded women is much greater in Bulgaria.

In 1829, Otto von Pirch crossed newly independent Serbia and visited Prince Miloš Obrenović; the following description of the prince's wife merits repeating: "She is the one who manages all of the domestic chores; she weaves, spins, she tends to the cooking, she also plays an important role in the education and the instruction of her children. . . . Around eleven o'clock, the bell rang announcing dinner. All the guests assembled in the tcherdak; this is the vestibule on the first floor in the principal part of the building. . . . The prince took his place, standing at the far end of the table. Then the princess presented the prince with a glass of rikija, which was followed by a short speech delivered by the prince expressing his wishes for the guests and for all the Serbian people. After this, everyone was seated. The prince was seated at the end of the table on a high seat in the form of a throne; the younger princes occupied the seats on either side of the prince. I was to the right of the eldest son. . . . On the left of the youngest were the archimandrite and the 'hospodar' Vaso. The remaining guests were then seated. The princess and her daughter remained standing, to the right and the left of the prince; I was surprised to see them remain at a distance from the table that I hesitated to seat myself. During the meal, they served the prince and his two sons, according to the old Serbian custom. Since the princess is the wife of Miloš, she has not once taken her meal at the same table as her husband" (Saint Rene Taillandier, I, pp. 145-155).

b) The wife must, at all cost, bear children into the world, especially boys, since this is one of her primary obligations as a spouse. ". . . the greatest misfortune that can befall a wife in this country, is to be sterile" (Blanqui, 1845, p. 268). The presence of children has been essential to all societies throughout the past. The cases where the number of children was limited are rare, since, in general, the more children there are, the better off a family is considered to be. There are additional motivations behind this desire: to assure old age, to assure the longevity of the household, to have someone to whom property could be left, and finally, to assure support from descendants during the difficult life beyond the grave. In addition to this list, military societies considered additional children to be a means of increasing the number of blood relations who could bear arms (Stahl P. H., 1981).

Within this framework, three types of situations present themselves: A woman who does not have any children at all, considered the worst of the possible situations; a woman who has children of both sexes; a woman who has children of one sex. The manner in which the last two situations are viewed varies a great deal. In most cases, when a couple does not have any children, they may adopt a child, if possible, from close relatives. If the wife gives only birth to girls, the situation is remedied, for the most part, by having the daughter's husband come to live with her family's house, thus forcing the marriage to become uxorial (Lodge, 1943, p. 255).

The husband's status, in this case, is inferior to a situation where his wife would have come to his house to live; not only does he lose his patrimony and adopt that of his wife's group (Trojanovitch, 1909, p. 176), but his authority is minimized. He is even given a special name, 'domazet' (Demelić, 1876, pp. 63 and 126; Kulišić, 1959, pp. 117-120). He can also be called by the name of 'prezet' (Drljača, Savković, 1973). Bogišić introduces us, in the code of Montenegro (article 670), to some provisions which provide for the wife of a domazet to have more property rights than a wife living in her husband's house. Mirko Barjaktarović (1976, p. 110) notes that a daughter in a household without brothers, married to a domazet, inherits her father's estate.

In Montenegro, with its tribal based military society, the scenario is a different one. The sterile wife, and even the wife who bears only girls, can be rejected: "Autocratic chieftains frequently drove their wives away because they bore female instead of male children, and then remarried" (Troyanovitch, 1909, p. 179). This testimony is easily corroborated with other testimonies of a similar nature which, however, will not be treated at this time since I have them elsewhere (Stahl, P. H., 1981; see also Djordjević, 1907; Krauss, 1885, chap. XIII).

In the past, the fact that a man could also be sterile, or produce only females, was not known. The general conception dictated that from the moment a man had normal sexual relations with his wife, he had done his duty and it was the wife who bore the responsibility of the birth and sex of any children that might have been produced. Only in a case where a man was sexually impotent was he recognized as being at fault and, in this case, one part of the Southern Slavs resorted to another man from within the domestic group, someone openly and publicly robust, to substitute for the impotent husband. This relationship continued until the wife bore one, or even several children into the world and, as is the case for ancient societies, the child was recognized as the legitimate child, not of his natural father, but of the woman's husband (Krauss, 1885, chap. XIII; Djordjevic, 1924; Filipović, 1958; Stahl P. H., 1982).

c) There are some cases where the woman appears to play a role in the household, cases which have been interpreted pejoratively as vestiges of the matriarchy (of particular note, see Gasparini, 1962-1963). Two situations which are subject to that type of interpretation are: the uxorial marriage (described above) and the case where certain zadrugas have a woman as their leader. In both cases, the situation in no terms represents an actual change from a patriarchal family system. In fact, marrige only becomes uxorial when, within the woman's group, there is no boy. In reality, these situations result from a typical crisis where biological nature render dispensation necessary in order to avoid the disappearance of the household, its property, and its name (Pavković, 1962). In this situation, the wife does not change status. She is simply functioning in the man's social role for one generation, since beginning with the next generation, it will be the boys of that generation who will inherit the property, their maternal grandfather's name and who will have their wives come and live in their houses. The same is true in a case where a woman becomes the head of a zadruga (Pavković, 1961), either because there is no man in the group, or because the men are underage and incapable of managing the group's affairs. Here also, the woman is merely substituting for a man; as soon as the boys grow older, her role diminishes and she eventually relinquishes her position to them.

Therefore, in summary, this last situation, does not represent any real change in a woman's status, but rather reflects once again the tenets of a typically patriarchal society. Still dominated by men, the woman who fulfills the role of the group's leader apparently serves as a missing link in a masculine chain of control. It is moreover absurd to imagine that a patriarchal society would suddenly become matriarchal, only to become, with equal suddenness, patriarchal once again. There are cases in Europe, however, where the woman has, with some degree of stability, rise to a place equal to that of a man's. But here again, these do not represent true matriarchal societies, but rather situations where, for example, in the Pyrenean-Basque society, absolute birthright functions, and the first born, male or female, becomes the head of the household and the sole heir of the estate of his or her parents. This is also the case in several Greek societies on the Aegean Sea (which will be treated below) where there is equal division of the rights among the first born, male or female.

### The evolution and the dissolution of the zadruga

Although quite strong in the past, the zadruga, little by little, does disappear everywhere. This is due to the pressure of economic changes brought on by the liberal economy which reach a climax under the nearly always decisive pressure of the collectivization of property. Significant political upheavals accelerate this process of change. The literature of the 19th century is full of information concerning the dissolution of the former social organizations of domestic groups and of the entire household. Some regretted the dissolution, others saw it as progress, but in general this dissolution seems to have been immediately followed by an impoverishment of the people and a weakening of family ties and of former signs of solidarity.

Various causes for the dissolution have been suggested, often pointing to arguments between women who pushed their husbands toward separation from their group, a separation facilitated by the putting in place of new law codes imitating Western laws. The Napoleonic Code, either the Belgian and the Austrian forms, served as a model to various Eastern European countries. These codes do not completely correspond, not even in the societies which saw them first implemented, since they ignore the former forms of property. They are evidently even less applicable to the realities of Eastern Europe (Bogišić, 1884; Stahl H. H., 1939, vol. I and 1958, vol. I).

Studies on the modern evolution of the former forms of the zadruga have greatly increased in recent times (Peševa, 1965; Hammel, 1972; Dilić, 1972; Halpern, Kerewski-Halpern, 1972; Kostić, 1958 and 1982-83). The last author mentioned analyzes the different family forms which were present in Yugoslavia after World War II. The diminished power of the husband, the improvement of the woman's situation, the evolution of the religious marriage, the opportunities for divorce, the limitation on the number of children, the disappearance of Moslem polygamy, all constitute fundamental changes to which must be added the change of the property system (even where there was no collectivization of lands). The same author gives information about the modern evolution of the property system in another of his studies (1966). Ruža First Dilić (1972) and Dinko Tomašić (no date) confirm, in part, these findings. Raina Peševa (1965) observes the same process in Bulgaria in the 19th and 20th centuries. To the idea of the differentiation separating Western Bulgaria (more traditional, and an area where the large zadruga were common) and the Balkans or the western part (where domestic groups had a smaller size), one must also consider the evolution brought òn by the changes effecting the full spectrum of social life which push toward a more and more accentuated division and resulting in the formation of the modern family as we know it today. In this respect, studies made by Petar Vlahović (1973), Dušan Maslevarić (1973) and Tomašić (no date) are useful.

Certain evolutionary processes date far back in history, as noted from the analysis of former Ottoman censuses. Interpreted with skill by Hammel (1972), they provide information as to the composition of the domestic groups and prove that they were varied, as early as the 16th century. The same findings also apply to the Armân (Vlachs).

The disappearance of larges family communities is obvious. It characterizes the time leading up to the 20th century, but the era is not uniform in this regard. In fact, family communities were widely known throughout the past in Europe, from the East to the West. It is in western countries, where the evolution of social life was more rapid, that they disappeared. Thus the rare "*communautés taisibles*" of France disappear toward the middle of the 19th century. The wave of modernism later reaches the regions of Eastern Europe and it must be noted that over and beyond these particular and individual causes which contributed to the disappearance of the zadruga, there is also the larger process of change to consider effecting all of social life. A study of other European regions confirms this notion. Vera Erlich's work (1966) provides insight into the parallelism which exists between rate of the disappearance of the large zadrugas and the progressive character of a particular region.

Throughout its history, the zadrugas, at one time or another, were divided. When domestic groups became too large and too difficult to govern, the members agreed to separate. These separations were not oriented toward domestic groups based on a single couple, but still toward groups who, in turn, had grown to the point of needing a new separation of groups. The group's arable lands were divided according to the principles of equality among the brothers described above. On the other hand, divisions which took place in modern times do not give birth to new zadrugas, rather they are linked to the origin of domestic groups based on the presence of one couple, known today as the modern family.

Following the listing of the general causes of a similar division, let us now look at several details concerning typical, individual cases. "What kills the zadruga is the love of change, the taste for luxury, the spirit of insubordination, the murmur of individualism and the so-called progressive pieces of legislation which were inspired from it. I have hardly seen in all of this any real progress," said Lavaleye (1886, I. pp. 132-133). The following words of an old woman of Siroko Polje also capture this nostalgia (Laveleye, 1886, I, p. 81): "In my youth, most of the families stayed united and together farmed the patrinomic domain. We supported each other, we helped each other. If one of the sons was called to the army, the others worked for him, and since he knew that his place at the common table would be waiting for him, he was anxious to return as soon as possible. Today, when the zadruga is destroyed and our young people leave, they are deciding to stay in the big cities. The home, with its evenings spent in the company of one another, with its songs and its feasts, no longer attracts them. The small families, those living alone, cannot survive an illness, a bad year, now that taxes are so great. If an accident occurs, they go into debt and wind up in poverty. Young women and luxury are to blame for the loss of our old and wise institutions. They want to have jewels, fabrics, shoes that are bought by the pedlers; to buy some of these things they need money; they get angry if their husband, working for the community, does more for others than for themselves. If he kept everything for himself, they surmise, we would be rich. From this attitude spring explanations, reproaches, and arguments. Family life becomes a living hell; the couple separates, with each one needing a fire, a cooking pot, a courtyard, a keeper for the animals. Then winter evenings come, and it's isolation. The husband becomes bored and begins to go to the cabaret. The wife, left alone, often times goes out as well."

Troyanovitch (1909, p. 173) points to the role played by the "osobina," individual property allowed within the framework of the zadruga, in definitive separations. Lutovac (1935, p. 35) brings to light the role of the liberation of territories formerly belonging to the Ottoman Empire, a liberation which accelerated the process of dissolution; he describes a separation in stages, since initially members began eating separately and ended up also separating real property (p. 39). The liberation of a particular region from Ottoman domination triggered an acceleration of the process of dislocation of the zadruga (Trifunovski, 1973; Kostov, Peteva, 1935, p. 192). The same situation even occurred after World War I and World War II (Vera Erlich, 1966, chap. II; Trifunovski, 1973).

I was able to observe a separation in stages among the Tartars of Dobro-udja, in Romania, who had formerly lived in numerous domestic groups and where at least the married brothers were still living together (Petrescu,

Stahl, 1956). This separation has also been studied by Liviu Marcu (1967). Demelić (1876, pp. 131-132) mentions among the causes of the dissolution, dissensions within the group, the exaggerated increase of the number of members, the presence of individual possessions, the despotic authority of the leader of the group, and the quarrels among the women. This last cause is mentioned many times as being a principal cause of the separations. Novakovitch lists among the causes, the intervention of public powers by the newly enacted laws; if the former Ottoman or Austrian laws favored the maintenance of the zadruga, those enacted at the time of the renaissance of the national states did not, so much so they penalized any form of community property. Novakovitch also affirms that the great domestic units were more successful in resisting the pressure of the Ottoman state; the appearance of outside sources of revenue in the zadruga, and subsequently the introduction of personal property, the questioning of the leader's authority, the jealousy which pits women against one another, the lack of economic success, all seem to him to be among the main causes which provoke the disappearance of the zadruga. But all these causes, real or otherwise, could have manifested themselves in the past without necessarily causing the disappearance of a zadruga. They must therefore be understood with the changed general framework of the social life in general. As for the intervention of the State, it is interesting to note that in the middle of the 19th century, under the influence of liberal ideas coming from the West, community property was pushed toward disappearance; a century later, due to the pressure of collectivist ideas coming from the East, it is the individual properties and what remained from former community properties which disappear.

## THE PHRATRY ("BRATSTVO") AND THE VILLAGE

Just as in our day, the rural settlements of Yugoslavia bear the village name ("*selo*"), a look back into history reveals to us rural dwellings designated by the name "*bratstvo*" –phratry. With time, one, or even a combination of several of these phratries, becomes a village. The blood-related group appears prominently within the phratry and, without totally disappearing, it fades and is replaced by the village name (Sicard, 1943, Part III and, in particular, pp. 329 sq.; Gluščević, 1967, p. 350). Hamlets inhabited by a lineage still exist (Pavković, 1961); in other cases, the lineage (forming a *"rod"*) or the phratry lives in a quarter of the village and even gives the same name to the quarter (Stojančević, 1980).

The *bratstvo* was a related group, linked by kinship, by the possession of common lands, by common religious celebrations, and by the fact that they bore the same patronymic. Friedrich Krauss (1885; see also Guidetti, Stahl, 9177, p. 73 sq.) even mentions eponymic legends concerning the formation of the *bratstva* and the origin of the name. Often, a dwelling (or a quarter) was designated by the plural patronymic of the group which was inhabiting it (Jankovitch, p. 103; Peševa, 1972).

How is a *bratstvo* formed? It is simply a question of the development of a patrilineal lineage which is descended or believed to be descended from a common ancestor. Troyanovitch (1909, p. 174) describes the situation for Montenegro in the following passage: "Sons of one father are called *Brats,* or brothers; their sons are *Bratuchtsi;* the sons of these are *Bratanitchi;* and, again the sons of these latter are *Bratsvenitsi,* and so on. Montenegrins count pure kinship down to the seventh degree, and consider that such kinship constitutes a single family, and intermarriage is therefore impossible. . . Down to this seventh generation all the members of a family belong to one Bratstvo or brotherhood, and often have one surname, and keep one *Slava"* (celebration of a patron saint).

The village is made up of one or several bratsvo (Stojančević, 1980, p. 34); occasionally the lineages having the composition of a bratstvo do not carry this name, but rather are simply called *"rod"*–lineage. They continue to consider themselves as related and they often recognize themselves by the common rights that they have to community property. In turn, they are composed of households, designated in general by the name *"kuča"* (house).

### The Arable Land ("baština") and the Common Fields ("komunica")

Among the Serbo-Croatians, the common name used to designate cultivated lands is *"baština,"* and *"bastinija,"* among the Bulgarians. This name designates a patronymic, a family property. The land included in this category are in reality property from the domestic groups and is passed on from one generation to the next through the male heirs, females intervening only where there are no males. Nobles, as well as the simple peasants, can own a *baština* (Novakovitch, 1905, p. 45 sq.).

The commonfield has various names, including the following variants given by Mirko Barjaktarović (1976, p. 112): *"domunice"* in Montenegro, *"gmajna"* in Slovenia, *"utrina"* or *"selina"* in Serbia, *"imovna opština"* in Croatia. They essentially include forests, pastures, high alpine pastures, meadows, in addition to mills, roads, hunting or fishing rights, irrigation systems, springs, and fountains. Depending on the individual case, some commonfields are found belonging to whole tribes, to villages, to phratries, or to lineages. Their boundaries are as strongly guarded as those of the cultivated lands, especially when pastures, or, in other words, any crucial aspect of animal breeding, is involved (Bogetić, 1972, pp. 551 sq., and 1966).

The access to commonfields is strictly reserved for members of the lineage, of the phratry, of the village, or of the tribe considered to be the owner; the members of the group know each othe well and the presence of a stranger does not go unnoticed. The right of access to the common-field first assumes the ownership of a house, of a courtyard and cultivated fields on the group's territory (Gluščević, 1967, p. 351; Grozdonova, p. 37; Novakovitch, p. 16). In this respect, the situation is the same as else-where in Europe and, as I have already mentioned, in Romania as well.

The commonfield belonging to tribes underwent a similar evolution to that noted in quite a few other countries; first, they are progressively divided among villages, phratries, and even later among the lineages. Their expanse diminishes continuously; lands formerly considered community, uncultivated, progressively become labor fields and form the *baština* of the village or family groups. One thus witnesses a continuous process of preparing virgin lands for cultivation or of clearing of forests, under demographic and economic pressures.

Each household has equal rights to the commonfield regardless of the number of its members. As in Romania, temporary properties may results; an area is enclosed (Jankovitch, p. 102), it is cultivated and then aban-doned when it no longer yields, while any land without fencing returns to the domain of community property. Admittedly, similar cultivation (which bring to mind what has been elsewhere termed "itinerant agri-culture") can not haphazardly materialize in any fashion and in any loca-tion (Novakovitch, 1905, p. 15). The resemblances to what has taken place elsewhere in Europe are striking.

The village can also jointly own arable lands that are divided among houses; these lands are enclosed, as are lands already entered as household property, in order to prevent the destruction of the crops by the animals (Arsitch, 1936, p. 75). An itinerant agriculture also developed among the Southern Slavs; the lands were developed in such a way as to be profitable, then left fallow. The system of cultivation which permits a more intense development of a land among the Southern Slavs is the system of two parcels of land, one cultivated, the other left uncultivated. Toward the west, one also finds the triennial system of crop rotation. This latter system requires people to have a piece of property in each one of the three parcels of land designated for the crop rotation (Winner, 1971, p. 134).

The forest played an important role and constitutes one of the principal parts of community property. It supplies wood needed for construction, for tools, and for fire, along with medicinal or food supplying plants. In addition, the forest plays a crucial role in agriculture and animal breeding.

The sentence "burning was employed as part of cultivation," (Yugoslavian Village, 1972, p. 44), Vacarelski (1969, pp. 11 sq.) refers to the fire, the "požar," which makes the land suitable for cultivation. In Bulgaria, "Nowhere is the land manured, whether it is by chance or due to the presence of oxen, sheep, and horses in the area. Burning is practiced occasionally, nearly always without discernment and too often to the detriment of the forests" (Blanqui, 1845, p. 224). "The land is only rarely manured," states Lutovac (1935, p. 33).

The clearing of the forests also allows for the obtaining of arable lands or pastures (Milić, 1958). The primitive wooden sowing plow was still being used in the 20th century along with other archaic techniques (Vacarelski, 1969, p. 11), primarily in the mountain areas. Milisav Lutovac (p. 33) states "cultivation was carried out with the prehistoric wooden plow, which barely penetrated the ground more than 12 to 15 centimeters. Instead of using an iron rake, a branch or a wooden stick was used to superficially cover the seed." Kostov and Peteva (1935, p. 195) offer similar statements concerning Bulgaria.

The animals are fed in the forest; pigs are fond of acorns, oak or beech trees (Lodge, p. 113; Yugoslavian Village, p. 44); the goats eat the young shoots and the sheep graze on the grass. Defoliation of the trees is practices in order to feed the animals, especially in winter (Kanitz, p. 239; Vučković, pp. 235 and 240). Certain woods must even be protected against fanatical development and especially against the devastation caused by the goats.

As for the forests' properties, if joint possession was the general rule, we have already seen that they end by being divided among the villages, the *bratstva,* and the *rods.* The mountain forests have the tendency to remain community property for the longest period of time. Olive Lodge (p. 114) notes that in the 20th century, property systems in the forest differ from one another: she distinguishes what she calls the *"srednjerit,"* (middle region, intermediate) where utilization is traditional, that is to say, where each group cuts as much wood as is needed; the *"zabranjena mesta,"* is the prohibited area, which is not developed since it must be left to regenerate. Finally, she outlines another system where forests have become household properties. There is a unique stuation involving the chestnut trees, which have a system unto themselves; each person knows the chestnut trees, which are not necessarily next to each other. Only the owner-group of a particular chestnut tree can pick its chestnuts; the entire village leaves together on a fixed date to go to the forest for this purpose (October 27–*Petkovdan*). The ownership of the tree is quite apparent when it is a question of a planted tree; the person who planted it is its owner and his rights are passed on to his descendants; when the tree does not yeild any fruit, it is cut down and the descendants divide up the wood (Primovski, 1975).

## Mutual Aid

Mutual aid for work takes on various forms and is widely practiced by the Southern Slavs. Most of the forms are based on reciprocity, found not only in the work domain, but also in other domains, including, for example, religion (Filipović, 1968-9, pp. 123 sq.). Georgevitch (1917, p. 46) distinguishes three forms: the first he terms *"spreja"*: "When a peasant is poor and his pair of oxen is not sufficient to plough his ground, or if, not being poor, he wants to speed up his work, he obtains the help of another peasant in the same circumstances and they work together. . . . A common interest binds them as closely as family ties. They considered themselves as related. The bonds of a sincere affection unite their respective families. They help one another on all occasions. It is very difficult to break the *spreja* since it lasts sometimes many years and is transmitted from father to son." It is thus an economic relationship which has a tendency to become a form of permanent neighborliness, uniting not only two people, but two households, and which therefore resembles a relationship of kinship. In the Montenegrin Code, where Bogišić loyally respected the principles of customary law, we find this practice written, called yoking society (*"sprega"*): "When two or several people combine their oxen for the purpose of work, it is assumed that they will use them to work all of the lands that the members (*"sprež-nici"*) have to work during the current year, without taking into account the differing amounts of land held by each" (article 446). Other points are also included which concern the alternative work on the members' lands, the number of oxen brought by each person, the land each person possesses and the animals' food. These principles, which govern traditional peasant practices, are recognized everywhere.

In a study devoted to work associations among the populations of Slavic origin, Kadlec (1905, pp. 64 sq.) describes the *sprega* (also called *"suvez"* in Bosnia and in Herzegovina). He reported that in Bulgaria, the members of a sprega (*"spreznaci"*) are associated, not only for purposes of working the land normally used for sowing wheat, but also for clearing virgin land. Several members bring their oxen, since in order to clear a virgin alnd, significant animal traction is needed. The land is therefore worked with four or five pairs of oxen, after which the corn is sown. During four years, the land will be jointly worked and the harvest shared by the members; this type of association results in the equal sharing of the jointly cleared lands (see also Kr'stanova, 1975; Kadlec, 1905, pp. 74-75).

The associations can also take on different forms, for example, the harvest of two or several people can be transported in one person's wagon.

A type of mutual aid, called *"pozajmica,"* presumes an exchange of work between two parties, and takes place primarily during periods of intense agricultural work and when extra help is needed (Georgevitch, 1917, p. 46; Pantelić, Pavković, 1964).

The *"moba"* has a different character. It is even allowed during holidays, when other types of work are forbidden: "Some houses, which can not finish their work themselves, call on people from other houses for mowing, harvesting, etc. on those particular days" (Jankovitch and Grouvitch, 1853, p. 109). The person who requests the aid of the others offers to feed them; often it is also a chance for the young men and young women, or even young couples, to sing and dance (Kadlec, 1905,

p. 74). The "moba is also practice also with special regard to old people, of invalids and of absentees—that is to say, for the good of all those unable to work themselves or unable to pay for the work of others" (Georgevitch, p. 46). A situation also arises where, a person who gives aid to a poor person does not expect to be fed. Bogišić also sheds some light on this situation (art. 345 of his code): "Each person who requests workers for gratuitous aid (*moba*) must, according to custom, feed them well, but he is neither obligated to pay them salary, nor respond to their call for help if asked by one of them." "When, with the consent of the village, of the phratry, etc., help is given to a widow, an orphan, a victim of a fire or any other indigent person, the person for whom the work is done, is not required, regardless whether the work is done on a holiday or not, to pay them, nor to help them in return (article 347).

It would be interesting to describe the animal owners' associations (especially sheep) which together place their animals under the care of a single shepherd, but which differ from the associations previously described. These associations bring up unique questions but will not be treated in this work.

Therefore, in summary, there is an association form for joint work on common lands which results in the sharing of the obtained products, an association where animals or personal labor is mutually lent, and finally there is work which is offered gratuitously, without responsibility of reciprocity, which is often "paid" by food, dance, music and which links work with the young people's celebrations. Sometimes, there is no expectation of being fed or entertained, when the aid is being performed for people deprived of resources.

## THE TRIBE—"PLEME"

The superior social unit to that of the phratry or the village was the tribe. At this level, one also finds a belief in a common ancestor having given birth to the entire tribe, and at the same time to its name. Generally, as is the case also within a lineage or a phratry, the group is exogamous, but not always. The tribe possesses a community property, fiercely defended, the possession of which often provokes conflicts with other tribes, especially concerning pastures and animals. The pastures are difficult to define and the animals are unable to know or respect community property boundaries. The tribe is already a mini-state, having a military organization and a leader, a voivode.

Southeastern Europe includes a rather large region which encompasses northern Albania, Montenegro and especially the neighboring regions of Macedonia. Some tribes of Albanian, Romanic, and Slavic origin live within close proximity. The region in question is marked by the presence of mountains with difficult access, far from the big cities and from large commercial roads, consequently enabling the region to maintain tribal structures up until the 20th century. The region was populated in ancient times by Thraco-Illyrian tribes which, being romanized in part, gave birth to the romanique populations. The arrival of the Slavs resulted in a large number of tribes, either of Albanian origin or of romanic expression, becoming Slavs, a process which actively continued into the 19th and 20th centuries. Toward the end of the 19th century, there were still tribes, part of which spoke Slavic and part of which spoke Albanian. In the same manner, there were Romanic tribes in the process of becoming Slavic (Cvijić, 1918, second book; Durham 1931, p. 155; Djurdjev, 1974, p. 298).

Montenegro, the most characteristic tribal region for the Southern Slavs, is typical in this regard (Barjaktarović, 1972, p. 147; Durham 1928, pp. 52 sq.; Durham, 1931; Glušćević, p. 355; Vukosavljević, 1957). In reality, it is historically proven that the tribes are often composed of populations of diverse origins; for example, a phratry can ally itself with an already formed tribe and "such a *Bratstvo* received a name *Pselitsa,* which means 'new-comers' who form a *Bratstvo,* and no longer belong to their consaguineous tribe" (Troyanovitch, p. 175). Cvijić (1918, p. 318 sq.) says it clearly: "There are within each tribe several former families related to one another, which form the nucleus. . . . It is rather through agglomeration than filiation that these tribes are formed."

Isolated individuals can also be received into the tribe. Mirko Barjaktarović describes the manner in which an outsider has access to the common property of the tribe: "Earlier, in the tribal commune of Drobnjak's anybody who wanted to participate had to take the general name of Drobnjak, to adopt Drobnjak slava St. George and to have a guarantee of one of the Drobnjak's that he is a constructive and a good man" (1976, p. 113). Novakovitch (1905, pp. 13-14) incudes among the conditions the necessity of becoming a relative of one of the members of the tribe, and his acceptance by the other members.

If penetration by outsiders is certain, it has not prevented the belief in a common ancestor from being strongly maintained at the level of the simple lineages as well as within phratries and tribes. The memory of ancestors sometimes is kept alive for several centuries; Mary Edith Durham (1909, pp. 86 sq. and 1931, p. 155) documents this practice for the Albanians and the Montenegrins and mentions Nopcsa who, in Albania, had found people knowing their pedigree back to the 14th century. She also explains this memory with regard to the necessity of avoiding incest, occurring when, out of ignorance, marriages take place between two related people. This type of memory is oral, a characteristic of societies whose culture is orally based (Kerewski-Halpern, 1977, pp. 141 sq.). The memory of the male ancestors is kept, in other words, those who count as being members of the tribe and who have access to its property. In this respect, a distinction is made between the ancendants and the descendants of the male line termed "thin blood"—"*debela krv*" and those from the maternal line, called "thin blood"—"*tanka krv*" (Simić, 1967, p. 88).

The Montenegrin tribes undergo a double evolution. The first focuses on the interior of the territory considered community where some sections begin to emerge as property of a certain group (Novakovitch, pp. 11, 14; Simić, 1967, p. 89). The cultivated lands are the first to become the property of a phratry or of a village. The communal territories, little by little, undergo the same change, as they also begin to be divided, even while maintaining community sections belonging to the entire tribe. In order to avoid abuses, the animals are taken to the community mountain pastures on the same date (Barjaktarović, 1976, p. 113). The process of the division of the communal territories among the phratries and the villages was already taking place as early as the 18th century (Gluščević, p. 352).

The second evolution that Montenegro undergoes results in a profound change in the character of the social units. The *bratstvo* becomes a hamlet or a village (Filipović, 1955); the tribe becomes a department—"*nahija*" (Jankovitch, p. 107); the leaders, little by little, becomes civil servants. This evolution, widely described by Sicard (1943), is already quite apparent in the 19th century, but double characters persist; thus, elements characterizing an archaic society are noticed, based on consanguinity, where solidarities are strong and are accompanied by vengeances which create long standing conflicts betweeen groups, where men are constantly armed, and where war and banditry constitute normal activities. At the same time, elements of a modern State are detected with, for example, a true system of justice; it was no longer acceptable for an invidual to apply his own ideas of justice, but the responsibility fell on specialized instruments of the law (Stojanović, 1974). In 1871 (Yryarte, p. 406), captains, leaders of the tribes (*voivodes*), begin to be replaced by civil servants or become civil servants themselves.

The code promulgated in Montenegro by Prince Daniel I in 1885, is characteristic of this phase of transition, faithfully depicting typical elements of the past mixed with elements relating to western justice (Delarue, 1862). Thus, the category of the "elderly" regularly intervenes in the settling of property disputes. If it can be said that the code tries to prevent people from attempting to take justice into their own hands, it also outlines circumstances in which the killing of a traitor, for example, would be justified. It is expected that needless killings will not occur, but which therefore implies that certain "necessary" killings would be allowed. The organization of the acts of banditry carried out by small groups (*"četa"*) upon the neighboring territories is forbidden, "but only in times of peace." Additional examples of thic concept can be found. (See also Gopčević, 1877, chapters VI and VIII).

## The Assemblies

At each level of social life—household, phratry, tribe—a leader is found and, above all, an assembly; in the past, this assembly functioned even at the leve of the tribal confederation in Montenegro.

At the village level, there is a an assembly formed essentially by the leaders of the households; it meets either on fixed dates, or because it has been convened by the leader. The meeting place, however, is not fixed; it can be in a house, out of doors, under a tree, near the church, or even in the middle of the village (Stojančević, 1980, p. 34). If possible, it is preferable to meet on a Sunday.

The name used to designate the leader of the village in Yugoslavia varies: Nikola Pavković (1961) records in the same region the names *"starosta"* for Christians and *"mukhtar"* for Moslems; elsewhere, he finds the name *"knez"* (Pavković, 1962), a name which can designate either a true prince or a simple village leader. For the evolution of this name, as for those names designating typical people of past Yugoslavian society, Friedrich Krauss' study (1885, the first two chapters) is particularly interesting. Jankovitch (p. 103) calls the village leader *"starešina,"* Saint Rene Taillandier uses *"knez"* (pp. 46-47). The head of the village is aided by the leaders of the households or, by the group of married men, or occasionally by a limited group of elderly or notables, designated by the by the name *"kmet."* The assembly itself bears the name *"zbor"* or *"skup."*

Among the Bulgarians, the name *"knez"* is found (Grozdanova, p. 44); it is aided by the older members of the village (Bobčev, 1935, p. 42), or by notables, designated by the name *"čorbadji"* (Bobčev, 1938, p. 431) and who received a stick as a sign of their office; they could also be called *"kočabaši"* (Grozdanova, p. 44). "The Turkish governments found that it was good and wise to have čorbačis elected by the people themselves to serve as arbitrators between the populations and the government. . . . Ordinarily, the term of a čorbači lasted one year, after which the same čorbači could be reelected if, due to his abilities, his honest conduct and his devoted services, he merited the voters' confidence . . . there were some čorbačis from the villages and small towns and čorbačis for an entire department referred to as *memleket čorbačis* (čorbačis from the district)" (Bobcev, 1938, p. 431). The čorbadji himself received a stick from the Turkish authorities, as a sign of his office. The Turkish kadi intervened primarily in the most serious cases, for example, those relating to a crime, leaving to the assembly the responsibility of passing sentences on others according to custom (Bobčev, 1935, p. 37).

The powers of the village assembles (apart from the relationship with the State authorities) are numerous since, in reality, these assemblies constituted a source of organization for the entire village, material as well as spiritual. Collectively responsible, the village also judged collectively (Pavković, 1980). Punishments that they inflicted were of a surprising inventiveness (Djordjević, 1948).

The elderly, the notables, or the assembly of all men were responsible for deciding the allocation and the collection of taxes. The taxes could moreover be set by village or by household; in the latter case, they could be set by door, or by smoke (*"dim"*), the tax itself being called *"dimnica"* (Yugoslavian Village, p. 41). But, whatever the means of imposition, the village intervened, trying to be as fair as possible in allocating the various responsibilities. Dates corresponding to religious holidays are chosen as fixed dates for the paying of taxes; either on Saint George or Saint Demetre's day, which regulated, moreover, the rhythm of still quite a few other things (departure and return of the herds and the shepherds, contacts, sales). Knotches are utilized to calculated the taxes or to serve as receipts (Kanitz, 1882, p. 108; Bogičević, 1953, Vacarelski, 1969, pp. 33, 143, 211-212; Koleva, 1972).

Managing assemblies are found at the level of the phratries or tribes; if the leader of a bratstvo can be confused with the leader of a village, the situation changes at the level of the tribe where the leader takes on the name *voivode* and above all is called *"zbor."* Also at this level, the powers of the assemblies are quite numerous (Vukmanović, 1964). Here, questions are discussed and attempts are made to resolve all issues that could not be decided at a lower level. It was also necessary to obtain unanimous consent on issues, since it was nearly impossible to impose a decision on the majority to which it was opposed (Vukosavljević, 1957, chap. V).

The abbot Fortis, known for his work on the Morlaes, a romantic tribe which became Slavic, published an account of his voyage to Dalmatia. He describes, among other things, the social organization of the Poglizza region where there was a society composed of different social classes: "This little republic deserves to be better known. Three classes of people make up a population of fifteen thousand souls. The first consists of twenty families who claim to descend from Hungarian nobles, who, in times of trouble, retreated to the country; a larger number of families, of the Bosnian nobility, make up the second, and the rest of the people, or the peasants, the third class. Every year, on Saint George's Day, the inhabitants of the province of Poglizza come together for an assembly which they refer to in their language as *zbor.* Each class camps separately in the Gatta plain. In this type of Diet, the Magistrates are elected or confirmed. The *Veliki Knez,* or the Great-Count, is the first person of the State, and is always chosen from the class of the Hungarian nobles. His voters are the lesser nobility, that is to say, the governors of the villages, chosen from the native Bosnian nobility, and who bring to the Diet the voices of their communities. While the lesser counts elect a great-count, the people divide into individual assemblies, which represent the inhabitants of the villages, and elect in turn the lesser counts for the following year, or confirm those deserving ones. At the same time that the first class is taking care of the election of a captain and two pro-secutors . . . (for the times of conflicts), the Judge visits the scenes, listens to the defense, seated on the ground on his spread out coat; he passes sentince before standing up, and ordinarily adjourns the proceeding in the field . . ." (Fortis, 1778, II, pp. 124-126). This organization, in cer-tain respects, recalls the traditional organizations of the regions situated more to the west, beginning with neighboring Italy itself.

When it is a question of societies where a neat separation of classes is not found, the rules change. Wilkinson (1848, I, p. 456) describes the as-sembly which convenes in order to decide affairs of the tribal confedera-tion of Montenegro, under the directorship of the State leader, an ec-clesiastic, the *"vladika."* "In a semicircular recess, formed by the rocks on one side of the plain of Tzetinje, and about half a mile to the south-ward of the town, is a level piece of grass land, with a thicket of old poplar trees. Here the diet is held, from which the spot has received the name of *'mali sbor,'* the small assembly. When any matter is to be discussed, the people meet in this their meadow of council; and partly on the level space, partly on the rocks, received from the Vladika notice of the question proposed. The duration of the discussion is limited to a certain time; at the expiration of which, the assembly is expected to come to a decision; and when 'the monastery's bell orders silence, not-withstanding the most animated discussion, it is instantly restored."

Some dozen years later, Yriarte (1878, p. 400) also attends such an assembly; this time the leader of the State is a prince: ". . . we saw the Prince leave, surrounded by a large, high-ranking staff composed of the president of the senate, senators, ministers, *voivodes,* guards and *perianiks,* in all about thirty people one after the other, all in their national costume. . . . Once in the plain, he sat down on the trunk of a tree; several indi-viduals had followed him, and one of them, walking straight toward him, stopped a few steps away and began a conversation. The prince was silent; he was listening, answering occasionally in monosyllables. . . . This is the manner in which he sometimes makes judgments. . . . Most of the time, provided that the season is beautiful, this process takes place under a great mulberry tree, near the well of the main street, or under a tree which stands at the door of the Monastery, where a circular bench is arranged for the purpose of rendering justice . . . . ."

If one goes toward the North, to Serbia, which was regaining its independence at the beginning of the 19th century, events unfolded in the following manner (Saint Rene Taillandier, pp. 305-306): "The 14th of February (1835) was the day of Purification; the Serbs willingly chose a great church holiday in order to inaugurate their *skupcinas* (assemblies). After their religious ceremonies, everyone assembled in the vast prairie where a sort of tent had been set up for the prince, the archbishop and the high ranking dignitaries."

One of the principal preoccupations of the village, phratry, or tribal assemblies was preventing the penetration of outsiders (Vokosavljević, p. 107) who, in order to be received, has to fulfill a series of conditions (Novakovitch, p. 13; Gluščević, p. 351). The most certain means of avoiding outsiders was the strict application of preemptive right, a right which functioned everywhere (Pavković, 1972; Grozdanova). Each time that a piece of land was for sale, close relatives, neighbors, or members of the same social unit had the first right to buy. Grozdanova (pp. 36, 39) notes that in Bulgaria even the right to withdrawal was in effect; if the member of a village sells his land to an outsider, the village can buy the property back by reimbursing the outsider the amount paid. In his Montenegrin code, Bogišić wisely maintained this practice to which the traditional populations were so strongly attached.

# CHAPTER III

## THE ALBANIANS

Numerous Albanians live beyond the borders of the Albanian State; above all, they are found in Yugoslavia (Islami, 1981, pp. 255 sq.), in Greece, and in Italy (Kellner, 1972). Given their estrangement from the central region where the majority of this population lives, marked differences appear among the diverse groups. These differences, however, do not prevent numerous elements from recalling a common origin and a common social organization from maintaining itself. Although some information will be given concerning the Albanians who live in the immediately neighboring countries (Yugoslavia, Greece), the essential part of the presentation that follows will be centered on the region in northern Albania, the tribal region, the region which, for the longest time, maintained the characteristics of the past which permit a comparison with the traditional Balkan societies described above. As with the Romanians or the Southern Slavs, the 19th and 20th centuries societies will be described. In fact, in all these countries, the change of the property system and, in general, the structural change following the installation of a political communist power, inevitably brought profound changes and it is necessary to go back in time in order to again find the former face of these societies. The new society which was born has not completely eliminated the traces of the past, but this question belongs to another study.

## The Household ("SHTEPI")

The Albanians designate their household by the name house—*"shtepi"* (Gjergji, 1982, p. 177) or *"shpi"* (Zojzi, 1977). Margaret Hasluck asserts (1954, p. 18) that this name is that of the orignal room of the house which also functioned as the kitchen. This situation corresponds to that of the other Balkan populations where the name of the original room, including a fireplace, later designates houses composed of several rooms (*"Kuča"* among the Yugoslavians, *"casa"* among the Romanians).

The presence of a house signifies the presence of a family; therefore, the terms *"votër"* or *"vatrë"*—family—are found among the Albanians to signify household (Georgescu, 1963, p. 80); the word is the same used by the Romanians, *"vatră,"* and constitutes one of the common words of the basis fond illyrothrac (Russu, 1959, p. 130). The words *"zjarr"* (family, fire), or *"tym"* (smoke) are also used. Therefore, all the designations of the household are used in southeastern Europe or elsewhere in Europe, but not the characteristic word having the unique function of designating the household (as the Romanian term *"gospod-ărie"*).

Gjecov's collection of customary rights affirms that "each house which emits smoke must have land" (Valentini, 1945, p. 111), which is to say that each inhabited house signals the presence of a social unit having rights to the property of the village, phratry, or the tribe. This brings to light once again the resemblance to the societies previously described, where the possession of a house installed on a particular group's land signifies membership to this group with all the obligations and rights that such a situation implies (Gjergji, 1982, p. 177). "Each inhabited house shares in the village possessions" (Gjecov, paragraph 215). "The house has a courtyard, a garden, vineyards and fields, meadows, hedges, paths" (Gjecov, par. 214).

When a new house is constructed, after having put on the roof, the first thing that must be done is to light the fire" (Dida, 1981, p. 194); afterwards, the trail of the smoke is observed in order to guess what the fate of the new social unit will be, while at the same time trying to avoid the extinction of the fire which would have brought bad luck to the group (Dida, 1981, p. 195). A group which separates, but still maintains close relations, asserts that it forms one single fire (Zojzi, 1977, p. 192).

When the last male representative of a household dies, which signifies the disappearance of his household since females do not have the right to inherit land, "the fireplace of his bedroom is demolished; where the fire was located, a bundle of thorns is placed" (Degrand, 1901, pp. 51-52).

Among the Southern Slavs, there is a characteristic word which indicates the fact that the domestic group is made up of several married couples, *"kuča zadružna."* The Albanian domestic group is also composed of several married couples; names which bring this situation to light are indicated. Mark Krasniqi (1971, p. 493) notes that among the Albanians of Yugoslavia, the name *"shpija e forte"*—the powerful house —is used; in the Polog plain, the name *"dere e madhe"*—great door—is found (Tufai, 1978, p. 431).

## The domestic group

"The second evening, we were invited by a certain Lhesch Mihidhi, a funny old man, full of prejudices. . . . His large family was composed of 35 people, all good Christians; he was an octogenarian. . . he had his house located on the top of a hill, next to an oak forest. Its location made it pleasant, and the vast courtyard surrounded by high walls, including in the interior, 12 or 13 cottages, a number which corresponds to the number of his married sons and grandsons who were living with him . . . " (Valentini, 1969, p. 136). This description, made at the end of the 19th century, is typical of households of the past in northern Albania; in fact, the domestic group is composed of several married couples living and working together within the framework of a single social unit. These domestic groups seem to be more common than those of the southern Slavs and they survived for a longer period of time. I was able to observe such groups in Yugoslavia in regions where Albanians and Slavs live as good neighbors; the numerous groups of the Slavs had disappeared (Tufai, 1978). Vera Erlich's survey is enlightening in this respect since it covers the entire territory of Yugoslavia; as for the question concerning the moment when the large domestic group disappeared, we see that the Albanian households are the last to be touched by the modern evolution. The great economic crisis of 1930 constitues the moment when this phenomenon also touches the Albanains (Erlich, 1966, p. 46).

The descriptions of the large domestic groups abound, several of which I will mention. ". . . in the great country of Haimeli, the largest of the Zadrima. . . families have 20, 40 or even 50 members. And, several years ago, there was one family, called Miloti, which included 102 people," affirms a priest in 1931 (Valentini, 1969, p. 259). Gopčević (1881, p. 317) tells of Albanian families made up of "50, 100, and even 200 heads," this last total probably being exaggerated since it has never been verified by another researcher. Margaret Hasluck (1954, p. 29) asserts that the domestic groups surpassing 20 people are numerous and mentions two in particular, one having 65 people and another 95. Mark Krasniqi (1979, pp. 237 sq.) mentions particular cases among the Albanians from the Kosovo region; for example, he describes a group composed of 83 people, including 16 married couples; in another chapter of the same work (pp. 250 sq.), he points out that in 1971, the average number of people per domestic group among the Albanians of the Kosovo region is 8, but one of these groups numbers 93. He also lists a complete series of large domestic groups in the same region (Krasniqi, 1982, pp. 27-36); two cases surpass 60 people, another 100 people, other cases have 80, 85, 30, 85, or 45 members (see also Krasniqi, 1971, p. 493).

The political changes that took place in Albania and the profound transformations within the society influenced the society. One of the most evolved characteristics is the number of people making up the domestic group. In most of the surveyed cases, the common presence of groups including three married couples is noted. The evolution toward groups of a single couple, or, of no more than two, is apparent. In a general analysis focusing on the evolution of the contemporary Albanian family, Alfred Uci (1970, p. 170) studies this question which confirms the above information. His findings are confirmed by Andromaqi Gjergji's surveys (1976, p. 93; 1982, p. 89) and by those of Naum Guxho (1976, pp. 104-106).

If one examines the structure of the domestic groups, one distinguishes the same existing categories among the Southern Slavs or among other populations organized in large domestic groups. There is a leader and a woman leader, male members having greater rights than those of the married women and girls, and finally, the children. They all work together on the same property, under the orders of the head of the group; they live together or nearby, in the same courtyard; they share their income. All the members are fed, clothed, and cared for.

Aside from the distinctions made between the sexes and between the leader and his citizens, the distinction that parents make between children should be noted. Among boys, the oldest is set apart from the youngest. Gjecov (par. 58-63) describes the rights of each one. It can also be added that similarly organized domestic groups are noted among lords (Krasniki, 1971, p. 492).

## The house

Two elements, among others, occur in the past which define certain features of the houses: the first is the fact that several couples live together under the same roof, and the second centers around the realities of an armed society where the vendetta and small scale local wars are endemic. Consequently, living situations which recall those of the neighboring Montenegrin society are found, and similarly structured.

Lucy Garnett (1917, p. 5) describes the most simple forms in the following manner: "The cottages of which they are composed are of one storey only, and contain but two rooms, one of which is used as a storehouse for the produce of the little farmstead, the other serving as a general living and sleeping apartment. The fire is made on the floor, the smoke escaping through a hole in the roof, the furniture being limited to a few mats and rugs, a *sofa*—the low stand on which meals are served in Turkish fashion, a well-scoured copper pan to mix the meal in, a wooden bowl or two, a few horn spoons, a copper *ibrik* and a brass lamp." These forms of construction, absent in the villages of the plains, maintained themselves longer in the mountain regions inhabited by shepherds (Krasniqi, 1979, pp. 380 sq.).

The presence of several couples can give rise to three different forms of habitation: there is first the form where the whole group lives in a single building, which can be of the type described in the preceding paragraph, requiring everyone to be crammed together, including the animals. Also, large, fortified buildings are found, which will be discussed below. A third form exists with a large, central house, surrounded by small, one-room houses, situated in the single courtyard, as described by a priest in the following: "It is the custom in these areas. When someone takes a wife, a wooden cottage, covered with dirt, measuring 2 by 3 metres, is built for him in the courtyard, and this becomes the wedding bedroom for the couple" (Valentini, 1969, p. 136).

A different living arrangement, appearing less frequently, is the one
where the rooms occupied by the various couples are installed under the
same roof, adjacent to the principal room, and eventually including a
bedroom for guests; this latter situation is common, given the role that
hospitality plays in the life of the Albanians (Krasniqi, 1979, pp. 453
sq.). "... each couple required a separate bedroom ... a number of
rooms were grouped together sideways, sometimes on one floor only,
usually on two, but rarely on more. In the second type one room was
built on top of another, as in a tower, for two, three or even four storeys"
(Hasluck, 1954, p. 18). "A housekeeper, who was generally elderly, cooked and baked for the whole family, swept the kitchen, the men's sitting
room, and her own bedroom if she had one apart from the kitchen, but
did not enter any room belonging to a married man, even if he was her
son" (Hasluck, 1954, p. 28). These bedrooms occupied by couples could
open directly onto the courtyard or first on to the gallery (Krasniki,
1979, p. 406); they are called *"kiler"* and the married couples sleeps
together with their non-married children (Krasinqi, 1971, p. 498). They
can be located on the first or the second floor, topping the storerooms
and the cellars (Mukha, 1979, p. 252; 1982, p. 221).

The fact that the people have to defend themselves gives rise to a typical, scattered living situation with houses, of a fortified nature (Bourcart,
1912, p. 178), situated in the middle of the land to be cultivated (Degrand,
1901, p. 125), on the highest points possible. "Each house is crenelated,
or pierced with loopholes amsked by an exterior coating, and are always
isolated, out of range of another habitation. The family of one party or of
a common line, by separating in collateral branches from the leader from
which they are descended, form levels of living quarters around a knoll,
or on a steep plateau, in order to be able to help one another without
dropping their guard against the enterprises of the people of their own
*phara"* (lineage) (Pouqueville, 1826, III, p. 246). These fortified houses
are common among peasant and lords: "In the mountain districts the
houses of the Beys, or chieftains, are complete fortresses, being surrounded by high walls, pierced with loopholes for musketry" (Garnett, 1917,
p. 5; see also Valentini, 1969, pp. 232 and 249).

The different couples forming the domestic group, in this case as well,
each occupy a separate room. This room can be included in the fortified
house itself (Thomo, pp. 106 and 108), called the *"koula,"* and whose
form often resembles a tower; in these koula, there is also a room for

friends and a gathering room for the group, one room alone serving both functions (Riza, 1976, pp. 171 sq.). It may also occur that the separate bedrooms of the couples are located in an adjacent structure to the koula, where refuge can be sought if needed (Kransniqi, 1979, p. 425; Mukha, 1982, p. 136; 1980, p. 221). Branislav Kojić (1973, p. 74) publishes such an example; the bedrooms are located on the main floor and on the second story; they open on to a corridor which leads to the main floor and the first floor of the tower; the tower moreover has a third floor. Jacques Bourcart (1921, p. 180) adds another piece of information which characterizes the relationship of this type of living situation to past social conditions: "... the brith of the kula is due to the insecurity that the vendetta creates.... The large kula of the Korča plain and of the Golloberda, northwest of the Ohrida lake... resisted systematic destruction by the Turks who lay siege after the death of Ali Pasha.... In general, only the first floor is inhabited, the whole interior is occupied by the staircase, whose defense by landings is carefully managed; the roof is covered with flat, very heavy rock, which are difficult for the attacker to remove. The kula is surrounded by flimsy buildings, sheds and stables; in several Moslem countries, in Mati, for example, the living quarters for the women, who are normally not involved in the vendetta, are next to the kula with large windows." In fact, during the vendettas, the men, who are exposed to the attacks of the adversaries, hold up in the tower and do not even come out for agricultural chores, leaving the women in charge.

Finally, there is a living arrangement which should be noted as a form which is apparently more recent. In the Polog plain, in the Albanian-Moslem villages, the houses are enclosed by vast courtyards, surrounded by high, massive, fences which allow no one to see into the courtyard. If in the past a single house was the center for everyone, it must be noted that with the most recent construction where several brothers are living together, each one of them will have his own house. It is therefore not a question of each couple having its own room, but an actual house, with two floors, where each brother lives with his wife and his children, regardless if the work is organized on a joint basis, on a common property, or if the cooking is done together and the children are reared in a single courtyard.

### The Head of the Domestic Group

The head of the domestic group is always a man; his authority naturally carries on the tradition of man's authority over women and children:
"The disdainful warrior believed himself to be demeaned by manual
labor; he waits for his family to do everything; taciturn, he holds the
stick of leadership in his hand; he demands attention, services and help
from those who depend on him; and he is never concerned with the details of domestic life except to trade or sell the surplus of produce. He
loads his wife with a sack full of food which she carries to the market;
he is the sole master of the earnings, and the keeper of the keys under-
which any valuable objects are locked. His occupation is to maintain his
arms, to provide care for his shoes, prepare his cartridges, maintain amun-
ition for war; and the rest of his time is spent smoking and vegetating."
This is a description taken from the 19th century (Pouqueville, 1826,
III, p. 272) and which includes characteristics also confirmed by other
authors. This descrption brings to mind man's place in the Montenegrin
society of the same era, with the exception that the rights of the leader
seem to be more distinct in Albanian society.

He is called *"zoti i shtepis"* or *"zot shpije"* in the Kosove region, which
means the head of the house (Krasniqi, 1982, p. 44); in Albania, the leader
is designated by the same name (Zojzi, 1977, p. 191), or *"plak"*—the
ancient one, the elderly (Zojzi, 1977, p. 190), *"tatzot"*—master father
(Zojzi, 1977, p. 190; Nova, 1977, p. 277), or *"babzot"* which means the
same thing (Zojzi, 1977, p. 190; the same, 1972, p. 28). He can sometimes have an aide or two (Krasniqi, 1971, p. 494). He is the leader for as
long as he is capable of leading the group; even though he is elected for
unspecified period of time, he can be removed from his position by the
members of his group. His office is sometimes transmittable, normally to
his eldest son or to the oldest male member of the group (Gjecov, par.
63). If the leader dies and there is no other adult male in the family, his
brother, who lives in another household, or his wife's brother, becomes
the head of the group in his place during a period of transition (Hasluck,
1954, p. 34).

According to Gjecov (par. 20), the leader occupies the first place in
the house, even if there are people older than he; he disposes of his own
arms, a horse; he manages the group's possessions; he sells, buys land,

animals, tools. he can lend or be a guarantor, construct houses, dependencies, arrange the work of the people of the house; divide the wine, brandy; punish the members of his group (by depriving them of food, arms, and by tying them up or imprisoning them in the house or even by banishing them). His actions must be conducted with the good of the household in mind, surpass the others in terms of work, be watchful that the land does not remain uncultivated and that the animals are in good health, obtain clothes for this group, be fair, unbiased, and purchase arms for the young men. If someone wants to enter the house, it is the leader that they call on (Valentini, 1969, p. 22). In the Polog plain, I was able to observe that, even in cases where it was known for a fact that the leader was not in the house, he is still the person called on when someone wants to make contact with the members of his domestic group. During ceremonies of a religious nature, the leader receives the largest candle (Valentini, 1969, p. 39).

The woman leader—"*zoje shpije*" (Krasniqi, 1977, p. 495) has more extensive rights than the other women (Gjecov, p. 22). She arranges everything dealing with domestic production, she has the right to give or lend wheat, bread, salt, cheese, butter, and the right to order the other women to look for water, and carry meals to the workers. She must prepare the meals, distribute the food, take care of dairy products, be fair to all, and look after the children while the other women work. She can neither sell nor purchase without the leader's approval. She is exempt from bread making, carrying water, wood cutting, working in the fields, and carrying meals to workers far from the house. She is sometimes called "*baçice,*" probably due to her role in preparing milk since the word, common to the Romanians and the Armân, also includes the idea of the head shepherd.

The other women do the work that the woman leader divides up for them and, in addition, take care of matters concerning their husbands and their children (Krasniqi, 1971, p. 496). Children begin work early by helping women or by leading small herds of animals into the fields near the house (Bourcart, 1921, p. 176). It should be added that, just as we have seen among the southern Slavs, specializations sometimes appear among the members of the group (Krasniqi, 1971, p. 496).

The domestic group shows solidarity in matters of justice or towards the surrounding society (village, tribe). In this respect, the role of the leader appears once again as dominant, his voice alone can represent the entire group (Gjecov, par. 559). At the inauguration of a new house, he is the one to light the first fire, a symbolic gesture having a great significance (Durham, 1920, p. 171); "When a new house is built and is ready for habitation the hearth has to be kindled for the first time ceremoniously. The fire is laid on the hearthstone; no person remains in the house; the family gathers outside; the house lord (*zoti i shpis*) strips stark naked, takes a loaded pistol and enters the house alone. He fires the pistol into the specially prepared fire, and, when it burns up, goes out, dresses, and the whole family takes possession of the house." Hecquard (1862, p. 339) confirms this religious function carried out by the head of the domestic group by describing a Christian ceremony which takes place during the month of May: "At this time of the year, each house, no matter how poor, makes a small chapel that is decorated as richly and as graciously as possible. Every evening and every morning, the head of the family recites the prayer and the litanies of the Virgin Saint there, in the presence of the children and the servants."

The domestic group is always perceived as a group, its members are not considered as isolated individuals but instead as members of their group; thus, they are collectively responsible for the deeds done by any member of their group (Valentini, 1945, p. 169). Cozzi (1910, p. 662) summarizes this situation: "The isolated individual, who has no economic power, no property of his own, and who is not worth anything except as a member of the family association, is neither alone in joy nor in pain. If the individual is offended, the entire group to which he belongs avenges him; if he is the offender, again the entire group assumes responsibility with him." And Cozzi adds findings (p. 673), confirming information about the Romanians and the Southern Slavs, findings which bring to light the preeminence of the household even with regard to consanguinity: "if someone kills a close relative, he is punished in the case where this relative has left the domestic group to which the responsible person belongs." Moreover, the solidarity of the group appears at all levels and not only at the level of the household (Valentini, 1969, pp. 24 sq.); the existence of the vendetta proves this affirmation in a striking manner. This principle dates far back in history and is late, and slow, to change (Nova, 1981, pp. 99 sq.).

Fines or taxes are paid per house; folklore says of a warrior:

> . . .a heavy debt imposed on the entire country;
> by fire and by house a sheep in taxes,
> by fire and by house a virgin in taxes . . .
>
> (Sako, p. 16)

In case of war, in northern Albania, each household furnishes one man, without regard as to the total number of members in the household (Hecquard, pp. 28 and 230). The church also considers the household as one unit in a number of cases; thus it can excommunicate the entire domestic group rather than one individual (Durham, 1928, p. 203). In the village assembly, the group is represented by one member; the rights to the commonfield belong to the group and not to individuals (Gjecov, par. 26). Lastly, the entire group, descended from a common ancestor, bears the name of this ancestor; in order to validate its rights to the community property of the village or the tribe, the male ancestors are recalled and mentioned by name (Zojzi, 1977, p. 195). At the level of the household, the members of the group are known by the leader's name.

The domestic group has its own assembly which decides the most important matters, normally meeting in the reception room (Krasniqi, 1971, p. 496). It includes only the men; rarely, on speical occasions, is the woman leader (*zoje shpije* or *bacica*) called to participate (Krasniqi, 1971, p. 495). The male members of the group can dismiss the leader or the woman leader; they carry arms and can dispose of them; they can not present themselves as guarantors without the leader's authorization, nor work outside without his approval. They are also prevented from buying and selling, and they must obey him and to go war if they are sent (Gjecove, par. 24 and 25).

### Women

"A woman, as long as she is in her husband's house, is considered to be like a small goatskin which bears up under weights and strains" (Gjecov, p. 29). She is "a living object meant to carry objects, have children, and look after the housework, while in her father's house, she is merely excess weight" (Nova, 1977, p. 278). At the time of her birth, "even the joists of the house weep," since she was not expected and because a boy would have been preferable (Nova, 1977, p. 278). "The code (of Lek Dukagjin) considers a woman as a superfluous object" (Gjecov, par. 20).

She does not participate in the household assembly; she can not figure as a witness, nor be a judge (Gjecov, par. 1227), nor vote, and she does not inherit anything (Zojzi, 1972, pp. 35-36). During a marriage ceremony, or another celebration, the women are grouped separately, dance separately; they have a separate area in the church or the mosque (Sako, 1970, p. 215). The bride is first congratulated by the men, classed according to their degree of kinship to the couple, and then by the women, always in an order which conforms also to their degree of kinship (Mitrushi, 1976, p. 158). The two sexes attend funerals in separate groups; moreover, "if the deceased is a man, he is mourned by his friends from all the tribes; if a woman dies, only close relatives grieve" (Cozzi, 1909, p 913). And as if that were not enough, there is no real mourning for a woman (Cozzi, 1909, p. 918). Her husband is allowed to beat, tie up, and punish her.

Her only apparent advantage is that she is not implicated in the vendettas: "She travels alone during the night or day, anywhere without fear of being offended in any way. In fights which pit tribes against another, and in which she participates with the men, she is sure to be spared by the enemy gun" (Cozzi, 1912, p. 311).

She is known as "her husband's wife" and bears his name (Hasluck, 1954, p. 33); she was known before as "her father's daughter," a situation which, in this respect, is the same in all of eastern Europe. Cozzi (1912, p. 323), asserts that she can continue, even after her marriage, to be called "daughter of a particular family or tribe," based on her native tribe.

a) At the beginning of the 19th century Hobhouse (1813, p. 145) affirmed: "Their women, who are almost all of them without education, and speak no other than their native tongue, are considered as their cattle, and are used as such, being, except the very superior sort, obliged to labor, and often punished with blows. They have, in truth, rather a contempt, and even, occasional inclinations, which can be said to partake of what we call the tender passion. Yet all of them get married who can, as it is a sign of wealth, and as they wish to have a domestic slave. Besides, as in most parts of the country, the females are not nearly so numerous as the other sex, the bride often does not bring a portion to her husband, but the man to his wife, and he is obliged to get together about a thousand piastres, before he can expect to be married. A young fellow, being asked by us if he was going to get a wife, shook his head, and said he was not rich enough. Some time afterwards he came to us in great glee with a letter in his hand from his father, part of which he read to us, couched in these very words: 'I wish you to come home—I have got a wife for you.' Just as if he had said, 'I have got a cow for you.'"

The purchase of the bride is frequently mentioned and is certainly a custom which must have been widely known. To this characteristic, it must be added that the marriage is often decided at the moment of birth of a boy or a girl, the case described by Mary Durham (1935, p. 93) being fairly typical; a Catholic from the Hoti region "He pointed to a swaddled babe in the cradle and said, with pride, that he had just sold her. . . . He would not send her away till she was sixteen. Some did at twelve or thirteen, but it was not healthy. Nor would he let a youth have a wife before eighteen, unless the houses needed another woman to do the work. Then a boy of fifteen or sixteen might be married. But it was better not. I met two men once who looked like brothers. They were father and son. The father was thirty and the son fifteen. The father said that when he was just fifteen he had been married to a woman of twenty-eight." Parents who decide the purchase, consider henceforth that their children are engaged: "children of both sexes are engaged in the cradle, without being permitted to see or get to know one another during the years of innocence, nor when they mature. It frequently happens that the engaged couple ignores the fact that they are promised, a similar disposition being deemed their parents' business and secret, who will inform their children of this prearranged marriage only when it seems appropriate. When the time arrives, usually around twelve years of age for girls and eighteen for boys, the future father sends one of his relatives to the fiancee's house to call for the conclusion of the marriage" (Pouqueville, 1826, III, p. 260). "The poor young girls, without knowing it, are sold by the parents like animals, to those asking for them. Quite a few irregularities result from this situation; among other things, the woman is considered a purchased object, and if her husband dies, she remains in the family a part of the inheritance" (Valentini, 1969, p. 11; see also p. 39).

The agreements arranged by the parents are not always respected, either due to the parents themselves or to the children. Girls especially reject, in different ways, a marriage that they do not desire. The most common form of rejection is to run away and seek protection from another family, which, given the Albanian custom, can not refuse anyone protection under its roof. A Catholic priest states in a report written in 1897: "Vat

Preni had sold a daughter as a bride to someone from Puka; but she fled and does not want any part of that husband, and if Vat Preni does not deliver her, he will fall in bloody hands," that is to say, fall victim to a vendetta (Valentini, 1969, p. 171).

In fact, the person who sells a daughter and who receives money in exchange, must deliver her to her future husband; moreover, he is even held responsible if his daughter, once married, leaves her husband, and flees, even if she does not return to her parents' house; they are obligated to bring her to her husband. ". . . the woman's family is obligated to justify before her husband her running away, or face the consequences of a vendetta" (Valentini, 1969, p. 181). "Often women who are tyranized by their husbands run away and live with someone else . . . resulting in vendettas, illegitmate children, a curse from heaven" (Valentini, 1969, p. 11; a comprehensive presentation is found in Dojaka, 1982, pp. 3. sq.).

Another aspect linked to the custom of selling daughters must be mentioned: ". . . young girls, already promised in marriage, frequently run away from their home and seek refuge with their finance, or even in another house" (Valentini, 1969, p. 191). The explanation of this is given later on in the same document: "The father does not permit the girl to go out of the house before the husband pays the entire agreed upon sum; and since the peasants are rather poor, following the engagement, eight or even ten years can pass before the full sum is paid and the marriage is finally celebrated."

It also occurs that the girl quite simply refuses to get married: ". . . the father of the poor girl, having agreed upon a price, sold her; and the husband took her despite her opposition, hoping that she would change her mind. Three or four months this unfortunate girl remained with the man she detested without changing her mind and still persisting in her refusal to marry him; she was cruelly beaten several times, but she remained firm in her conviction" (Valentini, 1969, p. 12). Another girl, whose brother had an implacable hate against his sister, who did not want to marry the person her brother had chosen for her, had run away to be with another man. For this reason, the situation gave rise to a questionof blood (a vendetta). The brother of the fugitive, who had kept her bride's clothes, had moreover obligated the husband to pay him a large sum of money if he did not want to be killed" (Valentini, 1969, p. 228).

It should be made clear that a good part of the money paid by the future husband will come back to him in the form of his wife's dowry

(Hasluck, 1933). Mark Krasniqi, therefore, does not see the situation as one of a true purchase, since the money received by the girl's parents will be used to buy clothes and presents for the bride and groom (1979, pp. 158 sq.). The Orthodox Church tries to intervene in these types of transactions by forbidding, or at least limiting, the price paid for a woman (Papastathis, 1974, p. 190); the Catholic church tries the same intervention of which numerous examples are mentioned by Valentini (1969). More rare is the situation where an exchange of women seems to have existed; for example, in 1900, the family of Pren Doci, "the most important family of Rienzi, rich, famous, including more than 35 people . . . was in the process of celebrating two marriages on the same day with another important family with which it had exchanged two spouses, one was coming, the other leaving" (Valentini, 1969, p. 213).

The case of kidnapped women should also be mentioned: "And this situation is at the root of the hate and crimes which reciprocally take place in those poor tribes (Nikai and Merturi), each one of which had stolen women from the other, married or not; and, being unable to find their women, resort to a gun and kill relatives or members of the abductor's tribe' (Valentini, 1969, p. 196).

In citing one of Cozzi's manuscripts, Valentini (1945, pp. 66-67) adds that: "The sons or the male members of a family can only marry, one after the other, by order of age, so that the youngest must wait until all of his older brothers are married, except in the case where the eldest willingly renounces his right." This situation is verified by Krasniqi's research (1971, p. 497) which affirms that the order is even respected by girls as well. "Apart from this manner, no one can be married except an orphan having neither mother nor father." Valentini (1945, p. 67) adds that in Scutari, the same rules are observed, except for the eldest child to whom the responsibility of th domestic group has been given and who must "wait to marry until he marries and appropriately endowed, at least his sisters, creating a situation where it is not rare to see these people marry at a later age." This practice is comparable to one observed in Crete, where sometimes the brothers wait until their sisters marry first, and, in addition, they are obligated to suitably endow them. Quite a few of these aspects of marriage in the past are reflected in Albanian folklore (Haxhihasani, 1977, pp. 207 sq.).

In an exhaustive study, Alfred Uçi (1970) studies the recent evolution of the family in Albania and the situation of women. In a survey focusing

on the wage-earners of an industrial firm, the following information is
noted: 20% of those polled had a free choice in deciding whom to marry;
18% said their parents took the initiative in arranging the marriage, and
62% of the cases reported matchmakers had intervened (p. 149). In the
village of Reshen, 44% chose their mate, 30%, the parents and 26% stated
their marriages were arranged through the intervention of a matchmaker
(p. 150). The expressed criterion of the choice also seem to have changed;
for example, 58% of those persons questioned place honesty and the moral
purity of life first among desired qualities for a spouse (p. 150). Marriages
uniting people separated by a great age difference tend to disappear (p.
155); the most common length of marriages is between 20 and 30 years
(p. 158). Yllka Selimaj (1982, p. 227) studies marriage in the coastal
plains of northern Albania, and among other things, the age of marriage
of young girls. The number of girls who marry between 16 and 19 years
old changed from 56.6% in 1950 to 24.3% in 1979, while girls marrying
between the ages of 20 and 24 jumps from 33.3% to 70% over the same
period of time. It is therefore a question of an obvious change which allows girls to marry later, a situation which moreover corresponds to other
peasant or urban societies in Europe.

Divorce, in turn, necessitates several remarks. In the past, it was above
all the man who "was authorized to cut (from his wife) a lock of hair or
a bow from her belt and send her away. . . . There are two causes for
which a woman may be killed . . . for adultery and for the betrayal of
a guest" (Gjecov, p. 31). The grounds for divorce change (Dojaka, 1982,
pp. 3 sq.), and also the procedure. Women also ask for divorce; in 1968,
the proportion is reversed, since there are 1007 men who request divorces
and 1056 women (Jejdiaj, 1976, p. 124). All these changes, as with the
changes in general affecting women's position in contemporary society,
are considered by Uçi as being due to general changes in Albanian society.
Thus, the fact that men change professions (and become workers, civil
servants), that farming, still dominant within the country, becomes collectivized (Uçi, pp. 143-144) and that private property and religious life
disappears (the same, p. 147) directly influenced marriage (see also Gjergji,
1970; Dojaka, 1977, pp. 217 sq.).

b) It is not possible to give a simple answer to the question of a woman's
situation after marriage. Three groups come into play, the first of which is
the idea of the purchase. A woman can be bought and paid for, but a good

part of the money received will be returned to the husband in the form of a dowry and presents that his family receives. Other observations seem to confirm the fact that the woman is not sold; the husband can only kill his wife if she violates the abovementioned cases, since in any other situation, he must justify his actions to his wife's family, who in turn will seek revenge on him or his group (Gjecov, par. 61). The son no longer can kill his mother while his mother belongs to her native group. The customary code collected by Gjecov (par. 61) affirms that if an outsider harms or kills a woman, her honor is avenged by her husband, but injuries and death by the woman's kin. The code moreover clarifies this point by stating that "the husband purchases a woman's work and a life to be shared with her, but not her life" (Gjecov, par. 28). Other recorded customs in other Albanian provinces confirm these findings (Zojzi, 1977, p. 190).

It is in this sense that I interpret the situation to be leviratic, a frequent occurrence in past Albanian society, inspite of the opposition of the church where Christians were present. "The consider the woman as bought; if the husband dies, she remains with the family as an inherited object and she is taken by the brother of the deceased or by another member of the house" (Valentini, 1969, p. 11). Admittedly, the fact that someone paid to have a wife and to benefit from her services, favors levirate. It should also be noted that a large number of men who die young in the vendettas, often put a group in a position to practice levirate. Degrand (1901, p. 166) affirms that only 30% of the men in Upper Albania die from illness or old age, the rest are killed. Several decades later, in 1929, Coon (1950, p. 27) notes once again the importance of violent deaths. Figures regarding several regions of northern Albania, collected for the years 1854-1856, and published by Hecquard (1862, p. 378) agree with what has just been said.

In their reports, Catholic priests of northern Albania often mention levirate, since, forbidden by the church, it does not allow for a religious marriage and gives rise to cohabitation. The opposition to custom and canon law results in numerous disputes with interminable endeavors and interventions by the Church and local leaders. The texts published by Valentini are eloquent (1969, under the term "levirato"). It was even more common among the Moslems (Durham, 1928, p. 202), and considered a normal situation since their religion did not prevent them from having, for example, a second wife; ritualistic differences separate the first marriage from subsequent ones. "Of the 213 families (households) that made up the Merturi tribe, more than fifty, or one quarter of the tribe, were excommunicated for having given their daughters to the Turks, or because they kept their sister-in-law, their aunt or another woman in a sinful manner (Valentini, 1969, p. 123).

The widow of a deceased brother, cousin or uncle can be taken (Durham, 1928, p. 203; the same, p. 461; Cabej, 1934, p. 223; Coon, 1950, p. 25; Valentini, 1969, p. 38). It is the closest relative of the deceased who seems to have the right to marry the widow (Durham, 1910, p. 461), but the fact that someone had not been married must have had a bearing. "If a woman is not married by one of the husband's relatives, she can not marry a second time in the same village without the permission of her husband's family, a permission which, in the mountains of Pulati, was never granted. If this was disobeyed, a vendetta would result, the mountain people considering it a disgrace to see the wife of one of their relatives taken by one of their fellow citizens" (Hecquard, 1861, p. 386). The wife, "upon the death of her husband can neither remarry nor return to her family without the permission of the family of the deceased, otherwise killings and terrible vendettas would result . . . there would be great displeasure and dishonor if she were to marry someone else, especially someone considered to be an enemy; thus, the family of the deceased takes her for itself, and consequently, there is no more need for additional expenditures in order to find another wife" (Valentini, 1969, p. 16; see also p. 120).

The fact that more boys are born than girls (and this is in an unusual proportion for other European regions) also explains why it is difficult to find a young man a wife and why the easiest woman to obtain is taken.

c) "The Albanians, in public, display a great indifference toward their women, and especially toward their own wife" (Cozzi, 1912, p. 310). For the husband, "he is not permitted by etiquette to show any familiarity toward his wife, who, in exchange, gives an impression of not being interested in her husband. Especially during the first years of marriage, the husband must use a master's tone when speaking to his wife, who shows that the sentiments she has for her husband are out of respect rather than affection . . . like the Easterners, an Albanian will never directly ask news about someone's wife; and if he is forced to give proof out of deference or friendship, he will not speak to her directly, but will find a periphase or a metonymy" (Cozzi, 1912, p. 312). The wife "refrained for several years after her marriage from speaking at all to her husband in public and spoke to him in whispers only in private, meanwhile keeping her eyes modestly downcast" (Hasluck, 1954, p. 31). She could not even call her husband by his name (Sako, 1970, p. 214).

A woman never eats next to her husband, especially when there are guests (Cozzi, 1912, p. 312). "No tribesmen eats with his wife; and the odd custom still prevails of a married couple never addressing each other by name. To eat with a woman seems to be thought very degrading. The men eat first and the women eat at up the bits left over afterwards at the other end of the room or, if Moslem, in their own quarters" Durham, 1910, p. 460). This statement is further enhanced by another character-istic indication taken from an account of Mary Edith Durham's travels throughout the Albanian regions, upon her stop in Vuthaj, "where they had never before entertained a strange female, there was a very long pow-wow as to the correct course to pursue. It was decided I was far too important to feed with the harem. I was to rank as a man and feed with the chiefs. But to satisfy their sense of fitness I was helped last of all, even after my horse-boy, and so honour was satisfied" (1923, p. 84).

In well-to-do Moslem houses, the receiving room often has a small room located next to the one where the men gather. During times of celebrations, the two sexes eat separately, the women can hear and even catch a glimpse of the men through a wooden wall made out of inter-secting lath which leaves small open spaces. In Christian societies, where men are served first, "while a man drinks, the mistress of the house or the most recently married of the sisters-in-law must remain standing with her hands on her chest . . . if the refreshments are brought by a servant, she presents them on bended knees. . . . " (Degrand, 1901, p. 27; see also p. 24). Pouqueville (1926, III, pp. 261-262) summarizes all of these find-ings in a short passage which describes the situation of a new bride. Once she has arrived in her spouse's house, "she bows in order to kiss his hand, and she places at his feet a sack and a piece of cord in order to express that she is destined to carry the loads and to keep the household sup-plies." During the first month after the marriage ceremony, she gains some privileges. "After this time, the privileges cease; and after having removed the nuptial headband, the wife is only allowed at her husband's table during special yearly celebrations, and can feed herself only with the leftovers from the meal. During the trips, with her back loaded with the cradle which holds the newborn, she follows her husband on foot, whose gun she also carries on her shoulder, while he, crouching down on his mule, smokes and meditates tranquilly" (the same, pp. 261-62).

The picture which has just been described strongly resembles the situation of the Montenegrin woman; the fact that the Montenegrin population includes numerous Albanians who have come under Slavic influences, certain tribes being part Albanian and part Slavic, the fact that these two societies are in direct contact and especially given that they have the same social organization, accounts for the similarities. The lines which follow only serve to confirm the parallels that one can draw from these two societies.

d) The woman's situation, even though it is difficult all throughout her life, does not show an obvious improvement at the time of the birth of a son (Cabej, 1934, p. 223).

". . .a good man, who as of yet had no sons from his marriage, begged me during a celebration of mass to tell him if a person who had no sons was really saved since, he said, everyone tells him that there is no way to be allowed into heaven without them" (Valentini, 1969, p. 17). Having a son is essential for life after death, since he is the one who will take care of your soul; and it is always the son who carries on with the life of the household; he also inherits the property, goes to war, defends you, and also avenges you. The birth of a daughter is not a happy event (Nova, 1977, p. 278; Mitrushi, 1982, p. 136): "If the birth of a son is greeted by the parents and friends with gun shots, a sign of joy, and all the neighbors overflow with congratulations to the parents and endless wishes for happiness for the newborn, the birth of a daughter is a true disillusion for the parents" (Cozzi, 1912, p. 314). Even the mother has the same attitude, since "she doesn't value her beauty as much as she does her sons, who consitute her sole ambition and who love her more than they do their father" (Cozzi, 1912, p. 325; see also Cabej, 1934, p. 219). Wishes expressed at birth are significant (Selimi, 1981, p. 149); for a boy, one says to the mother "bless you," "God is delighted with you," "may your son grow in fortune," "may your child grow old and bearded." For a girl, "be happy you're saved," "it doesn't matter, she who bears daughters can also bear sons." The information furnished by Krasniqi (1979, p. 30 sq.) and especially Coon's findings confirm that there are more boys born than girls.

A woman must bring children into the world, especially boys, since "so many men are killed before they reach maturity, therefore women must produce boys. The birth of girls is less important because they are not killed, and because they leave the family to get married" (Coon, 1950, p. 22). Fertility was, in the past, a condition sine qua non of marriage, because "the woman is a sack intended to carry (children)" ". . . everyday experience proves that the woman was judged first by her fertility, especially in giving birth to sons, and second by her self-effacement, her work, leaving last any consideration of her charm" (Valentini, 1945; p. 37). "As in other regions of Albania, also among the Lage of Muzeqe, a couple's sterility was believed to be the woman's fault" (Mitrushi, 1972, p. 135). This was a generally accepted idea throughout the past; the moment a man is able to have sexual relations with his wife, any absence of children must be attributed to the woman, male sterility being unknown.

The sterile woman is designated by specific names, such as *"beronje"* —sterile (Nova, 1977, p. 277), or *"barkthare"*—dry belly (Mitrushi, 1972, p. 135). Even if she bears girls, the marriage contract is not considered fulfilled. In both cases, total sterility, or the absence of boys, she can be sent back to her family and a second wife, or even a third, can be taken to replace her (Hahn, 1854, p. 150; Cabej, 1934, p. 223; Durham, 1935, p. 93; Mitrushi, 1972, p. 135; Nova, 1977, p. 277). "A man, also Orthodox, sent away his wife because she was childless, and married another. Then, pluming himself on his *"trumni"*—'fighting abilities,' he demanded the return of his first wife's bride-price, and failing to secure its return, threatened to shoot any man who tried to marry her" (Hasluck, 1933, p. 192). "Some reject her, however, and exact the return of half the bride-price, or another girl from the same family" (idem, p. 19).

There is also another way to procede; a woman is brought to the house and then everyone waits to see if she will bear children, especially boys (Cabej, 1934, p. 219; Coon, 1950, p. 24; Hasluck, 1933, p. 193). Mary Edith Durham (1910, p. 459) reproduces a passage taken from a report written in 1702 by an archbishop in the Catholic area of northern Albania: "Among the execrable customs of the mountain people, the wretched parents are in the habit of buying young girls for a price for their sons who are of tender age, and of keeping them in their houses till of age of cohabitation, and of omitting to contract matrimony unless a male child is born, even after fifteen years of sinful cohabitation."

One consequence of these practices is bigamy an even trigamy, forbidden by the Christian religion but practiced just the same, "Nue Luka has two wives, the second of whom gave two sons" (Valentini, 1969, p. 171); in a report concerning the Nijaj and Merturi groups, a Catholic priest states that "at present in our *bajrak* (territorial military organization), there are 45 houses where concubines are living" (Valentini, 1969, p. 197); a young girl left a widow is taken as a second wife by her brother-in-law (idem, p. 59); in one parish alone, there are 27 pairs of concubines (idem, p. 1). One of the reports written by priests and published by Valentini (1969, pp. 16-17) is explicit: "The mountain people considered it a great misfortune to have no sons, and they would pay anything, or would accept any proposals, in order to have the assurance that they would have someone to carry on after them. If the legitimate wife does not bear children, another one is taken, and then a third, if need be in order to fulfill this desire. If a wife can be found without going outside the house, for example, a widowed sister-in-law, it's all the better, she will be taken." Coon (1950, p. 23) includes in studies he made of the region where Moslems, those considered Orthodox, or Catholics had several wives and he also finds that those regularly practicing the three religions may have several wives. He also analyzes the reasons for this situation, in order to reach the conclusions already cited, the primary reason being that the woman has not born children, and the second that she has only born girls.

In order to conclude this chapter, a curious practice noted by Cozzi (1910, p. 674) should be mentioned: "In the mountains included in the Pulati diocese, there is this type of abuse, when a widow is pregnant following the death of her husband. Even after two or three years, in order to avoid dishonor, she declares that she is pregnant by the deceased, and the son who is born remains a legitimate child belonging to the family of the deceased husband. This practice is also found among the Moslems. . . . This physiological trick is only allowed for four or five years. This abuse which obviously serves to cover up immorality, is referred to in the mountains as 'bar vrane'." I am inclined to link this practice with a practice widely known in Roman antiquity, for example, where the widow takes up with a close relative of her husband and where the child who is born is considered to be a child of the deceased (Fustel de Coulanges, 1943, p. 53).

e) A particularly unique situation occurs when girls do not follow a normal destiny, that is to say, when they do not marry and bear children. They remain virgins forever after having taking an oath in a church or a mosque to never marry. They are referred to among the Mosles as *"sadik,"* a word of Turkish origin which signifies just, honest (Nova, 1977, p. 279); the most frequent name used is *"vergjinesha"* (Cozzi, 1912, p. 318) or *"virgjin"* (Gjergji, 1979, p. 13). Twelve cojurors, members of the same village or tribe, take an oath at the same time, as witnesses and guarantors (Durham, 1928, p. 194; the same, 1935, p. 93; Coon, 1950, p. 24; Gjergji, 1963, p. 290).

Once the ceremony has been performed, the girl leaves the rank of young girls and assumes a position which comes closer to that of the men. The reasons which prompt a girl to make this type of decision are varied: the desire to avoid a marriage arranged by her parents which does not suit her; the death of the parents and the responsibility which fall to her to take care of her sisters and younger brothers; the absence of boys and the parent's desire to have a helper live with them (Valentini, 1945, p. 29; Garnett, 1917, p. 24; Coon, 1950, p. 25).

Contrary to the other women, she can keep her paternal property during her lifetime; if she is the only child, she keeps the entire property, if not, she shares it with her brothers (Garnet, 1917, p. 24; Cozzi, 1912, p. 318; Durham, 1910, p. 460); she can be the mistress of the household (Gjergji, 1963, p. 290; Hahn, 1854, p. 183); she participates in men's assemblies (Degrand, 1901, p. 155; Nova, 1977, p. 179); Gjecov mentions the presence of virgins in men's assemblies but adds that they do not have the right to vote (par. 1228). They dress differently, either wearing men's clothing or only changing a part of their dress to resemble that of a man's (Degrand, 1901, p. 155; Durham, 1928, p. 211; Cabej, 1934, p. 223; Coon, 1950, p. 24; Gjergji, 1963, p. 290; the same, 1979, p. 13; Gjecov, par. 1228; Nova, 1977, p. 279); she carries weapons (Degrand, 1901, p. 155; Cabej, 1934, p. 223; Coon, 1950; Gjergji, 1963, p. 290; Gjecov, par. 1228; Nova, 1977, p. 279); she eats her meals together with the men (Durham, 1910, p. 460; the same, 1928, p. 211) and smokes with them (Durham, 1910, p. 460; Cozzi, 1912, p. 319; Nova, 1977, p. 279). She participates in war and even in vendettas (Bourcart, 1921, p. 205; Gjergji, 1963, p. 290; Nova, 1977, p. 279); sometimes, under a man's cap, she shaves her head like men (Cozzi, 1912, p. 319; Nova, 1977, p. 279).

Andromaqi Gjergji even mentions cases where the girl changes her name (1963, p. 290). The behavior of the virgins, just as the distinct sign of their dress, is not the same everywhere, differences according to regions appear even in their status. Mary Edith Durham notes the presence of these virgins among Montenegrin tribes of Albanian origin (1928, p. 211) and adds that pressures are exerted on them in certain cases in oder to prevent them from becoming sworn virgins (Durham, 1935, p. 94). Coon (1950, p. 24) evokes the eventuality where a virgin breaks her oath and marries, for which she is to be burned alive; but he immediately notes that no such cases are known to exist.

A separate situation exists in the Catholic region of northern Albania, especially in the neighborhood of the city of Shkodra (Cabej, 1934, p. 223). Degrand describes the situation: "There exists another situation offered to a young Catholic Albanian girl: she can become a *'monaca'* (tertiary); when she declares that she gives up her right to marry, and wants to become a monaca, the young girl is free to go out, to be present during visits by her parents, with whom she continues to live, and her semi-religious situation is indicated by her dress, for which jewels, embroidery and garish colors are strictly outlawed; she must oberve three days of lean diet per week, Tuesdays, Fridays, and Saturdays, for reading of various prayers, an obligation from which she frees herself rather generally. As for her rank, she comes after her mother and has a step on her sisters-in-law" (1901, pp. 31-32). More numerous details are given by Cozzi who also indicates that they have a particular name: *"murgesha"* or *"morga"* (Cozzi, 1912, p. 321). In a document that he found in the parish archives of Shoshi, it is stated that in 1715, several young girls, having decided to become nuns and to remain virgins, had their house that they had constructed destroyed by the Catholic hierarchy and were subsequently sent back to their homes. "Once this assembling was stopped, the custom of becoming a nun was not for all that wiped out. Numerous engaged young girls without their consent having reached majority, wanting to shirk an arbitrary marriage, died their clothes black, wore a cord like the former nuns of Santa Chiara, which causes a lot of comment among the people. . . . One day they presented themselves in church in the midst of a group of assembled people and took a vow of chastity" (Cozzi, 1912, p. 320). But the practice quickly vanishes, except in rare cases: "In the city of Scutari, there were many such *murgesha* clothed entirely in black, veiled with a shawl of the same color. The past year (1910), however, the leaders of the Christian community of the city came up with a law according to which it was henceforth forbidden for girls to declare themselves nuns, except for those who enter a convent. Those who are already nuns could continue to be such and to wear the black shawl; but the *murgesha* who went out of the house wearing a *čarčaf,* a little white sheet, instead of this shawl, were indicating to every-one that they wanted to get married" (Cozzi, 1912, p. 321).

### Property and Work

Two kinship forms are distinguished in relationship to sex: the blood tree (*"lisi i gjakut"*) which shows the kin of the men, and the milk tree (*"lisi i tamlit"*) showing those of women (Valentini, 1945, p. 24; Dojaka, 1979, p. 76; Tirtja, 1982, p. 81; Gjecov, par. 700 and 701). A testimony recorded in the northern Mallesies states: "If you put two children of two lineages together, and take a bone from the ancestors' tomb of each one of them, when a prick is made which draws blood, you will see that the blood of each one of the ancestors attracts the blood of his heir, not the other" (Tirtja, 1982, p. 89).

Sons and daughters are thought of in different manners; the son is the column of the house (*"shtylla e konakut"*), the daughter, simply a re-minder (*"teprice"*) (Zojzi, 1972); the man is "a shoot from the trunk," the woman is "the daughter of others" (the same). Once a woman ar-rives in her husband's family, she is "a foreign daughter" (*bije e hauj*) and to his original family, she is henceforth known as a "distant daughter" (*bije e dale*). "When death comes to the last male representative of a family, whose name dies with him, the fireplace in his bedroom is de-stroyed, and in its stead, a bundle of thorns is placed, a window in the house is boarded up, the trees in the garden are cut down, the flowers are pulled up" (Degrand, 1901, p. 52).

Property is tied to the blood line; in other words, to men; the entire explanatory system which justifies this affirmation, at the same time eliminates women who do not pass along the blood line, nor, as a result any property.

Despite the fact that the land belongs to men, women take an active role in farming and this is in addition to the work that they carry out in the house itself. Quotations concerning this issue abound: "The land is very carefully cultivated by the entire family, but above all by the women, with very primitive plows whose plowshares are wooden covered in iron" (Bourcart, p. 174). The wooden plow, still common at the beginning of the 20th century, is also mentioned by Cozzi (1910 B, p. 39). Hobhouse adds: "in may parts of the country the sowing and reaping of the harvest is delegated to the women, the old and the infirm, and only those labours which require the strength and skill of man, such as the felling of timber, and the cultivation of the vineyard, fall to the lot of the young mountaineer" (1813, p. 140; see also Pouqueville, 1826, III, p. 272; Gopčević, p. 308; Dojaka, 1976, p. 114). Clarifications concerning the divisions of agricultural labor between men and women are given by Margaret Hasluck: "Her husband did heavy work like ploughing, sything hay, or cutting oak leaves for winter fodder. But she must carry manure from the stable to the fields in spring, help her husband to sow and earth up the maize and, while he stayed indoors, reap it. She must carry home the hay and fodder and feed them to the animals. If grain was trodden out by horses or oxen, her husband drove them; if threshed with flails, she wielded them. If there was no miller, she conveyed the grist to the mill, ground it and brought back the flour" (1954, p. 26; see also Krasniqi, 1982, p. 47). Spiro Shkurti adds that it is especially in the regions of Orthodox and Catholic denominations that women take care of the harvest (1979, p. 58); he includes a map of Albania in his study on which a distinction is made between harvests carried out by a man, a woman, or by the two together (p. 71).

The fact that this society is one in which the vendetta is a reality is considered one of the factors which accounts for the women taking care of the farming, since the men are obligated to shut themselves up in the house (Bourcart, 1901, p. 204; Degrand, 1901, p. 165). The men "excused their comparative idleness by saying that, in Turkish times, when blood feuds raged, it had been death for most of their faces outside in the daytime. . . . They claimed that when blood feuds grew rare, they become more industrious" (Hasluck, 1954, p. 28). The situation of the woman who works more than the man continues, even if to a lesser degree (Gjergji, 1970, p. 205). It is interesting to note that the money earned is handed over to the woman who is in charge of keeping it (Gjergji, 1970, pp. 206-207), seemingly introducing a change from the past.

The fact that the woman must carry various things (food for the family or for the animals, wood, her husband's weapons, and so forth) establishes a connection in this respect with the Albanian and Montenigrin woman (Cozzi, 1912, p. 313; Degrand, 1901, p. 87).

Property includes, as seen elsewhere, two major categories: the arable land under the domain of the household, and the commonfield. The land is cultivated with techniques which resemble past practices in other Balkan populations. For example, the land is fertilized with animal dung; the herd sleeps during the night within a mobile enclosure which is moved from place to place during the day (Cozzi, 1910 B, p. 39), thus fertilizing the land at the time of their crossing. The alternation of crops is almost unheard of and the tools are of a primitive nature. Mutual aid is widely practiced by working, for example, on holidays, for free, helping someone who does not have oxen, or by lending them their animals (Cozzi, 1910 B, p. 40; Haxhiu, 1977, p. 303; Shkurti, 1979, pp. 53 sq.). The importance of mutual aid is so great, that one of the most dreaded punishments of the mountain people is civil excommunication, often mentioned throughout the past. These decisions made by the village assemblies, for example, place the group being punished in an almost unbearable situation.

Once the harvest is finished, the right of common grazing land comes into effect: "the grounds were transformed into common grazing land beginning with All Saint's Day (the 1st of November) . . . . In these zones, the 1st of November was the absolute deadline for the harvest . . . . After that date, if the yield is not brought in, the livestock can enter the fields, since 'late harvest is for the cows' . . . . The land served as common grazing land until Saint George's Day, a period when the strict property limits were reestablished. This custom was most strongly observed in northern Albania. It was less vigorous in central and southeastern Albania, but gains strength in Labërie and Çamërie, in the south. Here, also the fields, beginning with Saint Demetre's Day (October 26) were left for common grazing ground. This norm was so deep-rooted, that 'when the harvest is brought in autumn, the fellow worker can cut the hay and bring in his livestock, without being stopped, since you have already obtained its yield, and the ground is now considered to be common'" (Shkurti, 1979 A, pp. 59-60; Xhemaj, 1981, p. 91; Hasluck, 1954, p. 55).

The commonfield (*"kujria"*) includes forests, pastures, prairies, rivers, lakes, which can all belong to a lineage, phratry, village, or tribe. The rights to the commonfield are divided by households and not by individuals, for "each dwelling that emitted smoke" (Hasluck, 1954, p. 23). Individual rights are justified by the descent from the male blood line, for a common ancestor (Cozzi, 1910 B, p. 46; Zojzi, 1977, p. 195). Legends concerning the origin of the tribe justify the rights to a particular commonfield (Hecquard, 1862, pp. 181-182; Hahn, 1854, pp. 183-184).

The rights to the commonfield vary according to the land categories. Thus, irrigation canals, even though they are constructed by the man's labor, are considered common property. Gjecov (par. 351-386) mentions irrigation canals, among other things: "The trickle of water, from the fields as well as from the mill, is a collective possession" (par. 359). A priest describes, in 1890, the construction of a certain irrigation network: "In the country, there are two phratries, one belonging to the Thaci tribe and is the largest, the other, the Kabasci, is only made up of twelve families. If in these mountains, there is not irrigation, the entire country goes dry; each region has its canal, a waterway for irrigation. Its sources are the numerous streams and rivers which cross these mountains. The entire country takes part in this work, since the water will benefit everyone and often it must be obtained from great distances, through mountain slopes, over great obstacles; great care is taken to repair the canal each time that it is needed. Once the work is ended and the water brought to the region, it is shared. All the heads of the households gather in an open area and lots are drawn from watering days. Each one takes a small tree branch and gives it to the head of the country; he then mixes the branches in his hand and afterwards begins to lay them on the ground one after the other in the presence of everyone, who watches silently, attentively, to see which day will correspond to his personal branch. . . . If someone draws a day which will not work for him, or who wants to have his water use divided between two days, that agreement is decided with his fellow worker in private . . ." (Valentini, 1969, p. 46). It is interesting to note that the most ancient plan is recognized by all and no one can alter it without everyone's consent.

As with irrigation canals, the same rules apply for mills. Their canals constitute collective property whose use is also determined by the drawing of lots, each household having its day for using the mill (Gjecov, par. 331, 387, 464).

One statistic gathered in 1938 (Shpati, 1945, p. 74) allows us to state that Albania still had at this time 30% of its territory made up of pastures,

and 36% forests, underlining the importance of the commonfield throughout the past when its use was at its height, since pastures and forests made
up the essential elements of the commonfield. "These areas are not divis-
ible, because every family in a village has the right to the community
possessions of the village; every family of a bajrak has the right to the
community possessions of a bajrak. No one, without the consent of the
others, can sell the common patrimony. . . . On community land, no one
can sow, plant vines or gardens, without the consent of the village or
bajrak. Whoever plants a tree in these areas has some rights to it and can
cut it when he wishes. . . but the fruit cannot be gathered and eaten by
anyone, without the owner's permission" (Gjecov, par. 232-237).

The crop system for the commonfield is the same as the one described
above for the Romanians: "Whoever wants to install a stable on the
common pastures, by constructing cottages, sheep pens or by opening
a bit of a garden or a field, is allowed to do so, without anyone's inter-
ference; the chosen ground remains his property" (Gjeçov, par. 219).
This paragraph contradicts what has been stated above, but in fact, the
two systems were able to coexist, and a common land can be occupied
by someone else. Sometimes this process is stopped, but in general the
fate of the commonfield is to be progressively transformed into household property, sometimes even with the consent of the elderly who
manage the village (Hasluck, 1954, p. 23; Gjergji, 1982, p. 155).

The pastures constitute an essential part of an economy where animal
breeding occupies an important place. "By looking at the pasture, one
understands these places where only the inhabitants of a certain *bajrak*,
and not another, are allowed to graze their herds" (Gjeçov, par. 281).
Cottages can be built on the pastures (Valentini, 1945, p. 114), either
on common pastures or pastures belonging to households. "This pasture
(*Biescka*) is an entire mountain divided among the households of the
region which have each constructed cottages where they go each year
with their animals during the summer. But, because of the maliciousness
of certain individuals, the borders of these pastures have been moved"
(Valentini, 1969, p. 207); a conflict arises which pits people against
one another. Moreover, the conflicts were frequent, either due to border
disputes (Valentini, 1969, pp. 238 and 241), or due to the fact that
one household or another was trying to transform them into private
property. "Do you see those hills over there, and beyond them, the

other larger hills covered by rather large trees? Do you see these meadows and these plains which are not cultivated? All of that is the area we call *meraa*. Our fathers took care to endow each tribe and each country with *meraa* (commonfield), each one having the right to cut wood for himself and to graze animals on all these meadows without anyone having the right to usurp even a small portion of the ground. . . . Through the indifference of certain village leaders, and also somewhat due to their greed and connivance, several of the stronger families expanded in order to increase their neighboring lands with the forests and the meadows of the *meraa*. . . " (Valentini, 1969, pp. 238-239; see also pp. 253-254; Zojzi, 1977, p. 198; Gjeçov, par. 277 sq.). Cozzi notes that when collective pastures are to be set up, the different animal owners wait until everyone is present so as to set them up at the same time and avoid unfairness (1910 B, p. 43); these same precautions are also found among the Armân sheperds (Triantaphyllou, 1983).

Conflicts which arise over commonfield possessions sometimes end up with the forced occupation of a piece of ground by a group which is stronger than the others (Elezi, 1977, p. 237).

As is the case elsewhere in Europe, the forest offers multiple advantages for hunting, harvesting of fruit, wood, and honey from wild bees. But the two principal occupations of the past, the development of the agriculture and animal breeding also find their place in the forest. This explains why fires are set in the forests, in order to thus obtain land for cultivation or pasture use. Shepherds in Albania, it seems, destroyed many forests by fire. The animal herds "are guilty of worst devastation, destroying, like the carelessly lit fires set by the shepherds, the great Albanian forest, a great source of life and richness" (Bourcart, 1921, p. 177; see also Durham, 1928, p. 74; Cozzi, 1910 B, pp. 42-44). The goats destroy the forests by devouring the young trees and sprouts.

When observing the means by which property is kept, it must first be mentioned that the woman does not inherit real property possessions, and second, that her dowry does not include land. Gjeçov (par. 88-98) gives two reasons which justify this situation: the desire to prevent nephews from settling in the maternal uncle's house, and if there is no male offspring, a need to prevent confusion concerning the blood lines. The result is that blood related households will have their land next to one another, without an outsider coming between them. Next, preemtive right should be mentioned (Valentini, 1945, p. 115; Hecquard, 1962, p. 384; Gjeçov, par. 464); at the time of a sale, it is the close relatives, distant relatives, neighbors, and finally members of the phratry or tribe who have the right of purchase. Outsiders cannot buy property except in a case where no one from the above listed groups presents himself. In spite of everything, conflicts can erupt: "A Christian from Lufai wanted to sell his land, but before selling it to anyone outside the group, as proscribed by Albanian and Turkish law, he offered his land to insiders first; thus if someone wanted to acquire it, he was able to do so before other competitors. After having waited a month, and having had no response from within, he concluded a bill of sale with a group from Božić in an attempt to keep them from taking possession of the land" (Valentini, 1969, p. 249).

The belief that only blood heirs have access to property is so deep-rooted that one evisions that they are also the only ones who can discover a treasure buried by their ancestors (Degrand, 1901, p. 291). If someone dies without male heirs, the next male blood kin inherits his land (Gopčević, p. 302).

Despite all of this, exceptions exist, all the more so since it is a question of regions having lost their tribal nature. We see in these cases processes that have been examined elsewhere, adoption, for example. A sterile couple can, for instance, adopt a child from the husband's brother (Mitrushi, 1972, p. 135; Gjergji, 1976, p. 95). The son-in-law marriage is recorded, whereby a couple without boys sees the husband of their daughter settle in their house (Gjjergji, 1976, p. 95). In Scutari, daughters can inherit in the absence of brothers (Degrand, p. 52). Some domestic groups where there is an absence of consanguinity are mentioned by Mark Krasniqi in the Kosovo region; extremely rare, they are sometimes based on the fraternization of outside people who, through this ritual, which includes the mixture of blood from the two parties, consider themselves as true blood relatives (1982, p. 41).

*The Division of the Household*

The rules which decide the division of possessions of a household at the time of the separation of the domestic group are the same as those described for the numerous domestic groups of the southern Slavs. The reasons for which a group maintains its unity or decides to divide itself also parallel those of the southern Slavs (Hasluck, 1954, pp. 51-52; Krasniqi, 1971, p. 499). "The day of the separation was considered a day of mourning for the family, so much so that close relatives and friends came to offer their condolences, grieving as they would over a death" (Zojzi, 1977, p. 191). The group separates taking into account each person's ancestry; the descendants of each of the brothers of the first generation (forming a "*bark*"—belly) constitute a separate group. The property is divided according to the equal rights of the brothers of the first generation, each brother having the same share; the successors have rights to their ancestor's share, regardless of their number. It is not, there-fore, a question of an equal division of possessions among those people living at the time of the separation, since, at this level, the division appears as unequal; equality only existing at the level of the ancestors (Zojzi, 1977, p. 202).

This form of the principle of equality functions in the domain of inherited land, but does not function for land acquired in the mean time which is divided equally among all men living at the time of the division, since everyone had worked in order to procure these acquisitions (Hasluck, 1954, p. 61). Gjeçov calls those having the right to the division "those who bear arms" (par. 66).

The house and the courtyard must be passed on to the youngest of the brothers (Gjeçov, par. 65). This simple rule can be applied when the group separating is formed by father and sons; when it is a question of a larger group, a skillful division must regulate each person's rights (Muka, 1982, p. 210; Hasluck, 1954, pp. 55-57). If the father is living at the time of the division, he stays with his youngest son (Hasluck, 1954, p. 63 and 66), a situation which recalls the common situation for most of the Balkan regions. The cabins and the sheep pens are divided into as many equal shares as there are equal rights. The division of the land is accomplished first by measuring it, and then dividing it into equal shares taking into account the quality of the land. The youngest is the first to choose his share (Gjeçov, ar. 66); the oldest is the last (Hasluck, 1954, pp. 68-69). If the relationship between the brothers is good, the division of the plots is administered by the oldest son, alone or helped by the elderly members of the group if there are any adversities. The water of the irrigation canals is divided in proportion to the amount of land each brother receives (Gjeçov, par. 67); the right to use the mill is divided like the land, according to the rights of the brothers of the first generation (par. 68). The same principle rules the division of farming tools, household objects, and animals. On the other hand, produce from the fields is divided among the members of the domestic group, men and women, and even children older than one year (Gjeçov, par. 74-78; Hasluck, 1954, p. 59). The access road which leads to the fields is also divided (Hasluck, 1954, pp. 83 sq.). It is important to remember that there is a difference between the principle of the division of real property and animals on the one hand, and work related products on the other, this second category being divided among everyone equally, since everyone worked and everyone must survive until next year's harvest. Cozzi (1912, p. 239) adds that at the time of the repudiation of a woman, she is still entitled to receive her share of food and produce. Mark Krasniqi clarifies the division of property at the time of the separation of the groups of the Kosovo region (1971, pp. 493-497, and 502-503).

## THE PHRATRY (VLLAZNI), THE TRIBE (FIS), THE BAJRAK

The smallest social unit, the household, is presented throughout history, all the while changing its structure. The different collections of customs known among the Albanians prove this (Zojzi, 1956, pp. 144 sq.; Kostallari, 1972, pp. 18 sq.; Elezi, 1977, pp. 235 sq.; Frasheri, 1977, pp. 144 sq.).

The social unit which is immediately superior is, as seen in the Montenegrin region, the phratry "*vellazë rie*" or "*vllazni;*" a tribe is made up of several phratries. Rrok Zojzi (1977, pp. 197-8) who analyzes the structure of these tribes notes that their first division is formed by what is called great phratries ("*Vllazni te medha*") in Malessie Madhe, tribe feet ("*kambe fisi*") in Dukagjin, and units ("*çetë*") in Laberie. The number of ramifications of each tribe differs; each one has its patronymic linked to the name of its founder, real or fictitious eponyms, and is a name which situates them within the tribe itself. Thus they can be called the first foot, the second foot, etc. Exterior signs signal their presence; the Kelmend (or Klementi) combed their hair in the 17th century in four directions, tracing four braids which indicated the four large phratries of the tribe. The large phratries themselves can be divided into smaller phratries ("*vllazni te vogla*").

The superior social unit to that of the phratry is the tribe; its name differs according to regions. In the north, its usual name is *fis*, in the south, *fare* is used (Zojzi, 1977, p. 194; Pouqueville, 1826, III, pp. 245-247 and V, pp. 439-440; Ancel, 1934, I, p. 119). The tribes maintained themselves longer in northern Albania, conserving a certain autonomy vis-a-vis the Ottoman authorities in exchange for the obligation to participate in war if called upon (Kalesi, 1974, pp. 389 sq.). Just as the household or the phratry, the tribe constitutes at the same time a political, economic unit, with its own territory, the whole of which is linked to a common origin and to an ancestral eponym. The element which seems to dominate, at least in terms of beliefs and the explanations of life, is consanguinity, as is the case for Montenegro.

The idea of consanguinity is expressed in terms of kinship; thus, in the household, the men call themselves brothers even if they are not (Hasluck, 1954, p. 30), a situation which brings to the mind the Montenegrin household where cousins even call themselves brothers (Durham, 1928, p. 152). The servants who live in a household consider the master as their father and the daughters as sisters (Hasluck, 1954, p. 34). Among the Albanians, second and third cousins are always called brothers or sisters; elderly people are called by the name uncle and aunt and the young are called nephew and niece by the elderly (Hasluck, 1954, p. 30). This reminds us of the Romanian custom of calling each elderly person in the village uncle (*"unchi"*) and aunt (*"mătușă"*); the young people are called nephew, niece ("nepot," "nepoată"). The custom of calling old persons uncle and aunt is also prevalent among Greeks and Southern Slavs. Mary Edith Durham reports that the members of a tribe, descendants of a single ancestor, consider themselves brothers and sisters (1928, p. 15).

The fact that a person considers himself as blood kin, even if he is far removed from the common ancestor, is normally accompanied by the idea of incest and the banning of any marriage between descendants of the same ancestor. Marriages between members of the same phratry or tribe are therefore forbidden.

Marriages also occur within the mother's original group, called *"gjini"* (Dojaka, 1979, p. 74) but it is a kinship by milk and not by blood. Thus custom forbids marriages in the paternal line much farther than the announcement by the Church, yet marriages are allowed which would be banned by the Church on the side of the maternal lineage, because they are too close. (Dojaka, 1979, pp. 82-83). "Engagements within the *fis* did not take place because they were considered scandalous. Within the *fis*, you are brother and sister; within the *fis*, you are together for holidays, together for funerals" (Dojaka, 1979, p. 80).

The society jealously keeps watch over these bans; in Rapsha, there was the custom of "not contracting marriage with a person of his own tribe, even if it meant with someone one hundred times removed . . . but some from Traboina, from the Hoti tribe, knew a young Moslem belonging to the same Hoti tribe; she ran away with him to Montenegro, where she was baptized and then her marriage was blessed by the Church. The Hoti, instead of rejoicing in this conversion, considered themselves offended because the old Hoti practice of not contracting this type of marmirage had not been upheld and they hunted the young man down with the intention of killing him, obliging him to keep away from his tribe" (Valentini, 1969, p. 225; another case is found on page 258). Rare exceptions, however, do exist: "The phratries of Beriscia and of Merturi formerly constituted, according to tradition, a single tribe, they therefore had a common origin; but through the years, the two phratries grew so apart in terms of kinship, that for several years, the people of Beriscia and of Merturi have been marrying one another as if they were from different tribes, even though in other tribes there is no custom for intertribal marriages since members are considered as brothers with whom one shares the same blood line" (Valentini, 1969, pp. 131-132).

The absolute ban on marrying within the same tribe (Durham, 1910, p. 458; the same, 1935, p. 93; the same, 1928, p. 15; Krasniqi, 1971, p. 501; Dojaka, 1979, p. 76), was observed in numerous regions (Dojaka, 1979, p. 76); it occasionally pertained to several tribes at once, who were considering themselves as descendants of a single ancestor (Dojaka, 1979, p. 77). This rule weakens in towns (Krasniqu, 1974, pp. 34 sq.) and weakens in general as time passes: "Marriages are not granted in the *fis*. In former times, even if the distance between the two families was one hundred generations, this alliance was forbidden. In our day, a limit of 6 generations was set for paternal filiation and for maternal filiation" (Rrok Zojzi, in Dojaka, 1979, pp. 79-80). "In Senice in Delvine, marriage was permitted after seven generations of paternal filiation and five generations of the maternal filiation. In Bolene, on the contrary, marriage was permitted after 6 to 10 generations of paternal filiation and 3 maternal" (Dojaka, 1979, p. 80). At the beginning of the 20th century, the three groups from Mirdites (Orosh, Spac, and Kushnen) did not intermarry considering themselves to be related. "They therefore called an assembly to study the possibilities of marriage, considering that they had adequately distanced themselves from each other for the future. During the debate, a woman from Spaç passed through the neighborhood and greeted them with the name 'brother.' The men who had gathered together for the assembly immediately put an end to their discussions; 'if she calls us brothers, how could we take our sisters as wives?'" (Dojaka, 1979, p. 78).

Forbidden between related tribes, marriage thus becomes preferential with other tribes (Durham, 1928, p. 21; Dojaka, 1979, p. 77).

As is the case elsewhere with societies of the same type, the names of supposed ancestors of the group are kept in memory, and sometimes the names of the ascendants up to the founder are recited by memory. Margart Hasluck affirms that twenty generations of names are remembered for the paternal line and two or three generations for the maternal line (1954, p. 25). This difference is normal if one recalls that kinship is based on the masculine blood line and that rights to property are justified according to each person's position on the male family tree within the entire tribe. These ancestors' names may be mentioned in priests' prayers prayed during the commemoration of the dead, in order to arrive at the founding eponym (Durham, 1909, p. 87).

Several eponymic legends collected in the 19th century were published by Hahn (1854, p. 183), Chopin (1856, pp. 131 sq.) and by Hecquard (1862, pp. 171 sq.). The group of descendants bears the name of the founder in the plural (Hecquard, 1862, p. 177). Certain of these legends start with a common ancestor who gives the name to the entire tribe and continues with his descendants, who, in turn, each given his name to a branch, a region, or a village. The common origin of a tribe is regularly invoked and the authors treating the subject are numerous (Hahn, 1854; Gopčević, pp. 562 sq. and 569 sq.; Durham, 1910, p. 458; Garnet, 1917, p. 21; Bourcart, 1921, p. 205; Zojzi, 1977, p. 189). As is the case for Romanian villages or for the phratries and the tribes of the Southern Slavs, if the common origin includes a portion of the truth, it also includes an element of imagination, even more so when a large group is involved. Common origin is, in fact, first a justification for the solidarity of the group and a justification for the rights to community property.

The facts which prove whether the practice stems from beliefs, where the true and the imaginary intermingle, are numerous; despite everything, men of science also believe in their pure faith (Durham, 1928, p. 15; Zojzi, 1977, p. 190).

Certain tribes believe themselves to be descended from the national Albanian hero, Scanderbeg: "Even though the history of Scanderbeg is well known, the tradition maintained among certain mountain tribes around their genesis is rather interesting, because they claim to be linked to the Kastrioti, a noble Albanian family of the Middle Ages. The Albanian mountain dweller thus brings to light one of the most important factors of his psychology when he links his tribe's origin to well-known names of authority, or to eminent historical figures" (Krasniqi, 1979, p. 276). A parallel can be drawn between this belief and the Romanian legends of Moldavia, where the greatest prince of the region, Stefan cel Mare, appears as the founder of a great number of villages, if not from a biological point of view, at least from a political one, villages about which sometimes the previous origin is known up to the time when this prince reigned.

There are tribes whose multiple origin is clearly known; powerful tribes accept weaker, less numerous groups, and consider them henceforth as brothers; the smaller group considers the most important ancestor of the group as its own ancestor (Dojaka, 1979, p. 80; see also Valentini, 1956, pp. 217-218). The same situation is noted in Montenegro and in similar forms among the Romanians who invent an imaginary ancestor, a relative of their own ancestors, in order to justify the rights of newcomers. Cozzi (in Valentini, 1956, p. 95) mentions cases where a tribe is formed by human groups having a diverse origin: a) "Several of them belong to ancient, primitive inhabitants who occupied a region or a country, and who were later dominated by another tribe which arrived in the area. A good example can be found in the Plani (Plandi) tribe where the local population of Boksi is more ancient according to tradition, since it represents the natives of the region. Seven families from Gjovukajt in the Shoshi tribe are remnants of the primitive inhabitants who, following wars and fights with the Mirdite, abandoned their ancient territory in order to settle in Molik de Rjeka near Gjakova, while two Mirdite brothers gave rise to the current population of the Shoshi. b) Some families descending from other lineages came to settle in the middle of already formed tribes. c) Other families can have their origin from women born in the tribe, married elsewhere, and who, following the death of the husband, return to their original family together with their sons, who once married, give birth to new lineages. Thus according to tradition, thirty families from the Gjani tribe descend from a woman of the tribe, married in Shkreli, and who subsequently returned with her sons to the paternal house. But these cases are rare because children normally remain the property of the husband's family. There are also some tribes which mention more than one founder of the lineage. For example, the Kiri tribe recognizes two founders, one from Peja, the other from Kuçi, in Montenegro; they gave rise to two principal lineages which divide the population of Kiri."

In an excellent study on the remaining tribal customs among the Albanians, Rrok Zojzi (1977, pp. 185 sq.) tells of several concrete traditions. For example, the Mirdites included 4 "feet," first division of the tribe, 28 phratries, 165 *"bark"*—belly (lineages) and 2000 houses. Shale counts four feet, 24 phratries, 82 bark and 600 houses (p. 199). These figures alone justify the practice of imaginary figures. Thus, the founder of the Mirdites, had had four sons who gave four feet; we can rightly presume that he also had some daughters (who are never mentioned in eponymic legends since they neither play a role in consanguinity nor in property), thus the founder had 8 children, to which must be added children born dead and those who died at a young age and before they had the time, in turn, to have their own children. The founder must have been prolific since he therefore presumably had 12 children, a figure which begins to appear exaggerated. As soon as the second generation is reached, we see that each founder of a foot gave birth to an average of 7 phratries (28:4 = 7), therefore, each one had seven boys, to which you add seven girls and seven children who died before giving birth to a lineage, for a total of 21 children. The supposed proliferation here takes on a normal appearance for mice, but certainly an imaginary one for humans. According to the same considerations, the third generation which gives birth to barks, had 18 children on the average per bark founder. These imaginary genealogies are found elsewhere as well, among the Romanians, for example. It should also be added that if these genealogies are taken seriously, one can see that they date back to one or two centuries, which brings up the problem of the non-existence of populations for entire regions (Stahl H.H., 1958, pp. 54 sq.). This obviously becomes false when the eponymic legend has the origin of the village dating back two or three centuries and historic documents prove the existence of the same village much earlier. Hecquard (1862, pp. 234-235) mentions a clear example for the Albanians: "If the Mirdites claim to be descended from the sons of Lech Dukadgini, whose laws bear his name, their tradition has only conserved the memory of a leader existing about one hundred years ago. From that moment on, their tradition reveals a succession of uninterrupted facts and a genealogy without, however, giving one precise date."

A part from the three units mentioned above—household, phratry, tribe—where the idea of consanguinity is accompanied by other elements which make them complete social units, there exist other notions which express consanguinity and give birth to social units, but whose outline is imprecise. One example is the notion of the "*gjini*," already mentioned which designates the relatives on the mother's line, and the "*gjak*," designating the masculine blood relations (Valentini, 1956, p. 87). The name "*bark*"—belly—also indicates the descendants of a single ancestor; the name seems to have had various meanings concerning the number of people that it designates. In fact, the word can refer to an entire phratry, or an entire tribe since they also are descended from one ancestor; but the word also refers to the male members of a domestic group who are descended from a brother of the first generation, the descendants of each brother constituting a bark. In this last case, each *bark* will have one third of the property of the group upon separation if in the first generation there were three brothers. Within a bark, all are considered brothers and sisters, and therefore marriage is forbidden (Cozzi, 1912, p. 316; Valentini, 1956, p. 88). The word "*kushrinija*" (from "*kusheri*"—cousin) always refers to a group related by blood (Valentini, 1956, p. 88) and recalls the Armân word "*cusurin*," similar to the latin, "*consobrinus*."

We find, therefore, a complete series of words referring to groups related by blood, several of which are well defined, and because they concern property matters, the groups have a leader and a name which distinguishes them from others. We should now include some social units, and whose archaic nature is evident. These new social units maintain the idea of consanguinity (sometimes they are even confused with the preceding social units), but the territorial element becomes apparent. It is therefore a question of an evolution which parallels that of the southern Slavs where the phratry becomes a village or a quarter of a village, and where the tribe becomes a department. The transition between these two categories does not take place at a precise moment in history, but is rather the result of a long process which unfolds at different moments, varying according to regions. A distinction must be made from the beginning between the social units constituting this second category; a first group is the result of the internal evolution of Albanian societies, an spontaneous evolution; it is the case of the social units known as "*katun*" or "*mahalla.*" A second group is the result of the intervention of Ottoman authority which gives rise to the "*bajrak*"—flag.

The word *katun* designates a village or a hamlet and is used by most of the populations of south-eastern Europe. The word *mahalla* can refer to a quarter of a village, town or even a small region having a dispersed living arrangement. The two social units can conduct themselves as such, having their own leader, territory, political unit, a property system with commonfields and a preemptive right. Occasionally the *katun* corresponds to the parish and has a church, a cemetery, and a patronal holiday (Valentini, 1956, pp. 155 sq.). The *katun,* like the *mahalla,* can in reality cover one social unit based on consanguinity, one phratry, for example, or several (Whitaker, p. 258; Durham, 1928, p. 16); they can include one or more lineages belonging to a phratry which has representatives in other regions as well. The grouping of houses by related groups is as common in the towns as in the villages (Andromaqi Gjergji, 1982, p. 161; Zdravković, pp. 351 sq.). In the town of Gostivar, in the Polog plain, related Albanian families have adjacent houses and courtyards. Hecquard gives a description of the town of Shkoder around the middle of the 19th century (1862, p. 16): "Scutari counts 4500 houses, of which 3000 are Moslem, 1400 Christian (Catholic) and 100 Greek (Orthodox), covering an area of ground whose circumference is more than four miles. They are divided into ten quarters (*mahalla*). . . . Tradition has that between Tabachi (a large quarter in those days, for the most part inhabited by the beys, but which today is nearly entirely destroyed following a revolt) and the other quarters, there existed, for a long time, a fierce war. Each party had established demarcation lines that were only crossed bearing arms. Even though this state of hostility has ceased, there still exists a hate which is easily brought to the surface and translated into frequent assassinations. Each quarter is divided into streets or Bay-racks having at its head an *alfier* or *Bayrackter"* (flag bearer).

The *bayrak* — flat — is a territorialized military organization, imposed by the Ottoman administration; the word eventually refers to a district. The warriors from the different local formations fight under a single flag and under the supervision of a flag bearer (*"bayraktar"*); this organization experienced an evolution which tends to supplant the former social units. But, like the katun or the mahalla, the bayrak can hide one or several other social units, like the phratry or the tribe (Ulqini, 1977, pp. 617 sq.; Gopčević, pp. 188 sq.). The cases where the bajrak corres-ponds to the geographical unit are numerous.

A final notion should be mentioned which, in spite of the frequency with which it appears, does not have precise outlines. This is the notion of the mountain (*"mali"*) which can refer to the region of northern Albania, to a part of that region, or even, on occasion, to a single moun-tain inhabited by a tribe, in which case the name of the mountain refers, in reality, to a tribe. Several "mountains" can make up a community of mountains, understood to be a community composed of several tribes. The "mountain" follows a similar evolution to that of the other notions already analyzed and, belonging to the ancient level, it becomes, in time, a bayrak, or a department (*"nahije"*) (Frasheri, 1977, pp. 251 sq.).

No better words than those of Gjecov can be found for the summation of this chapter (par. 19): "The family is made up of the domestic group of the house; several united families form a phratry, several phratries a lineage, several lineages a tribe, several tribes a bajrak, and all these groups together, having the same origin, the same blood line, the same language, habits and customs, constitute this great family which is called a Nation." The only reservation that can be made is that the lineage can be located at any level, including the levels of the domestic group, the phratry, or the tribe since, in all of these cases, the group itself is one which is de-scended from a single ancestor.

### The Assembly (*"kuvend"*)

Just as there is an assembly made up of the male members of a house-hold, there are assemblies at all levels of social life; the Phratry has its assembly, as do the village, the tribe and the bejrak. Intertribal assemblies can also take place. At each session, questions of a common nature are discussed, questions which can be numerous. The assembly members judge, make laws, put an end to a vendetta or declare war, and resolve the multitude of questions concerning property matters. They decide when to hold a meeting when they see each other, for example, at religious ceremonies. The meetings can be announced by communicating from a distance: "they have, in the mountains, a complete system of telegraphy by shouts; in very little time they can be called together" (Degrand, 1901, p. 262). A herald announces the decisions sometimes by going from door to door (Gjeçov, par. 1213).

Meetings are preferably held in the morning (Hasluck, 1954, p. 150), in the church courtyard (Degrand, 1901, p. 129; Gjeçov, par. 1112) and, among the Moslems, in the courtyard of the mosque (Hasluck, 1954, p. 149). Gjeçov (par. 1112) gives a list of the meeting places of the Christians of northern Albania, including, for example, the church courtyard, near the ruins of some sacred structure, in the center of the country. Most often, the assembly gathers out of doors so that everyone can find a seat, sometimes under the branches of a tree, an oak, for example (Hasluck, 1954, p. 151; Coon, p. 30). The location can be called *"log"* (from the Latin *"locus"*), fairies themselves presumably having a meeting *log* (Sako, 1964, p. 134). The Kabash village fair takes place on Palm Sunday; a general truce is declared on these occasions, a truce guaranteed by the notables of the Kabash lineage. The Moslems and Christians of the lineage gather on this occasion to discuss common business (Meçi, 1979, pp. 291-292). Hecquard (1862, p. 228) notes the meeting of tribes on a religious holiday, Easter. These two cases mentioned enable a distinction to be made between meetings held on a fixed date, and those more numerous meetings determined by circumstances which change from one year to another. The fixed date meetings can coincide with a religious holiday and with the organization of a fair.

The *katun* has an assembly whose purpose is to resolve problems which occur at this level. The "old man" of the katun convenes the assembly (Valentini, 1956, p. 161) but he is not the one to make decisions, because he is only the president of the assembly (the same, p. 179). A good number of the problems discussed at this level deal with agricultural life, especially the commonfields, which belong to everyone. Much of the discussion centers on the problems posed by the irrigation canals, the forests, the pastures (Hasluck, 1954, p. 156), or the date on which each person can send his animals to the mountain pastures and the number of animals that can be sent (Hasluck, 1954, p. 162). Gjecov refers to these assemblies as partial assemblies (par. 1108).

It is again Gjecov (par. 1111) who clarifies the actual makeup of the assembly: the "elderly" and the "under-elderly," the leaders of the lineages or of the villages, the "brave," a name which refers to the heads of the households. Each household is obligated to participate in the assemblies, but can only send one representative, regardless of the number of men making up the household. The heralds also participate, as well as those in charge of collecting fines *("djobars")*. A special place is reserved in the region of northern Albania for "the house of the Gjormakaj of Oroshi."

The people are seated in a semicircle so that each person can see the others; the leaders then face them and those persons stating their problems are in the middle of everyone (Gjecov, par. 1113); outsiders are excluded (par. 1115). The tribal assembly is called *"kuvend"* or *"medjiliss"* (Durham, 1910, p. 464; the same, 1928, p. 74). In Maltsia e Madhe, the assembly includes the *bajraktar,* two *voivodes,* twelve elderly members and 72 heads of households. In the following passage, Hecquard describes an intertribal assembly (1862, p. 368): "At last, an assembly bringing all the mountains together is taking place, either to deliberate general interests, or to oppose orders received from the Turkish authorities, orders that they believe unfair. In these reunions, the *bayrak* of Hotti always presides and occupies the place of honor. The absence of a family at the convened meeting is punishable by a fine. In the assemblies, the leaders and the elderly members meet in a circle; the people then arrange themselves around them. The bayraktar of Hotti, when the assembly includes all the mountains, or the village person considered to the the most important among the tribes, takes the floor and explains the goal of the meeting. After a discussion in which those present may take part, the *djiobars,* in the Scutari mountains, and the *dovran,* in the Pulati mountains, retreat to summarize what has been said, and to make proposals which, upon their return, will be put to a vote of the population. . . . It is also during these assemblies that judgments are made concerning crimes committed against the community, crimes punished by supplying animals for a family feast that is prepared in a house designated in advance, and to which one person per family must take part."

Rrok Zojzi's description is much more detailed since it brings to light the strict hierarchy of groups claiming their orign from a particular ancestor. Each tribe is composed of feet or of large phratry (see above); they are divided into phratries, barks, and then into houses. The eponymic founder of the tribe, "the elderly member of the *fis*, passes on the right to be the first person of his tribe to his eldest son, who, in turn, passes it to his own eldest son, and so forth. The eldest son becomes the "elderly member" of the foot; he is the founder of the first food and receives the title of *voivode*, a word of Slavic origin which refers to a tribal leader, or a war leader. His eldest son becomes, in turn, a voivode, and so on. To the extent that the tribe divides, leaders appear for each social unit. Thus, the foot divides into phratries, which each have a great captain (*"krenet e medhaj"*) as their leader; the phratry then divides and the leaders of these sub-divisions are minor captains (*"krenet e vogjel"*), offices which are passed on from eldest son to eldest son. "During the assembly, each person has his designated seat, a seat which can not be occupied by someone else. The seat was designated on the basis of primogeniture or birthright, not on age or wealth" (Zojzi, 1977, p. 200). A parallel can be drawn between this strictly followed hierarchy and the hierarchy observed on other occasions, for example, for the marriage procession, where each person's place is fixed in advance and strictly observed (Gjecov, par. 51).

The military force of the tribe is called youth (*"djelmni"*) and it is composed of one man from each household; each tribe therefore includes as many "guns" as there are households. Each person places himself and fights in the order described above, in relationship to the group to which he belongs. "In order to respect the interior democracy of the *fis* and in order to prevent the concentration of forces from falling into one hand, the rule was such that, if the supervision of the *fis* was passed from eldest son to eldest son beginning with the ancestor (founder), then the supervision of the youth was passed from second-born son to second-born son (Zojzi, 1977, p. 201). "The youth took part in war in the name of the *fis* and the victories were considered joint. The symbol of the community was a piece of cloth referred to by the population as *'pece'* (cloth or flag). It was under Turkish influence that it began to be known as *bajrak* (banner) which bore as its emblem a hand with five open fingers. It symbolized the hand of the ancestor, the first person of the fis. . . . Wherever this pece or bajrak is set up, bearing the hand of the first ancestor, the site becomes a common piece of property" (Zojzi, 1971, pp. 201-202). "Just as the leadership of the *fis* is passed by inheritance from eldest son to eldest son, and that of the *djemni* or youth from second-born to second-born, the task of *bajraktar* or banner carrier was passed from third son to third son . . ." (the same, p. 202).

A contradiction appears between this description and the organization of the bajraks as they have been observed in the 19th century, because, in many cases, the bajrak included several tribes, not just one.

## The Leaders

The elderly people must be mentioned in first place among the leaders of the former Albanian organizations, a situation which parallels the previously mentioned organization of the Balkan populations. At each level, there are "elderly people" and these elderly persons are considered to be the founders of the blood related groups. The word itself *"plek"* or *"plak"*—elderly—has, like the Romanian word *"moş,"* two meanings; an older person and an ancestor. Gjecov (par. 1161-1166) characterizes the elderly members of the village in the following manner: each village has its elderly members of the lineage; these elderly can convene a village assembly; but they can neither denounce nor impose fines on someone without the assistance of the under-elderly and of the assembly itself; they are not exempt from collective responsibilities within the village nor from participation in war; they are punished by the fellow citizens if they commit a crime. The elderly member occupies a place of honor at the table, receives the head of the animal and is the first to get his coffee (Hasluck, 1954, pp. 132-133). Kristo Frasheri describes the two typical figures of the patriarchal society, the elderly member (*"plak"*) and the head (*"kefali"*), or military director of the community (1977, p. 254). Coon (1950, p. 30) notes the presence of the elderly whose office is hereditary, but also of elected elderly. One of the elderly members is a elderly leader (*"kryeplak"*), a title which can be hereditary or the result of an election (Hasluck, 1954, p. 131).

The elderly are also found at the level of the tribe or of the *bajrak* (Valentini, 1956, pp. 113 sq.). Hecquard (1862, pp. 227-228) describes the organization of the Mirdites in the following passage: they "recognize a leader to whom is given the title of captain; the Europeans call him prince. His offices are hereditary, but the leader's powers are very limited and his authority is directly related to the influence he has had over the population. Each district has a banner (*bajrack,* a name given to the mountain district), a *bajraktar,* who is in charge of it during war, and its elderly who, under the presidency of the captain, administer justice and deal with business . . . like the office of the leader of the tribe, these positions are also hereditary." In a footnote, he further states "that the elderly are called the leaders in charge of administering justice and protecting the assemblies, the interests of the village or of the tribe. Named by election in the other mountains, they are hereditary among the Mirdites, and this name elderly is the designation of offices which were formerly filled by the eldest men" (pp. 228-229).

The elderly are in charge of accompanying the bride to her husband's house (Hecquard, 1862, p. 320); the elderly person of a household is responsible for beginning the harvest (Shkurti, 1979, p. 57).

If the word elderly has, with time, evolved to a point of designating a political office, it still, however, maintains some characteristics which recall the position of older people in the traditional society. It brings back, in all points, the position of the elderly in Romanian and Southern Slavic societies. The Albanian elderly, correspond to the *"dobri ljudi"* of the Slavs and to the *"oameni bătrâni şi buni"* of the Romanians, old and good men, with the wod good meaning someone worthy of confidence. We also find among the Romanians, not only the *"pleks,"* but also the *"sterplek,"* which correspond to the Romanian words, *"moş"* and *"strămoş),* it is clear that the person is an ancestor of an ancestor, a distant figure in the past and one who lived at the time of the group's origin.

## The 12 Witnesses

One of the most important functions of the elderly is to judge. Gjecov (par. 991-1016) defines the elderly judges in the following way: they are elected among the elderly of the phratries, or the heads of the lineages and their word is the basis of the law; without them, no new law can be made, nor can any case concerning a phratry, lineage, village or bajrak be

judged; those who are renowened for their caution and their long experience in judging and deliberating are also called elderly; they have the right
to settle conflicts, prevent a crime by use of force, with the village's aid.
They can resort to the armed force of the bajrak; they convene the village
and for minor situations, only the elderly of the village or of the phratry
are called; they bring differing parties together, judge, and administer
justice. This right falls not only to the elderly who know the laws, but
also to the elderly whom Gjecov refers to as the *"straplek;"* once chosen
by an arbitrator, they can no longer be replaced. The elderly of the bajrak
can not judge without being assisted by the elderly and the under-elderly
where the incriminated person is located; if the whole village, along with
its elderly, rebels against the decisions of the bajrak, then the elderly of
the bajrak and of all the phratries and lineages and all the people unite
in order to resolve the issue; if the village declares war against the leaders,
the elderly, the under-elderly and their own bajraks are called together
to subjugate the rebellious village (see also Hacquard, 1862, p. 118). It
should be remembered that the elderly intervene at all levels and that
the term *straplek*—archelderly—is also a word which changes its original
meaning and eventually ends up designating an office.

The number of elderly and witnesses is not without importance, since
it is always in relation to the number 12. Elezi (1977, p. 240). further
states that the officially chosen (*"poroniki"*) are always chosen in part
by the tribe, in part by the accused, and are between a number which
varies between 4 and 24. The Albanians, use the number 12 as do the
Southern Slavs and the Romanians, where the witnesses, the jury, and
the elderly make up a group in relation with the number 12 (4, 6, 12,
24, 48). Cozzi (1912, p. 330) mentions twelve witnesses who intervene
in conflicts between husband and wife; Coon (1950, p. 30) notes the 12
elderly members of the village; Valentini (1945, p. 34) distinguishes
cases where a crime committed by a man is judged and where 24 witnesses are needed, while crimes committed by a woman only required 12.
The notables of the lineage of Kabash are its 24 elderly (Meci, p. 291);
in the country of Kastrati, 24 elderly make new laws in the presence of
leaders (Gjecov, par. 308); Valentini (1969, p. 166) tells of 6, 12, or 24
jurors: ". . . a petty thief stole a gun, and accused of having taken it,
denied it, and under oath swore to his innocence. But since no one wanted
to believe him, he was asked to prove his innocence by having 24 witnesses swear in his favor. This means of swearing of 6, 12, or 24 witnesses

is common among the Albanians and is called *'me baa be n'parod'*. . . .
In this case, while the 24 witnesses were giving their testimonies, one
after the other, basing them on the assertions of the young man, one
of those present stood up and said: 'Stop, don't go any furrher, since
you are all swearing falsely; I am a witness to the theft and he proved
it."

If 24 witnesses are needed for a case, and if one of those persons also
testifying holds the office of an elderly member, his testimony alone is
worth those of 12 others; thus, in order to obtain the necessary 24, 12
witnesses are called plus one elderly person, maing a total of 24 witnesses (Hasluck, 1954, p. 133). Gjecov confirms this assertion but applies the same rule to the leader of a bajrak (par. 1049) and adds that
the oath of a priest and his testimony are worth 24 other testimonies
(par. 1048).

Besides the offices of the elderly and the under-elderly, there is the
office of the leader, of the *voivode,* and of the *bajraktar,* which have been
previously outlined. Several observations, however, should be added at
this time. The fact that someone is the first born or that he has the best
qualifications has an effect, from the smallest to the largest of the social
units. This is true for the head of the household, of the village, or even
of the tribe (Hasluck, 1954, p. 10). Gopčević adds that the fact that
someone is the brother of the former leader also has an effect (p. 317).

Gjecov describes the leaders of the lineages and of the tribes, hereditary offices, whose rights and obligations are equal to those of the other
members of their group (par. 1146 sq.). But the leaders of the *bajraktar*
of the Nikaj and Merturi mountains, those of Hash and Krasniqe, have
the privilege of an additional turn at using the irrigation water (par. 1160).
Rrok Zojzi (1977, p. 204) goes even farther with the observation: "The
aristocracy, which at one time had no symbolic advantage, like, for instance, assuming the first place in meetings, having the lamb's head at the
table . . . the first portion of fines and the spoils of war, etc., began specu-
lating about its position and about popular traditions. Thus began acts
of favoritism, bribes, underhanded schemes, and under the counter pay-
ments in the judicial assemblies (assemblies where judgments are made).
Thus were instituted secret and illegal revenues outside customary rights.
Otherwise, the silver buttons and the silk scarves that the leaders used in
the 17th century could not be explained."

Leaders are also found in the cities along with the organization based on consanguinity within the framework of the *bajrak,* here merging with that of the quarter (or *mahalla*). Thus, for example, in 1897, "the city and the province of Djakova is governed by a commission made up of the leaders of the various quarters of the city and of a civil servant bearing the title *kaimakam,* who represents the government of the Sultan, but who only has nominal authority since in fact the commission does everything" (Valentini, 1969, p. 184).

The *voivode,* head of a tribe or phratry (Valentini, 1956, p. 114) will be more and more in competition with the *bajraktar,* head of the bajrak. The evolution parallels one which saw an organization based on consanguinity evolve into one based on territoriality. Valentini (1956, p. 194) draws a parallel between the office of the voivode, military in the beginning and which, little by little, becomes civil and that of the bajraktar, who, with time, obtains more extensive civil functions. Cozzi (in Valentini, 1956, p. 182) states that "in ancient time, the voivode was the principal head of the tribe; but with time, a portion of his authority was passed on to the bajraktar who, for a half century, has come to be considered as the true leader of the tribe. In the beginning, the office of bajraktar was simply that of flag bearer who led the tribe in times of war for the Sultan."

As we have seen above, the flag bearer belonged to a certain lineage and his office is passed on hereditarily (Durham, 1928, p. 16; Hasluck, 1954, p. 116); in the absence of a son, it is passed on to the brother or to the closest cousin. The flag itself is conserved in the lineage (Valentini, 1956, p. 141). Among the various bajrak, there is a hierarchy and Hecquard mentions such an example: "Each one of these three villages has its particular bajrak; however the Hot bajrak is the main one and functions as such in times of war, at the head of all those from the Albanian mountains, located on the right bank of the Drin. During general meetings, the leaders of the Hot also have precedence, and it rarely occurs that a decision made by this bajrak is not implemented in all of the other mountains" (1862, p. 162).

During combat, the bajraktar is accompanied by four young men,each one belonging to another "foot" of the tribe. If he is killed, the banner is taken by one of the young men, and will remain henceforth the possession of the phratry to which this young man belongs. These assertions, made by Rrok Zojzi (1977, p. 202) are accompanied by an observation which contradicts those made by Mary Edith Durham and Margaret Hasluck, since he asserts that, among all of the offices of the fis, only that of the bajraktar was not hereditarily transmittable. Conflicts can even occur over the right to keep and carry the flag. Rrok Zojzi later adds that the bajraktar, who descends from the third born son of the ancestor of the entire tribe, occupies the third position in the assembly and at the hand washing which precedes the meals; but, as his influence inceases, the third phratry acquires first position (p. 205).

The description of the former social structures of the Albanians can not clarify all the details since there are so few materials available. The contradictions that I have mentioned on several occasions can be explained accordingly, but not in all cases; for example, it is evident that the Albanians did not have a unique form of organization and that often the contradictory descriptions of a particular social fact are, quite simply, the reflection of different social realities. Regional differences appear in the *kanun,* collections of customary right; they are the result of evolutionary level differences, where exterior pressures are reflected in Albanian society.

# CHAPTER IV

## GREECE

For each of the populations studied in the preceding chapters a typical social structure can be introduced that covers the entire population. This is not the case for Greece. In fact, it is not possible to be acquainted with their social structure by describing a single society and a single property system due to the important variations that appear. It is therefore necessary to describe the various typical forms separately, thus constituting a difference with regard to the presentation of the preceding chapters. A second difference is found in the fact that I will primarily be using data collected by my students and myself since they cover aspects needed in order to make a comparison with the other populations. Research which is ongoing is not included in this exposé.

## THE MANI REGION

The Peloponnese ends in three peninsulas in the south; the central one is called Mani. The region is divided into several sections, the most characteristic of which in terms of pertinent facts for this study is the interior of Mani, or Messa Mani. It distinguishes itself neatly by its social organization from the other regions of Greece, all the while paralleling the northern Albanian society of Montenegro. A discussion of the origin of the Maniote society, as well as any discussion of the eventual influence

138

of the populations which established themselves next to Greece in the Peloponnese, first including the Slavs, followed by the Albanians, goes beyond the limits of this present study.

## The household ("famelia")

The domestic group is essentially composed of a married couple and its unmarried children. In addition, one or two of the husband's elderly relatives may be included in the group, especially if the husband is the youngest child in his family. Thus characterized, the domestic group of the Greeks from Mani resembles the organization of the Romanian domestic group and distinguishes itself from the Slavic and Albanian populations, as well as from the Turks. What distinguishes the Mani from the Romanians is the fact that the lineage is important in a different way in Mani. Here the household is established in immediate proximity to households belonging to the same lineage; the element of kinship based on the masculine consanguinity plays a principal role. Members of the household always settle next to their nearest blood relatives thus avoiding the penetration of any outsiders; close by, there is a tower and other elements which are considered the common property of the lineage. In a study devoted to marriage in Mani, Anargyrop Koutsilieris (1960) discusses arguments which prevent someone from settling in the middle of "outsiders," in other words, among anyone except one's own blood relations. Thus, the outsider risks being caught up in a vendetta involving the lineage which surrounds him; the lineage itself risks having in the midst of its living arrangement an eventual enemy.

Like the other populations we have seen, the household property is made up of the arable property of the lineage. Property is not owned by individuals, but rather belongs to the domestic group. Like the Romanians, the father, who at first glance seems to be the owner, is only the administrator of the possessions of his group. He cannot sell what he has inherited from his father without the consent of his sons. He is also not allowed to disinherit one of his sons and must divide the property into equal parts which are given exclusively to the boys (Andromedas, 1968, p. 64). When he passes the property on to them, the father calls "three appraisers and his sons, and all together they walk the land and estimate its value. If there is only one piece of property, they divide it into as many parts of equal value as there are sons. They each take small sticks of differing lengths which each represents a definite section of the land. The sons, in turn, draw a stick, thereby choosing a plot of land for themselves. But since it is rare to have a property made up of a single section of land, this practice is carried out for each of the sections, thus enabling each son to have a plot of equal value in each one of them (Didika, 1977, p. 110). If the couple has no children, the property will be passed on to the husband's closest blood relatives (Didka, 1977, p. 110).

The father proceeds with the division of property of his sons' endowment at the time of their marriage; he can also do this later, but this sort of delay appears to be rare. He can carry out the division in two ways: first, he can divide all of the land among his sons with the understanding that they will in turn take care of him and his wife, or, second, he can reserve a section for himself which will be divided among his sons upon his death. In this respect, we note resemblances with the unfolding of the transmission of property among the Romanians.

The daughter does not receive any land; her dowry consists of a trousseau placed in a chest. At the wedding, "after the dinner, the spouse receives his wife's dowry made up of herds and furniture from his father-in-law" (Stephanopili, II, p. 8). Koutsilieris (1960) adds, that this is interesting as well as being typical for the region, that at the time of marriage, boys are primarily looking for native girls from powerful families. The fact that a girl has brothers, many brothers, makes the group powerful and insures that the dowry will include fabrics. If, on the other hand, the girl has no brothers, the dowry will include animals which compensate for the lack of brothers.

Only when the couple has no boys can the daughter inherit land. The girl heir (*"xaklirospora"*) thus poses serious problems to the lineage since a similar situation implies the arrival of a foreign husband (*"soghambros"*) who settles in his wife's house, thus producing a uxorial marriage. The solution to this problem is double; if according to the general rule marriages between members of the same lineage are forbidden (Didika, 1977, p. 51), such a marriage becomes possible when a girl has not brothers (Andromedas, 1968, pp. 67-68; Didika, 1977, p. 60). One of the members of the lineage publicly announces that he will marry the girl while firing shots into the air, or by cutting a lock from the girl's hair. A second solution is to have the husband come from outside the lineage but this then becomes a matter which involves the entire lineage. The assembly of the elderly of the lineage meets: "The more strategically located the girl's property, the more difficult the decision is to make" (Didika, 1977, p. 103). The lineage can even decide to buy the land from the girl, or exchange her property for another whose location and strategic importance are less dangerous. The *sophambros* thus assumes an inferior position to that of a man who marries under the conditions of a normal situation and he loses his identity by adopting the patronymic of his wife's father. His situation is therefore similar to a man whose marriage is uxorial in the societies described in the preceding chapters, with the exception of the Albanian marriage which is always virilocal.

The local house goes through several stages. The most ancient constructions are very simple and Guillet de Saint Georges (1676, I, pp. 100-101) who visited Mani about the middle of the 17th century describes them in the following manner: "Whoever sees the architecture of one, sees them all. About 10 or 12 steps from each one there is a high wall built dry, where they stage an ambush when it is necessary to attack the passer-by and behind which they take refuge when they need to defend themselves. Each house has one story. It is entered by a grade of three or four rocks, dryly placed one upon the other. There are no other windows except the door. In the middle of the bedroom they have a raised wooden scaffold which serves as their bed. They sleep there, fully clothed, the voluptuous or the ill adding some straw mattress to the wood. They descend the scaffold to the right and to the left by two ladders, one of which leads to a fireplace where the cooking is done, and the other to a stable for the goats. Since they have an obvious hate for one another, and since normally their nearest neighbor is their greatest enemy, every night someone from the family is on sentry duty near the roof of the lodging." There is also the stone house made up of one room without windows, a single door, where men and animals live together. This same type of house is seen elsewhere, primarily in the Balkan regions near the Adriatic and Mediterranean Seas.

The study of the former living situations of Mani allows us to find traces of similar constructions which stand out because of the thickness of their walls. In new living arrangements, innumerable towers surrounded by houses are seen, either attached to the towers, or surrounding a tower. The towers themselves are often lived in on a permanent basis; they include an excessively simple interior, with rudimentary furnishings and a single room on each floor. The necessary elements for everyday life blend with those items needed for defense. A terrace overhangs the entire structure and often a water tank is hollowed out above the ground level. Mobile, interior staircases permit the passage from one level to another. These towers are the visible, material expression of a society in a constant state of war, where men are armed, where the vendetta rages. Once again, as we have seen in northern Albania and in Montenegro, there is a correspondence between the type of construction and the social organization.

## Women

The position of women, in this case, is also typical for the general structure of the society. It is a position which must be known in order to understand the household and even the lineage. Several problems present themselves which strangely recall situations already described for other populations.

An important difference separates men and women, a difference which has been maintained up to our day. Didika Niki (1977, p. 73) mentions, among other things, that in 1907, in the region of Messa Mani, 49% of the men knew how to read and write, compared to only 5.47% of the women. A woman is called by the name of her native group before marriage, and by her husband's name after marriage; the custom is so strongly adhered to that the great majority of women marry even within the same canton of Mani (Andromedas, 1968, pp. 12 and 58).

Her situation vis-a-vis her native lineage and that of her husband's corresponds to the situation previously described for the Albanians. A woman belongs to her native lineage. Within her husband's lineage, her role seems to be one of bearing children into the world and working. During a vendetta which opposes her husband's group and her native group, she is obligated to support the latter (Andromedas, 1968, p. 63); if she is attacked by her husband's enemies, she lodges her complaint with her native family and not with her husband (Koutsilieris, 1960); if she betrays her husband, the subsequent dishonor falls, not on her husband, but on her native group; her father and her brothers are her natural protectors, and they are charged with punishing her by death if she is found guilty of adultery; when there are no brothers, then the closest, blood cousin kills her (Didika, Niki, 1977, pp. 70-71).

The purchase of the bride seems to have been practiced throughout the past (Andromedas, 1968, p. 44), but has not been in recent times. The engagement is important because it links from that moment on, two groups, the boy's and the girl's. If ever the finance dies, she then belongs to the youngest brother of the finance. If she is widowed and has children, she remains with her husband's family to raise the children since the children belong to the husband's family; in the case of divorce, the children remain the husband's property (Stephanopoli, 1798, II, p. 11). In the eventuality the widow desires to remarry, she can only do so with the consent of her family-in-law (Didika, 1977, p. 79).

The woman works more than the man and does a good portion of the tasks normally considered a man's responsibility. She actively particpates in the cultivation of the land (Andromedas, 1968, p. 32), often for reasons which recall those put forward for the Albanians, including the need for men to shut themselves up in the towers in order to escape the consequences of the vendetta: "During the continuance of these feuds, which, with the interval of an occasional truce, often endured for generations, the women were allowed to go free and unmolested, to carry on their domestic avocations, to cultivate the ground (though at times the hostile party would come down upon the fields, and carry off the harvest) and even to convey food to their husbands, who were shut up in their towers" (Carnarvon, 1869, p. 146). The women of our day carry the wood to the house on their backs: "There is nothing more normal than to see a Mainote woman coming from the fields with a bundle of wood behind her back, and, underneath the bundle, the cradle of her infant, the entire load is so well arranged that she has enough freedom of movement in her arms to allow her to spin cotton along the way" (Stephanopoli, 1798, I, p. 295). If a woman is alone and she has children, mutual aid functions regularly: the members of her lineage help her by assembling on a certain day which is convenient for all. Moreover, mutual aid not only benefits women who are alone, but everyone, being based on the idea of reciprocity.

Even if the women are spared during a vendetta, they are not strangers to fighting and there are many examples which support this idea: "The women in Maina often gave proof of a valor and of a consistency worthy of the ancient Spartans; how many times were they seen fighting with intrepidity beside their husbands or loading their firearms?" (Comnene, 1794, pp. 118-119). And in order that the resemblance with regard to the

Albanian and Montenegrin tribes be complete, I am duplicating the following passage that, as is, could be found in descriptions of both of the preceding societies: "They would sometimes walk in front, and their husbands would skulk behind them, until the men, themselves unseen, came within gunshot of their enemy, and levelled their deadly aim" (Carnarvon, 1869, p. 146).

A woman must bear children into the world, especially boys. "The birth of a boy is announced by a gunshot fired by the father. Upon this signal, all his relatives and friends display their joy by discharging their firearms" (Stephanopoli, 1798, p. 293). The birth of a girl appeared as a misfortune, especially if it were not the first (Didika, 1977, p. 72). The birth of a boy assures the position of the wife in her husband's household; on the other hand, the sterile woman is discredited. A man without children is called *"xakliros,"* and a man without boys is referred to as *"akliros,"* meaning, without heirs (Andromedas, 1968, p. 66).

How do the people react to these type of situations? In rare cases, it is obvious that the absence of a child is caused by the husband; in this case, a child is bought *("agorasto")* who is adopted and who will pass along the name of the father's property (Didika, 1977, p. 75). The same process takes place when sterility is attributed to a wife originating from a powerful lineage in order to avoid the split with this lineage due to the rejection of the woman. But the most common procedure is to seek a second wife, called *"syngria."* This second wife can be a widow who has proven her fertility, or even a young girl who comes into the man's group often with the consent of the first wife. The negotiations take place secretly and the new wife arrives discretly at the house where her presence is, in the beginning, also discreet. Afterwards, she can either find herself in a situation equal to that of the first wife, or remain in a position of subordination. Didika Niki (1977, p. 76) adds some interesting details to this idea. For example, before taking a second wife, the advice of the native group of the first wife is sought: if the *"syngria"* gives birth to a boy, her place can equal that of the first wife. Sometimes, "the newborn is brought in, with his head down, under the shirt of the legitimate wife, and holding him by the neck, he is allowed to slip down to the ground. This gesture symbolizes the birth of the child by the first spouse. Next, he is placed on her knees and thus he becomes her child. She is the official mother but his real mother takes care of him as a nurse would. But, if the legitimate wife is older, the syngria assumes the role of the mother with her child, while the spouse took the place of the stepmother which re-established the natural order of things."

Since I am not introducing other Greek societies where a second wife is added to the original couple in order to bear sons, I will include here a parenthesis. Dim. A. Petropoulos (1952) groups interesting information together concerning this question; he finds the same practice elsewhere especially in Crete, where past society recalls, in certain respects, the Maniote society. In contradiction to its rules, the Church participates and grants the husband the right to take a second wife, and eventually to divorce the first, but he must provide her with the economic means needed to support herself. In Mani, the Church also intervenes, it seems, by blessing such unions which are, in reality, illegitimate marriages. Lord Carnarvon, who visited the region in 1839 (1869, pp. 198-199) described just such a case: "The man was already married, but having had no children by his wife, he was permitted, with her consent—and, it is affirmed, under the sanction of a priest—to be united to another woman of the place. It is said here that if he should have a son, by this second union, that the son would in the Maina be considered to be legitimate, and the first wife could be repudiated. On my asking some further questions, it appeared that his first marriage had indeed given him three daughters; but my informant repeated his statement 'that there were no children'—so completely are girls counted as nothing in this country. One of my muleteers clinched the argument by the additional question of 'how could a man wish to have anything to do with a woman who brought him no sons?' " The bishop of Gytheion noted about thirty *"syngria"* in the Messa Mani in 1864 (Andromedas, 1968, p. 67) at the same time that he condemned them. Didika Niki (1977, p. 56) points out the case of an old man to whom his wife had given five girls and who remarried in 1865 a girl only sixteen years of age, belonging to an inferior lineage; the marriage took place only after the young girl had given birth to a son. This is therefore an example of the trial marriage, customary for the Albanian and Montenegrin tribal societies.

### The Lineage

The superior social units of Mani are difficult to grasp since they are in perpetual movement. The terms which designate them are *"genia,"*

*"ikogenia,"* and *"dhikologia."* The first, *"genia,"* has the broadest character and refers to a blood related group formed essentially of men; the
three notions are related to consanguinity and primarily involve men.
The purity of the blood line is assured by keeping a close watch on the
women; virginity is required before marriage and fidelity afterwards.
The clear-cut distinction between the man's lineage and the woman's
among the Albanians also appears here, even though the forms are less
accentuated; the group of relatives on the mother's side is called *"manogenia."* The group is seen as an allied group and the Maniotes say,
"Mother's milk is sweet, as is the manogenia" (Didika, 1977, p. 56).
*"Ikogenia"* and *"dikhologia"* are sub-divisions of the "genia," and may
be called sub-lineages. In reality, all these notions have common characters in the sense that they are blood related groups, they have a common
ancestor, a common name, common rights to the community property,
and demonstrate solidarily during war and before the law. The lineage
is added to the patronymic of the sub-lineages. A sub-lineage can, in time,
become a lineage, just as a lineage can diminish in number, lose its importance, and fall to the rank of a sub-lineage. This perpetual movement
of the groups makes their classification difficult.

Mani is particularly interesting in this regard since, until the 19th
century, there was a permanent evolution of the groups taking place.
Didika Niki's study made of the village Vathia is clear and offers a series
of concrete cases. She notes a significant difference in the classification
of the lineages; there are the sub-lineages which belong to a lineage, referred to by the phrase "they are from the X." To describe the sub-
lineages who associate themselves with a strong lineage and mix with
that group by taking its name, the phrase, "they are considered to be like
the X," is used. To this distinction, a second is added, that of purity;
there are pure sub-lineages, less pure ones, and those termed "fertoi"—
brought; but no one admits to being less pure or "fertoi." Social memory
has therefore maintained a distinction between groups considered blood
related since the beginning and groups added later whose consanguinity
is imaginary. For example, in the village of Vathia, the sub-lineage of the
Xypolitianoi, which was a member of the Aravouchioi, allied itself with
the Carambatianoi. The people did not say that they were of the Carambatianoi, but rather "for us, they are from the Carambatianoi," or, "they
are considered to be like the Carambatianoi." By offering their services

to the Carambatianoi and by receiving land that these people had given them they had become "fertoi."

The local living arrangement accounts for the presence of hamlets inhabited by a lineage or a sub-lineage. The presence of villages or of several lineages co-existing is observed at the same time. But here the village unit, such as it was seen among the Romanians (where the village plays an essential role and forms a perfectly joined social unit) does not exist since separation by lineages is so strong, making it very difficult to organize a truly, common life. Even if among the Romanians the entire village has one eponymic legend, here the lineages each have an origin linked to another eponymic hero. In order to further complicate the social landscape of the region, it must be added that the principal lineages have ramifications in several villages and that these ramifications, in spite of their territorial separation, do not show any less solidarity among themselves. True alliances which tend to restore an equilibrium or, on the contrary, to obtain a substantial advantage, join together and break up. Marriages (Didika, 1977, p. 53) or the fraternizations accompanied by transfers of land are common. Questions over land possession provoke violent fights pitting blood related groups against each other and even more so those who are not related. Often, a powerful group does not even have to fight, it merely asserts its claims to a piece of land and the weaker ones withdraw, resulting in a change in the configuration of the properties. This allows us to understand why the penetration of an outsider is avoided as much as possible and why the pieces of land belonging to a lineage are grouped together. This distribution of land by lineages is clearly perceived even in our day from the ground; sometimes a simple observation of the material traces left on the territory allow a reconstruction of the face of an entire lineage; its arable lands, houses, towers, cemetery, church, roads, in fact its entire enclosed area separated from the commonfield can be detected.

The right to common grazing ground is practiced on the "nomes," the cultivated wheat fields; "the last day of the harvest, when everyone had finished, the church bells rang and it was announced that the next day there would be 'ampolisia.' That meant that all the animals of the village would be allowed to roam freely in all the fields without distinction" (Didika, 1977, p. 85).

Besides the arable land possessed by the households, the property of the clan includes pastures, towers, high mountain pastures, rocks near the sea for gathering salt, churches, and ovens. Andromedas (1968, p. 71), who offers a description of Kitta, counts as many chapels, squares, and priests, as there were lineages. The lineage hires a rural policeman and thus assures the safety of the towers. In Vathia, each lineage has, in addition, its cemetery (Didika, 1977, pp. 132-133) while in Kitta, the cemetery is a common one; the inhabitants affirmed the fact that, in spite of the existence of this one cemetery, each lineage has an area of its own where they bury their dead.

Assemblies appear at each level and they keep an eye on the running of the group's activities. Each sub-lineage or lineage has its assembly in which the elderly have the place of honor and whose word is respected. There is no written law; the law is based on custom and the customs are known by the elderly. "The elderly are respected; their pieces of advice are oracles; the young men and women never approach the elderly without displaying some sign of profound veneration. . . .Decisions involving the expenses needed by the cult for the maintenance of fortified areas, for the purchase of powder, balls, in short, any measures dealing with the safety and protection of the country are settled by the elderly in the synods. The means by which agriculture can be increased and outlets multiplied for the exportation of products are also discussed" (Pouqueville, 1805, I. p. 197). They judge and arbitrate; they rigourously apply preemptive right; at the table, they are seated in the place of honor.

The assembly has a name, "*gerontiki*" ("*gerontas*" − elderly), a name which does not necessarily indicate that they are truly the oldest persons of the group, but rather that they are individuals holding the office of elderly. Each lineage has a leader, the "*protos gerontas*" (Andromedas, 1968, p. 75) or "*protogeros*" (Comnene, 1784, p. 102), first elderly. He is also called "*kephalari tis genias,*" or the head of the lineage (Andromedas, 1968, p. 75) and "*sofos*" − wise (Didika, 1977, p. 134).

Finally, there is one last aspect which has not been made clear. In addition to the reputation and power of each lineage, another notion, that of nobility, must be considered. Within the Maniote society, there is a distinction made between the Niklianoi, considered to be the most noble, the Achamnomeroi, occupying an intermediary position, and the Famegii which are in the lowest position. The Niklianoi habitually intermarry; the two other categories are their allies, with the distinction that the Achamnomeroi can also rise to a important military position and own towers, while the Famegii cannot. Discussions concerning the relationships between these three groups, as well as their origin, are still going on. Even if the Niklianoi are considered to be like nobles, they cannot be classified as lords, nor the Famegii, for example, as serfs. The latter do render them services, but we do not find evidence of the typical, regular relationships, the tithe and statute labor, for example, which link lord and serf.

Although the Maniotes are opposed to one another at each level of their society, they unite each time their region is threatened from the outside. The Turks in the 18th century tried to impose upon them a unique type of administration which had a Bey for its leader, who would be aided by captains chosen from the local lineages. But this authority, however, remained weak, the former local structures having the greatest weight.

In order to answer all the questions concerning the entire Mani unit, it would be necessary to analyze other aspects as well. I have noted in fieldwork the presence of elements which go beyond those of lineages and even of villages. For example, the region has a road which crosses it from one end to the other, which, in reality, is a wide path paved with stones, bordered by fences; intervillage water reservoirs appear here and there; mountains mark the center of the peninsula including high mountain pastures which are the common property of several villages; there are joint pilgrimages to the churches located at the summits; towers occupying strategic positions defend the entire region. In documents from the past, political or military agreements made between the Maniotes and powerful foreigners, the Venetians, for example, can be found.

## ANOYA, A MOUNTAIN VILLAGE ON CRETE

The data which follow are based on the research of Françoise Saulnier carried out during the 1970's. She studied the village of Anoya, located at an altitude of 750 meters in the Cretan mountain, a region which has always maintained a spirit of marked independence. Together with the region which surrounds Chora Sfakion, the village is renown for its warlike spirit. The population, which includes about three thousand inhabitants, lives in a region where the traditions of antiquity blend with those of the Middle Ages and of modern times. The area formerly sheltered one of the most important sanctuaries dedicated to Zeus.

Man-made terraces aided and still aid in the practice of agriculture, an agriculture which is not profitable. In our times, the abandoned terraces around the entire village are easily detected and are testimony to the fact that cultivation of the land has only been maintained in areas offering the most favorable conditions. Today, only 30% of the households rely principally on agriculture for the resources (Saulnier, p. 77); this number increases somewhat in cases where farming is a complement to animal breeding. An obvious division marks the farm land; the inhabitants have small parcels in several locations, often even going beyond the limits of the village territory, extending to land which borders the sea. Equipment is rudimentary; for example, wheat is separated from the shaft on threshing floors, with the aid of the animals. Both men and women work but, an observation of the vegetable gardens, which constitute an important part of the farming activities, reveals that women are more active.

The village consists of two areas for habitation; the lower, where farming is practiced, and the area situated on the neighboring mountain, where animal breeding is carried out. The importance of animal breeding is great, since 60% of the people practice it; out of a total of 500,000 ovines and caprines on the island of Crete, 80,000 are located in Anoya. The people practice transhumance; in October, they take their herds down to the plain, leading the animals on foot, and returning to the high mountain pastures in the Spring. I have noticed traces of agriculture in living areas even at the level of the region of the mountain pastures, but not one of these areas was cultivated.

Lineages play an important role in the village. As we have with other lineages, here the people also bear the same patronymic and claim to be descended from a common ancestor. Even if at the village level, where farming is practiced and property is divided by households, at the mountain pasture level, something of the former community life exists. The pastures belong to the lineages, each one having its territory, often with a chapel dedicated to a saint who is the protector saint of the lineage. On the day set aside to celebrate this saint, a celebration is organized where the entire lineage participates, accompanied by its friends and allies. "The baptisms of the newborns of the family are often celebrated in this chapel. On the altar, a list of the members of the lineage, dead or alive, allows the priest, on the holiday, to pray for the rest of the souls of the deceased and for the health of those still living" (Saulnier, p. 105). The borders of the lineage pastures "are not marked in the soil, but they are known by everyone: landmarks include differences in the level of the ground, paths, rocks, and isolated trees; the least known nooks of the mountain have a proper name known by all" (Saulnier, p. 104). In addition, each lineage has several sheep pens, whose appearance and technique of construction dates far back in history. They are made up of circular shaped huts of dry stones, covered by a stone dome, with one door and no windows. Stone enclosures surround them and close off the areas where the animals are penned. Oaks and other trees dot the landscape, remains of what was at one time a true forest.

The existence of lineages is even recognized in the village itself by the close proximity of the related households. Another indication is found by noting the threshing pens which serve several related households. It is no longer possible to know within the present situation of agricultural land if the land of one lineage was grouped or not in the beginning. The living arrangement has four sections, each one with several quarters and sub-quarters, each occupied by a lineage and bearing the name of this lineage. Often it is the church which gives the quarter its name, usually based on the name of the patron saint of the church.

The lineage is called "*soi;*" the consciousness of belonging to a particular group is very strong. A person refers to his own lineage by saying "ours;" others are "the outsiders" ("*xenous,*" also referred to by the name "*dikologia*"). The lineage is divided into lines called "*genies*" which group close relatives. The word "*siggeneia*" or "*siggenoloi*" (kinship) can also refer to the lineage or the line. The heads of the households are called a name which is common for various regions in Greece, "*o nikokiris*" — the master, and "*i noikokira*" — the mistress. A great knowledge of the patronymics enables each person to be situated within a particular group and, in this respect, the memory of the Cretan peasants recalls that of all the other populations for whom the knowledge of the kinship system is essential.

It is interesting to note, since this underscores the importance of the lineages to life in Anoya, that the most important lineages each have an eponymic legend which dates back to a founder, a founder who was the first to have arrived in the region and who would also be considered the founder of the village. The eponymic legends collected by Francoise Saulnier (pp. 124 sq.) are significant in this respect and they express the desire of each lineage to affirm its importance vis-a-vis the others.

The care taken to keep the lineage's property and to avoid alienating it is evident. Women's rights to property are limited; their dowry primarily consists of personal possessions (fabrics, furniture, silver, jewels). The land endowment alloted girls, more common in recent times, is less important than that of boys; moreover, these pieces of land are located in peripheral positions in order to avoid affecting the main property of the household and its integrity. The property included in the girls' dowries can neither be developed nor sold without the consent of the girls themselives. When a woman dies, if she has no children, her native family can reclaim half of this property.

The division and transmission of property takes place by and large at the time of boys' marriage; the father divides the property in an equal manner while keeping a section of land for himself which will serve him in his old age. He can also choose to divide up the entire amount and live with his youngest son on one of these sections, thus recalling the situation in Mani and in Romania , all the more so since they youngest son inherits the paternal house. But it is possible for the division to take place at the time of the death of one of the parents. The written will or the last wishes which are conveyed orally carry equal weight.

The position of the woman of Anoya is not as hard as we have seen in the tribal societies, nor is it similar to what we find in Romania and Bulgaria since the women of Anoya nevertheless live in a society where questions of honor with respect to women are considered quite serious, causing them to be closely watched and their liberty to be entirely relative. In this society, the vendetta has been widely practiced and the oppositions between lineages can take on violent forms. The theft of livestock which characterizes other Mediterranean societies (the Sandinian, Sicilian, Calabrian, Corsican, for example), competition among lineages, small wars over the possession of pastures are all situations which create a climate where gunshots are quickly fired. The village of Anoya can be considered as typical for European Mediterranean; it seems to be, as far as a social structure is concerned, situated between the two poles formed by the Romanians on the one end and the Albanians, the Montenegrins, and the Maniotes on the other.

## THE VILLAGE OF ELYMPOS ON THE ISLAND OF KARPATHOS

While visiting Greece and the regions inhabited by the Greeks in the first half of the 19th century, Georg Ludwig von Maurer (1835, I) noted, in a brief but precise manner, the judicial customs adhered to in particular regions; this enables us to see that in certain regions of the Aegean Sea custom differs profoundly from that on continental Greece. If everywhere else a women's role is inferior to that of man, with the family name and property being linked to the latter, there are, in the regions of the Aegean Sea, societies where the woman occupies a position equal to man and where the principle of equality concerning property, a principle dominating eastern Europe in general, is no longer followed. Mihail G. Mihailidou-Nouarou published in 1926 a work rich in information on just such an example, the island of Karpathos. His work, which has been followed by other publications, presents the history and the custom of several of the islands of the Aegean Sea by means of comparison (Tsenoglou, 1983).

Since the question deserves to be understood as much in terms of its scope as well as its structure, several research projects done in my seminar focused on the regions of the Aegean Sea. Here I am presenting one project which ended up being in the form of a doctoral thesis, and which describes the village of Elympos; it is the fruit of the work of Sophie Capetanakis (1979 and 1981). The same village attracted the attention of Bernard Vernier who studied its matrimonial and property systems for one part of the village population (1977). In addition to these works, the study by Demetrios Agamemnon Philipides (1973), which insists primarily on the relationships of this society to its space should be included. Here I am summarizing the essential aspects noted about Elympos, beginning with those aspects which facilitate a comparison with the previously described societies.

The village of Elympos is located north of the island of Karpathos (from the group of Dodecanese) situated at an altitude of 300 meters, the island has the appearance of a mountain village. The island succeeded in maintaining a certain independence under the Ottoman occupation, with the administrative affairs being formerly under the jurisdiction of three notables: a *"proestos"* aided by two *"dimogerontes,"* elected by acclamation for a year.

The village is marked by the presence of two professional groups, one linked to agriculture, the second to animal breeding. The two groups are complimentary since animal breeding requires land belonging to the farmers and because agriculture needs the presence of the animals which fertilize the land with their dung. Thus, the technical process of agricultural cultivation and animal breeding, which, in other societies involve the same group practicing the two professions simultaneously, is in this case practiced by two distinct groups. The agricultural land is divided into several quarters, limited, and fenced; the quarters are cultivated according to a triennial system which allows one or more of these quarters to remain fallow; it is primarily on these areas of land that the shepherds' sheep and goats come to graze. During the two other years, they are planted with wheat and barley. The right to common grazing functions on a regular basis; once the harvests have been transported to the lofts, the shepherds' herds can roam freely everywhere.

The group of farmers presents a particularity concerning the transmission of property and it is this particularity which characterizes the local society. In contrast to all of the societies of the Balkan regions, on several of the islands of the Aegean Sea, property is not divided. Moreover, here property is divided into two categories: property associated with men and property associated with women. The first born son, *"kanakaros,"* and the first born daughter, *"kanakaria,"* children of a couple who were also first born children, inherit the property at the exclusion of all their brothers and sisters.

The eldest female heir receives the whole of the mother's property, which she, in turn, had inherited from her own mother; the eldest male heir receives the whole of the father's property, that he had inherited from his own father. The property is neither divided nor sold, it is passed on in its entirety to the individual deemed by custom to be the sole heir. An heir (or an heiress) can only marry an eldest child. It therefore appears that feminine property, whose composition in principle does not change, is allied for a generation with the masculine property, which also does not change in principle; subsequently both of these properties are going to be allied with a property of the opposite six for a generation.

The terms *kanakaros* and *kanakaria,* which refer to the eldest heirs, come from the verb *"kanakevo,"* meaning to care for, to cajole, to over-protect a child (Capetnakis, 1979, p. 20). These words express the privi-leged situation of the eldest children, a situation which assures them a superior social status to that of their brothers as well as vis-a-vis the entire local society. The youngest children have an obviously inferior situation, resulting from the consequence of the order of the birth.

At the time of the transmission of property, a given name is also transmitted. Each feminine and masculine lineage disposes of two names; if the first generation bears the name A, the second the name B, the third will again bear the name A, and the fourth the name B. Each man and woman thus bears the given name of his or her grandfather or grand-mother, according to his or her sex. Every two generations the given name returns to the lineage, as if the grandmother or grandfather had been brought back to life. This rule is strictly observed, the simultaneous possession of the patrimony and grandparents' name being obligatory.

A second rule is followed: the second born son receives the maternal grandfather's name (and not the paternal, like the eldest son) and the second born daughter the name of the paternal grandmother (and not the maternal, like the eldest daughter). A third son receives the maternal or paternal uncle's name, according to the degree of influence of the two groups.

The existence of rules concerning the transmission of the given name appears everywhere in Europe. These rules, which are just now being well-known, bring to light several elements which frequently appear, for example, the grandparents' name being transmitted to nephews and nieces, a certain order in the transmission of these names taking into account alternately the lineages of the father and the mother and lastly, the name of a recently deceased parent being given to a newborn. But nowhere is this transmission of given names accompanied by the trans-mission of property, except, of course, on several islands of the Aegean Sea.

Due to the whims of fate concerning the birthrate, not all of the *kanakares* couples are fortunate enough to give birth a male and a female child each generation, nor are they exempt from having only boys or girls. If, for example, the girl is absent, the women's patrimony is passed on to the second boy, who takes the maternal grandfather's name. He is

not, for all that, the founder of a new lineage of *kanakares,* but strictly
a link which passes on feminine property from one feminine generation
to the next, since the property will inevitably be given to a girl. When he
passes on the property to his daughter, now heiress, he also passes on his
mother's given name, and the daughter of his daughter will receive his
grandmother's name (Capetanakis, 1979, p. 63). Thus, if his grandmother's
name is Maroukla, his mother's Vastarkoula, and his Pavlos, the succession
of names would be as follows:

Maroukla
Vastarkoula
Pavlos . . . . . . . . . . . . . . . . . . . . . . (youngest son of Vastarkoula,
Vastarkoula                                          bearing the name of the
Maroukla                                             father of Vastarkoula and
                                                     who is replacing a female
                                                     Maroukla)

The same situation occurs if the couple only has girls, in which case
the second daughter takes the place of the rightful male heir for a generation in order to pass the entire inheritance (name and property) to her
eldest son. Other situations can arise, for example a couple which only
has one child. Here, this only child (called *"diplokanakaris"* or *"diplo-
kanakaria"*) passes on both patrimonies and both series of names to his
first born children, boy and girl.

Orkis                                    Foula
Minas                                    Marinia
Orkis . . . . . . . . . . . . . . . . . . . . . . only child
Minas                                    Marina
Orkis                                    Foula

The same situation occurs when the only child is a girl, a girl who receives,
for a single generation, the whole of the two properties and who will
pass on the names of the two lineages.

Another case which presents itself involves the death of the eldest
son or daughter. In such a case, the second son or daughter passes on the
land patrimony and the name of the masculine or feminine lineage. It also

occurs that at the time of the death of the eldest son, the name of the youngest is changed to that of the eldest which is in turn accompanied by the transmission of the property (Capetanakis, 1979, pp. 70-71). The changing of names is practiced in cases where the deaths of the eldest son or daughter occurs at an advanced age of the parents, thus supposing that they would not be able to give the name of the eldest child to a newborn.

Finally, there is the possibility of the couple remaining childless. In this situation, a double adoption, that is of a boy and a girl, becomes imperative. The children are chosen from among the proper blood relations of the couple and, if possible, from those already bearing the necessary name.

The property of a *kanakare* includes several things; flat fields, suitable for farming, a stable situated on the best of the agricultural quarters, cabins in each of the agricultural quarters, pastures rented to shepherds, a windmill, a garden planted with vegetables, beehives (an occupation exclusively reserved for the *kanakares*), a small boat, a chapel, and a team of oxen. The heir, in addition, takes possession of the paternal house, and the heiress the maternal house. Both are located on the highest place in the village, where only the *kanakares* have houses (Capetanakis, 1979, p. 158).

The transmission of the patrimony takes place at the time of marriage, at which time the parents retire to a house belongong to the father and live on a small part of the land (*"geromdomiri"*) that they cultivate for their substenance and that of the younger children. By transmitting the property, they are at the same time passing on their position as *kanakares* with all the honor that term brings. The *gerondomiri* is linked to the death of the parents to the patrimony of the *kanakares*. Marriage is uxorial with the man coming to live in the woman's house. When the parents retire to the paternal house, formerly inhabited by the grandparents, the latter will now be dislodged from that location and will separate and live in the line corresponding to their sex, the grandmother with her new *kanakaria*, and the grandfather with the new *kanakare*. In addition to the patrimony mentioned above, there are also gifts received at the time of marriage, gifts which follow a special system but do not change the essential makeup of the property.

What happens to the younger sons? The boys are condemned to emigrate: those who do remain establish themselves as artisans or masons. The younger daughters do not leave the village; they can live with their parents on the gerondomiria, but upon the death of their parents, the younger daughters are divided among the eldest children (boy and girl) who are already married and who will employ the younger ones as agricultural workers. The division of the younger daughters is determined by the name that they bear; if the name is one taken from the father's side, they will join the family of the eldest brother; if it is taken from the maternal family, they will live with the domestic group of the eldest sister. A good number of the younger daughters marry people having an inferior social status, for example, shepherds or small farmers.

The shepherds form a separte group, separated from that which gives the *kanakares*. Their profession requires them to have relationships with the latter, but since their status prevents any marriage with the *kanakares*, we see marriages formed between them which are based on baptismal relations. It is therefore a form of kinship accessible to groups between which marriage is forbidden, for example, between Christians who are forbidden to marry Moslems. In this case, Christians and Moslems, form relationships of special kinship that of the first haircut, a form which is not recognized by the Church. But since nothing prevents the shepherds from having godparenthood relations with the kanakares, these relationships developed themselves all the more so since the kanakares avoid godparenthood relations with other kanakares. This is explained by the fact that godparenthood relations brings about marriage bans, and the kanakares being so few in number wish to avoid these bans as much as possible (Capetanakis, 1979, pp. 214-216). Special relationships are woven between godparents and godchildren, where visits, gifts, and contracts often come up and take care of the interests of each person.

Since the shepherds' rights to one part of the land of the kanakares are stable and transmittable to their children, a sort of right to double property appears; the right of the kanakares to rent their land and the right of the shepherds to use it.

Obvious changes intervene in the village organization: younger sons who have emigrated become wealthy, kanakares become poor, and the land loses its value. Changes also come into play in the basic land itself; kanakares sometimes marry people who are wealthy but who do not hold the status of the kanakares. The whole of these changes results in the fact that the position of the kanakares is no longer the same as it was throughout the past; thus, the principal village church, each kanakaia had her "*merees,*" a stone slab on which she seated herself which attending a religious service; the slabs were destroyed. The same was true for existing stalls in the church on which only the kanakares seated themselves; these too were demolished.

The superior situation of the kanakares which makes them different from the rest of society also expresses itself in customs. In his study on the two islands of Tilos and Kassos, Zacharoula Tourali (1980) describes similar situations to those of Elympos. On Kassos, the first born children, those who have the greatest rights to the land, are called "*kanakarides*" (men) and "*kanakares*" (women); they number twelve couples, the origin of this number probably being the result of an intended action and not the result of a free process of evolution of the local society. On Tilos, they are called "*protoyios*" or "*protokori;*" on the other islands the names vary, "*nkiolyris*" and "*nikokyria*" on Nysiros, "*protonikokyris*" and "*protonikokyria*" on Halkis. In all cases, they occupy a preeminent position; they administer their collectivity; they marry among themselves. In order to come back to the custom of the eldest being the sole heirs, the same process of the loss of the former, distinctive signs is observed in the contemporary world in the division of property, wealth, or honors.

## THE TRANSHUMANT ANIMAL BREEDERS

Three groups of transhumant shepherds used to travel the roads of the Balkan regions; the Youroucks of Turkish extraction, who left Europe after the appearance of the national Balkan states; the Saracatsans of Greek extraction, part of who still live today in Bulgaria where they are refered to as Karakatchans (Marimov, 1964), but whose majority lives in Greece; and finally, the Armâns, refered to by the other Balkan populations as the Vlachs, of Romantic extraction, related to the Romanians. In opposition to the first two groups, the Armâns not only include the shepherds, but the sedentary groups as well, whose occupations are not linked to animal breeding. Between the two groups of animal breeders, the Saracatsans and the Armâns (Vlachs), the resemblances are striking; discussions as to the origin, primarily of the Saracatsans, aimed at discovering if they are Armâns which have come under Greek influence, or of nomadic Greeks, do not yield a satisfactory answer due to the lack of information concerning their past. However, this problem is not a focus of this study. In the passages which follow, I will be content to describe the principal units of the two groups in order to situate them within the whole of the populations of South-eastern Europe.

The Armâns are the descendants of the former romanized Thracians and Illyrians; in antiquity, they lived everywhere in the Balkan regions, on occasion forming the majority of the population. The survivors of this population, whose medieval history was important, live in Yugo-slavia, Albania, Bulgaria, and primarily in Greece, where a good many of their most important villages are located. While they lived within the framework of the Ottoman Empire, the animal breeders of Romanic extraction were easily able to travel from one end of the empire to the other; once the national states were formed and the modern borders closed, their former roads were cut off and the direction of their trips changed (Beuermann, 1967). Cut off from one another, they blended in with the population which surrounded them, so much so that there were no schools anywhere in their language.

If the Romanic population living south of the Danube can be under-stood within the framework of the Armân denomination, it is probable that throughout the past, true tribes were distinguished among them, each one bearing a name. Only one of these tribes can be considered today as still constituting a tribe. They are the Fârşerots referred to by the Greeks as Arvanito-Vlachoi, Albania Vlachs, because a large part of the group lives in Albania and because they speak Albanian as a second language. In contrast to the Albanian or Montenegrin tribes discussed above, this tribe presents an important distinction; if it can be said that the former occupy a precise territory where they all meet, a territory which belongs to them, the Fârşerots, which recognizing the fact that they form a single group, are spread out over a large territory, and move on to new pastures in different directions. And although the preceding tribes have an assembly, a leader, this is not the case of the Fârşerots. The same is true for the Saracatsans who, while recognizing themselves as mem-bers of one group, do not have a territory of their own; they do not live together, neither do they have an assembly nor a leader.

What are the elements which enable us to consider some of them as tribes? First of all their awareness that they form a unique, endogamous group, bearing the same name, the same customs, and the fact that they consider all others as outsiders, even if some, the Saracatsans, feel close to the Greeks and others, the Armâns align themselves with other Romanic populations. In the second half of the 19th century, Ioan Neniţescu offered this description of the Fârşerots "... even if they are living near other Armâns, near Voscopole or near Gramosta, they do not inter-marry; they do not take their girls for their wives and do not give them theirs. Their national sentiment is close to that of the other Armâns, but their family is distinct. If a young Armân from Voscopole,from Gramosta, of from another region of Olympus is in love with a Fârşerots and only after having adopted their dress, their customs, their beliefs and their language, will he be able to marry his heart's desire and be received into his father-in-law's family who, according to Fârşerots custom, is the leader of his daughters-in-law, his sons-in-law, and his sons" (p. 175). This quo-tation enables us to understand what characterizes the group; the fact that custom is mentioned above all is not surprising since it has played such a prominent role in other past societies as well; added to that is life style.

Even if the entire tribe is not consolidated by the possession of a common land or by another common, economic element, these elements are found in the smaller social units. At the lowest level, that which corresponds to the household, we find the social unit called "*fǎmeli*" family (Capidan, 1926, p. 38). The domestic group is essentially made up of the couple and its married sons (Capidan, 1942, p. 51); they live together under the authority of the father and of his wife, their mother; they work together and jointly own their property, essentially made up of sheep. They separate upon the death of their father or when all of the sons are married, even though they can still continue, for a certain time, to form one social unit'

The girl's situation is typical for this domestic group, as we see in this passage taken from Ion Neniţescu (1895, pp. 175-176): "... the family of Fârşerots includes sons and daughters; upon his marriage, the eldest son has his wife come to his parents house where she is received as a daughter. But all the household responsibilities fall to her; she cooks for everyone, brings water, and makes bread for everyone, which is a difficult task, in short, she must do all of the household chores, since her mother-in-law crosses her arms, looks at her and gives her orders. When the time comes that a second son marries, a new daughter-in-law comes to the house. The first one begins to find some rest, and the second takes on the various responsibilities. The same scenario occurs for the third and fourth, etc. When the daughters born in the house are of marrying age, if the father is an important person, the newly weds will settle in her house. In which case, it will be this girl's turn to serve her sisters-in-law, since the domestic responsibilities always fall to the most recently married bride." The new bride does not address her husband by name; if she has something to say to him, she says it to his parents and when she speaks about him, she uses the word "him."

Where the Armân population is established in a stable manner, in wealthy and well-constructed villages, we find communities which have a stable living arrangement established on the mountains, and where different professions live: animal breeders (who regularly make the trip down to the plains), jewelers, fashion designers, builders, and various other craftsmen. A communal counsel oversees village life; it has a leader, the *"auş"* from the Latin *"avus"*—elderly, aided by a counsel of elderly— *"auşauet"* (Capidan, 1942, p. 70). If we were to observe the animal breeders, we would note several families grouped together which constitute a *"fâlcare"* (from the Latin "falx, falcem"—sickle). This name is probably given to the group because the living situation at the level of the high mountain pastures, under tents, takes the semicircular shape of a sickle. The group is lead by a leader known as *"čelnic,"* name of Slavic origin which dates back to the Middle Ages when the term referred to a high ranking civil servant in the court of the Serbian king (Capidan, 1942, p. 71). The čelnic is hereditary and is passed on to the same lineage, either to the eldest son, or to the leader's brother, according to wealth, prestige, and/or the candidates' knowledge of a similar office. The čelnic is required to defend the whole group, which shows solidarity before the law; the leader also takes care of any matters dealing with the outside world, for example, the paying of taxes and the following of trials. There are many conflicts which arise during the course of the group's activities, conflicts which can be said to be normal considering the fact that important groups, accompanied by tens of thousands of sheep, goats, horses, mules, and dogs, make their way through long itineraries on lands belonging to numerous owners. The čelnic rents pastures, sells everyone's products, divides the revenues, hires helpers, judges, puts an end to vendettas which are common for an armed population (Noe, 1938, pp. 19-21). Caravans are organized using the groups' transportation animals, caravans which travel far, linking the peninsula from north to south; they advance under the direction of the čelnic (Noe, 1938, p. 20).

If we examine the domestic group of the Saracatsans, we find the same composition as that of the Armâns; the father lives together with his sons, administering jointly one property. Sometimes the group is larger (Kavadias, 1965, p. 150). The reasons for the separation of the group are analyzed by Campbell (1964, p. 80); he notes either the death of the father or the marriage of the boys as the significant moments. The group is strongly organized into a hierarchy: the father—his sons—the mother—the daughters—the children. The position of the new bride is the same as that of the Armân group: "The essential fact is that the new bride is subordinate to all other adults in the extended family. Even the five-year-old tries with varying success to boss the 'new bride.' As a worker her services belong to the whole group. She is, as they often say, 'our bride.' Not only does she care for the comfort of her own husband but she is responsible for washing, mending, and darning the clothes of all unmarried brothers" (Campbell, 1964, p. 64). "During the early months of the marriage the young husband gives the minimum of overt public attention to his bride... For her part, a bride will never address her husband before other members of the family. If she requires anything she arranges it through her husband's family" (p. 65).

Kavadias adds some characteristic elements (1965, p. 141): "The young couple... settles in the hut where the husband's paternal family lives. Given the fact that the Saracatsans' huts do not have walls and that everyone sleeps on the floor of the house, it is easy to understand that the wedding night takes place amid family!" In this manner, the paternity of any future children will not be in doubt.

The superior social unit, made up of several domestic groups, is directed by a leader referred to by the same name as the čelnic of the Armenians, the "*tseligas*." This name gives rise to the name of the unit which he commands, which is called the "*tseligato*." "The elements of the tseligato are also organized into a hierarchy; at the head we find the tseligas and his family. Next, on an equal footing, are associated families and isolated shepherds. This is true from a contractual point of view; in reality, the families organize themselves into a hierarchy according to their importance in terms of size and herds, with isolated shepherds occupying a subordinate position" (Kavadias, 1965, p. 182). By analyzing the responsibilities of the tseligas and the motives which compel people to organize themselives into a tseligato, Kavadias finds the elements described above for the *fălcare* of the Armâns. Many more aspects, common to both groups, of Greek or Romanic expression, can be listed, but this is not the object of this chapter. The life of the two transhumant groups is in the process of changing rapidly and will soon be clarified; Irwin Sanders (1962, pp. 97 sq.) describes with sensitivity several aspects of their contemporary life (see also Beuermann, 1967).

* * *

Before concluding this chapter, I will add that the work which is on going in my seminar brings to light other differently organized Greek societies; I will mention three of them. First there is the society described by Ioanna Beopoulou who finds a division of the local patrimony between men and women in the village of Trikeri (in the Pilion); the men have property which are linked to the sea and their property focuses on any relationships dealing with the sea. The women are linked to that which deals with the land, and with agriculture (Beopoulou, 1981). On the island of Skiros, the society is divided into several categories which are easy to perceive due to the difference in dress; the *archontes* (nobles, land owners); the farmers who live on the archontes' land; shepherds; craftsmen; the Church with its property intervenes as a fifth factor; each group occupies a separate quarter. The island of Skiros is not the only one to present a similar structure. Lastly, the group made up of the father and his married children, which appears to be an exception, appears more and more as a group characterizing various Greek regions, not only the Saracatsans. Lambros Liavas (1982) describes just such a society on Eubea and the information which I have at my disposal allows me to presume that probably throughout the past these types of domestic groups were more common.

We find familial and economic associations between father and son, or simply between brothers, and also among Armâns who practice a profession other than animal breeding. For example, the Armân jewellers of Kalarytes (Calari) who today have come down to Joannina, still maintain the former tradition concerning the organization of workshops (Triantaphylou, 1978). The merchants of the past, Greek or Armân, whose trade linked them to far off eastern or western societies, often saw the father and his sons working together. Other examples can be found, but all these cases are still waiting on their monograph. What seems to me to be a decisive element for justifying the composition of a domestic group is the necessity itself of their profession. The animal breeders offer a good example to illustrate this point; a sheep owner does not have a single herd, because the rams, sheep which have given birth, sterile sheep, and sheep under one year of age, form different herds and each one requires the presence of a shepherd. The same is true for the companies of merchants working in various cities, which require the concommitant presence of several associates, the closest relatives also being the best colleagues.

# CHAPTER V

## COMPARISONS AND HYPOTHESES

The social units described above have several elements which insistently appear and which define them: a human group, a habitat, a property, and a common life. These elements have been presented for each of the units and now another aspect which has not been treated, the spiritual element, will form the basis of this next chapter. We will come back to several of the ideas which seem to ensue from the preceding chapters.

### Family or Household?

Men of science who study domestic groups are insistent upon using the term "family," which suggests the idea of kinship, in order to designate the smallest social unit. The word appears in the langues of south-eastern Europe as a neologism of relatively recent origin, developed under the influence of the western cultures. The peasants themselves and the people of past cultures in general do not use the word, but rather use terms which have another meaning and another significance. We find

166

two categories of notions in the vocabulary of the peasants and people of the past; the first includes words which clearly refer to the smallest social unit, for example "*gospodărie*" for the Romanians, "*nikokirata*" fro the Greeks, "*household*" for the English; the French had the word "*maisnie*" but which has now disappeared from modern French. The second category includes words having a double meaning, of which one is that of household, as in the case of words such as "house," "fire," "household," and "smoke."

This difference between men of science and peasants in the designation of the smallest social unit creates language imprecisions which result in interpretations which have no relationship to reality. The word family is imprecise, since it refers to persons living in a household; it also refers to people outside this household; moreover, it exclusively suggests the human group and not the others which make up a household. The limitations of the notion of the family cannot be fixed since in the term family the reference can either be to a couple or to the someone's large parenthood.

If we want to refer in a precise manner to the people living in a household, the notion of the domestic group must be used, a notion which facilitates the understanding that these people live together, work together, have the same property, the same religious holidays, without eliminating the idea that they are related. As soon as the member of the family detaches himself from his domestic group, he forms another social unit, all the while remaining a member of his native family; this separation from his domestic group is of prime importance and appears as a dominant element as much within peasant traditions as in past laws. Taxes, the vendetta, solidarity before the law, all change for a person who detaches himself from his domestic group, even if from the stand point of kinship his relationships remain unchanged with his native group.

This is why I have not used the word family in my analysis, and have chosen the terms household or domestic group, thus following the normal thought processes of people that I have studied.

A second manner of envisioning things, which also seems to me to be erroneous, is the following: numerous studies record the number of people making up a domestic group. They then pass on to a classification which, according to whether the domestic group is made up of two, five, ten, or thirty people (I am using random numbers), they classify the groups into such and such type of family. Without doubt, the number of people who live in a household is an important indication when studying a household, but this is only one indication, nothing more. In order to classify a domestic group, it must be remembered that the human group lives together, works together, has the same property, passes on this property in a manner that is characteristic for the group and forms a spiritual unit; therefore, we cannot make an abstraction out of these aspects. Finally, a human group undergoes an evolution, it passes through different phases in its life, changes the number of people which make it up, without, however, changing its character. How, then, do we arrive at a classification which takes into account what has just been said?

During the second half of the 19th century, Baltsar Bogižsić's article is entitled "De la forme dite inokosna de la famille rurale chez les Serbes et les Croates" (Paris, 1884). Bogišić contends that each domestic group passes through various phases without which we would have to assert that in each case each phase was another type of "family." He thus writes down for the first time the foundations of research which will be reinvented almost a century later, after the second world war, a research involving the different phases of the development of a family. His example is clear; the domestic group of the southern Slavs is normally based on the existence of several couples living together on the same property, a group which bears the name of *"kuča zadružna"* — house with many workers. He records this name and notes first that the name "zadruga" proposed by Karadžić is not used; despite all of this, the term zadruga has been the word utilized in scientific literature. His demonstration concerning the *kuča zadružna* has also been forgotten; this latter can, for various reasons (sickness, departure, war, division) witness its members who formerly were many in number be reduced to the presence of a single couple. In this situation, the *kuča zadružna* becomes a *"kuča inokosna,"* a house with few workers. In spite of this, it is the same type of domestic group and the same type of household because its rules of operation are the same, and the *kuča inokosna* becomes once again a *kuča zadružna* when the boys marry and have their wives come to live near them and their parents.

To come back to my demonstration, I will offer a clear example. If in a survey we find a domestic group composed of one couple, they are classified as a nuclear family. This means nothing, or almost nothing, since in reality nothing is said except that the "family" is few in number. But this couple can function in a different manner:

a) The couple has children: at the time of marriage, the boys receive their share of the land, they detach themselves from the parents and establish separate dwellings; the youngest son remains with his parents; this is the typical domestic group for the Romanians and for certain regions of Greece, and also a group that is found elsewhere, in eastern and western Europe;

b) The couple has children; the boys, at the time of marriage, have their wives come live with them and their parents, the separation and the transmission of property taking place upon the death of the father or upon the marriage of all of the boys; this is the characteristic domestic group and household of the transhumant shepherds described above, but also representative of various Slavic agricultural populations, and of others as well;

c) The couple has children; upon the marriage of the boys, they have their wives come live with them, and their grandsons do the same; the group can thus become quite large; the transmission of property is not related to death or marriage and takes place when the group splits into two or several different groups; this is the domestic group represented by certain southern Slavic or Albanian populations, but they are also found elsewhere in Europe;

d) The couple has children; only the eldest girl and boy receive the parents' property at the time of their marriage, while their brothers and sisters receive nothing and the parents retire separately, turning their position over to the eldest children; this is the society of certain islands of the Aegean sea;

e) The couple leaves property entirely to the first born, the sole heir, either boy or girl, who continues to live with the parents and the younger brothers and sisters, married or not; this is the case of the Basques or of other population French or Spanish populations, for example.

More examples can be mentioned, for example, by choosing a case where the domestic group is made up of about ten people, the evolution

only and the unfolding of the life of this group alone can give us an indication as to the type of group this is. Without knowing when a group
separates and how property is transmitted, a true classification cannot
be made. The key question of a survey, one which will easily lead to a
hoped for response, is the latter; what do the children do, especially the
boys, when they marry or when the father dies, and what becomes of the
property as a result of these changes? Other questions concerning the
house, the common life, the division of revenues, religious holidays are
needed in order to complete this initial sketch of a response.

The number of people that make up a domestic group is frequently
noted and we find that they are composed of two, five, or even ten people,
etc. etc. Next, the few in number are classified as nuclear families and
those more numerous in joint family—extended family, as if it were surely
a question of different types of families. In reality, it can be often a
single household form but which has been recorded at different times
during its evolution.

Here, I am limiting my study with the conviction that pseudo-classifi-
cations are going to continue to be made; Bogišić's example and the
oblivion into which the fundamental things which he wrote have fallen
is eloquent and justifies my reservations. In fact, paradoxically, his study
is most often interpreted as having proved the existence of two types of
family, *kuča zadružna* and *kuča inokosna,* in other words, the opposite
of what Bogišić proves throughout his study, since he considers them as
two moments of the same family.

It would be interesting to undertake a more careful analysis of the
people who detach themselves from the domestic group: the father and
the mother; the leader and the woman leader; the eldest and the youngest
sons; the elderly. Each one has a role and would allow parallels and com-
parisons between the various European societies to be made. I say European because too often European specialists forget to compare the European societies to one another, all the while using obtained results from
primitive and distant populations in comparison to Europe.

*Property*

If we put descriptions of the various property systems of south-eastern
Europe together, we find elements which repeat themselves in all the

societies, elements which are also found elsewhere in Europe. For example:

a) A distinction is made between land regularly used for farming and the commonfield. Farming land, along with all the crops worked regularly by a domestic group, are the property of this group. This land comes from the original community property of the village, phratry, or tribe. These are the pieces of land which most quickly led to individual property or property associated with small groups.

b) The commonfield essentially includes forests, pastures, high mountain pastures, sources of water; they continuously diminish in scope, being gradually eroded by cultivated fields as the population increases and the need for wheat becomes more apparent.

c) Property is linked to the men, except in the case of several islands in the Aegean Sea where property can be equally possessed by the first born boy and the first born girl. The general rule, when there are no boys in a domestic group, follows that the girl takes the place of a boy, without this being in anyway associated with the matriarchy (see also Pavković, 1986). The society of the northern Albanians is the only one where a girl can never attain property.

d) The possession of a house or of an arable piece of land on the territory of a village, phratry, or tribe gives access to the rights of the commonfield, but more and more exceptions appear as we approach modern times.

e) The rights to the arable land and to the commonfield are calculated by referring to each individual's geneaology. Sometimes this geneaology is traced back to a founding ancestor, often a hypothetical one, whose role is to justify the group's solidarity; this relationship also justifies kinship and rights to the property that originally belonged to this ancestor. The consequence of this is that being a member of the blood community gives a person rights to the common property. The people adhere to this practice in such a strict manner that, in order for rights to be accorded to newcomers, a fictitious ancestor related to the ancestors of the former inhabitants is invented for them; or, the newcomers quite simply adopt the forbearers of the former inhabitants.

## Kinship

Although kinship makes up a vast and extremely interesting chapter in south-eastern Europe, it is not the main focus of this study and will be treated more thoroughly in another publication. I must, however, bring up several aspects of kinship which will clarify the problems discussed in this study, beginning first with the forms of kinship in which the peasants of this region believe.

a) First of all there are forms of kinship which are also recognized by the Church: consanguinity, marriage, adoption, sponsorship. In addition there is a form of kinship on which the Church has not taken a clear stand, that of fraternization, sometimes disputed or sometimes accepted by the Church.

b) Forms of kinship which are not recognized by the Church play a role: fraternity my milk, kinship recognized and codified by Islamism; kinship by the midwife; kinship by baptism water; kinship of people born on the same day of the week, the same month, or those who have the same name.

c) All forms of kinship have effects on marriage in the sense that they give rise to bans. These bans can be very precise when the Church sets down written rules concerning them, but, despite all this, exceptions often appear; the bans take on a vague and changeable form involving forms of "pagan" kinship, where the bans are fixed according to oral tradition and especially when the forms of kinship in question are disappearing. These bans are in linked to the organization of the society making up a chapter of great interest; for example, in cases where the element of consanguinity plays an important role (in tribal societies), the prevention of marriage extends to infinity between persons believed to be descended from the same ancestor and bearing the same name.

d) Of all the forms of kinship, consanguinity is the most closely linked to property. Fraternization, which includes in its ritual an exchange of blood between two parties, also gives access to property.

e) Sponsorship is the form of kinship whose study had the most spectacular development after World War II. Like marriage, in addition to the rules imposed by the Church, other rules are added which have nothing to do with the Church. In 1936, Henri H. Stahl studied sponsorship in the Romanian village of Drăguş, in Transylvania, opening the way to modern research since his study focused on the relationship between sponsorship and the household. He notes that sponsorship is a stable relationship which is woven between two households and not between two isolated individuals; that baptism sponsors will serve as sponsors for marriage, and that those sponsoring marriage will also sponsor baptism, that these relationships unite in reality two households and are passed on from generation to generation. These findings are further developed and confirmed by Eugene A. Hammel in 1968 concerning villages in Yugoslavia; the clearest aspects are those which he puts forward among the Romanians (that he refers to as Vlachs).

f) Marriage, fraternization, and sponsorship play a particular role in tribal societies; alliances are formed, wars ceased, vendetta ended by marrying a boy belonging to a group to a native girl from a rival group; or by choosing a godfather from one group and godson from another; or by arranging fraternization between members of different groups. In all these cases, the concerns of kinship are based on reasons which can be called political, reasons which are lost in a modern village setting where other reasons take precedence.

## SOCIAL STRUCTURE, RELIGIOUS STRUCTURE, MAGIC STRUCTURE

The elements which link individuals by homogenizing and consolidating diverse social units seem to be consanguinity and other forms of kinship, as well as common, economic interests. In addition to that list, spiritual elements taken from religion and magic must be included. These last two, which have not been presented in the preceding chapters, are present in all cases without exception. Each society, for reasons of internal cohesion, needs a spiritual tie which links together the thoughts of those people related by consanguinity. I mention this last element because it is considered to be both spiritual and material. Without over emphasizing the point, it must be said that, for the people of the past, the blood was the soul, it was life itself. For the Orthodox Church, for example, blood comes from God and returns to him after death. The chapter on the religious and magic structure of the social units is vast; here again, I am unable to make a complete presentation of the question since such a study requires another context. However, certain elements must be introduced in order to complete the image of the social units in this particular analysis.

### The magic and religious structure of the Romanian village territory

The study of Romanian rustic life brings to light the existence of two fundamental social units: the village and the household. The village concept, such as it has been understood by the peasants themselves and as it should be understood by men of science who if they want to understand traditional life, includes several elements: a group of people, who consider themselves related, established in a single living situation and making use of a community property, known as the village territory. The men, along with their living arrangement and their territory make up a unit which cannot function unless all these elements are present. The same is true for the household. Traces of these two social units are recognized everywhere on the territory.

What are the material elements which symbolize the spiritual unit formed by each one? For the house, it is the icon, present in all houses, and which defends the domestic group, its animals, and property. For the village, it is the presence of a single village church, in addition to a priest for everyone, chosen and supported by the peasants.

When we go back to the level of the "country" ("*ţara*"), village confederation, the only living and well-studied example of the 20th century is the Ţara Vrancei. Here again, there is an icon for each house, a church for each village, and a monastery for the country, property of the country's village community. The entire region is thus based on a double cohesion, that of consanguinity above all; its inhabitants would be the descendants of seven brothers, children of a mother having received in her country the most brilliant prince of Moldavia, Ştefan cel Mare. The general assembly of the country came together to decide measures to be taken concerning the monastery (Stahl H.H., 1958, p. 174): "The actions setting this small convent against the State in order to have its rights respected are particularly interesting. In reality it is not a question of just one monastery, but of a sort of asylum for the old and poor inhabitants, a foundation for the entire country of Vrancea. All the villages of Vrancea formerly contributed to the maintenance of the monastery . . . it is a free creation of the peasants themselves, a creation in which no one could intervene and whose well-being depended not on the poverty of the neighboring villages, but on their wealth. Consequently, the monastery comes under the protection of the *epitropes/administrative* council of all of Vrancea. When I saw this monastery for the last time in 1934, an epitrope had been named by the State, a second by the House of the Church (*Casa Bisericii*); a third continued to be chosen by the village delegates . . . . The villages came together every five years for an assembly meeting, electing three delegates per village, delegates who, in turn, met in the village of Herâsträu in order to elect the *epitrope* of the monastery."

This is the clearest form of a spontaneous element, linked to the organization of a village confederation and not the result of a State or religious hierarchical decision. Another form is noted in the Dâmbovnic region (Economu, Stoianovici, 1942, p. 484); several neighboring villages which formed a related group, construct their churches so that these churches consolidate the intervillage cohesion. For example, the interior of the churches presents unitary elements, with the iconography being influenced by those who ordered it, that is to say, by the village assemblies. More evident still is the fact that these villages chose the same patron saint for their church (*Inălţarea Domnului*).

The icon, the church, the monastery, all are visible testimonies to the spiritual unity of the social units themselves. Just as the household and the village stand out among the Romanians, their holidays take on an even greater importance. In an old *Encyclopédie Theologique* (Migné) published in 1853, we find: "Each house has its patron saint in honor of whom a holiday called the '*sânt*' is observed. It is a custom for which each family bars no expense, no matter their level of poverty. The entire house is readied, the utensils are washed and cleaned, and the table covered with the most beautiful linen that the mistress of the house is able to obtain. Relatives and friends are invited to the celebration, and the memory of deceased members is venerated with a special devotional. They are even invited, by means of fervent prayers, to come join the celebration; empty seats at the table are reserved for them, with dishes, vases filled with wine, salt and bread, with the bread symbolizing peace. Apparently this is an perpetuation of the honors rendered by the Romans to the Lares or gods of the house" (p. 1941).

The household celebration can coincide with that of the saint represented on the icon that is located in the house; this icon, in turn, can be linked to the saint whose name is borne by the head of the house, but also to his profession, for example, that of the shepherd; in the shepherds' houses, icons of Saint Georges, patron saint of animal breeders, is often represented. Most often, it seems, the celebration of each household coincides with that of the patron saint of the village which is the same as that of the village church. Ion Pop Reteganul (pp. 275 sq.) describes the village celebration known as the "*nedeie*" in the region of Transylvania: "The *nedeia* is a brillant celebration, a day of great joy accompanied by games, banquets and religious celebrations in which acquaintances and relatives participate, even attracting people from distant villages to come and take part in the meals." Preparations begin a week in advance; the house is repainted, washed, and cleaned along with the courtyard and decorated with green tree branches and flowers; everyone dresses in new clothes. The table is placed in the middle of the reception room of the house and everyone goes to church; after mass, the people return home and invite passers-by to come into the house, only the Gypsies remain outside to beg. A dance is organized, musicians are invited, and toasts are offered.

It is interesting to note that the name "*nedeie*" also refers to another category of celebrations. Peasants from the regions of south-eastern Europe have gathered since remote times on the summits of mountains for religious celebrations. The summits are considered sacred by everyone, even if the divinities that are celebrated are not the same. Among the Romanians, the *nedei* are located along the Carpathian Mountains; here, I am focusing only on that aspect of the nedeie which interests me for the development of this chapter, namely their relationship to the social units. For the nedei taking place on the high mountain pastures, it is difficult to define in a social manner the society which participated in them since so many people came from distant areas. As a rule, primarily the neighboring villages of the mountain go up to the mountain pastures for a day. Can we therefore, at least for the distant past, speak of homogeneous social units including villages located on various mountain sides, villages which together organized the nedeie? What does appear evident throughout the observations that I have made up to this point is that, in the past, the mountain was not a barrier, a border, an element of separation, as is the case for the modern world, but rather was a unifying element. This is a subject which merits a separate presentation which I am unable to present here.

If we focus our attention on the territory, we first note that the territory differs in terms of criteria of the natural environment: forests, rivers, plains, mountains. The peasants value them according to the economic role that they play in their lives; for example, the forest yields wood, fruits, and edible and medicinal plants. Another series of elements introduces an even more marked social character: arable land, plots of cleared forest, fountains, roads. These aspects have been described in the first part of the book.

Nature and society exist side by side in a relationship of close interpenetration whose modes and historic evolution are just now beginning to be understood. My interpretation would be incomplete if I omitted the processes concerning magic or religion, elements which are associated as much with the organization of the environment or of the society as with their relationships. The materials available today on rites, ceremonies, beliefs, and superstitions are abundant. However, it is not their description which interests me here, but rather their structuring. My hypothesis is that there is a systematic interpenetration of the three levels of nature, of society and of magic, or, rather, of the supernatural.

In spite of their number, the publications on the subject are incomplete thus requiring me to resort often to personal observations. Moreover, only the facts presenting a general character and involving a large number of villages will be considered.

### The Territory

The peasants use the same term, "*hotar*," to refer to the limits of the village territory and the land included within these limits. Some intervillage territories, previous to the written documents of the 13th and 14th centuries, separate the villages from each other. Two or more village groups meet on their borders in order to clarify them because each group has an equal interest in assuring that these borders are respected. The administrations of medieval principalities had among their essential powers the organization of the agrimensural operations fixing or reconstituting these limits as well as the settling of disputes between neighboring peasants.

The plans, once established, acquired the character of magic borders; within the interior, where the human group lives, the space that the border must protect against outsiders, against the unknown person, is located. Destined to protect the entire village group, the defense of the border is every member's concern.

By what means could we recognize the double character of a border, which was once "social," but now becomes "magic?" Above all, the operation of demarcation itself assumed a special character; carried out by adjacent villages on their common border, this operation was accompanied by curses against possible smugglers, those who try to deceive the surveyor or who then clandestinely displace the borders. As we see in ancient documents, the resorting to these curses was a common, legal process. The priests wrote up the papers that the judge or the arbitrator carried on him in order to obtain the truth from the parties involved. The effectiveness of this system was great, proven by cases where the witnesses refused to stand up for a false case for fear of the consequences. The individual who dared displace the stones placed by the surveyor marking the border was the victim of serious annoyances in this life or in life beyond the grave.

The possible dangers which can threaten the collectivity from the outside are kept out by the village border. It is here, for example, that the plague, imagined as a woman with a hideous face travelling through the world spreading death, must be stopped. That is why peasants make use of the "plague shirt," a shirt made in one night by a group of women which is then placed on a doll standing on a stake and placed on the border facing the direction from which the plague may arrive.

Processions intended to cause a rainfall or to stop the rain went as far as the border that the cortege, led by the village priest, did not cross; the hoped for result was only valid for the village territory. This was true for the ringing of the church bells (or other processes) which protected the village from hail; hail still fell on neighboring territories. Various magical operations were practiced near the borders; for example, the heart of a deceased who had become a vampire, being capable of causing an excessive rainfall, killing people, or stopping the lactation of the cows, was removed from the corpse and thrown on the other side of the border. Supernatural beings themselves took these into account; this was the spot where they gathered to fight.

Most of the regions inhabited by the Romanians were covered with forests, cleared little by little in order to make room for pastures and farm land. The vast majority of villages made use of three categories of land, each one having a different economic function: the forest, the meadows, and the farm land. The forest, even though it was a part of the territory, is considered the mysterious zone, still wild and untamed. Animals live in the forest, and beliefs concerning them are numerous, but the essential element seems to me to be the forest itself, the trees.

The forestry zone was the last to remain community property; individual property begins as soon as a task is complete. For example, felled trees or simply those waiting to be so, or cleared land utilized for a certain period of time are all considered as private property. Trees are living beings and the relics of dendrolatry have relentlessly maintained themselves up to our day (Stahl, P.H., 1959). The tree talks, it houses living beings, it can be angry or happy, it can help, bring health or misfortune. The tree replaces the young bride or groom for young people who die before marriage. It accompanies the young bride and the nuptial cortege, it defends the courtyard, the animals, and the house; confessions are made to the tree, it pardons sins. Its role is, in principle, good, but you must know how to take advantage of it. Wood is cut following precise rules. Even though "the mother of the forest," a mean, ugly, old woman, lives there, the forest does appear in songs and in oral literature as a loved species whose advantages outweigh its inconveniences.

The meadows and the glades appear less clearly defined: these are the areas that the fairies prefer for dancing, and it is not advisable to fall asleep there because of the risk of waking up ill. The animals which come to graze in the grass are protected by magical processes which are widely used.

Much more clear is the situation involving the farm land, the more strongly humanized space where the farmer takes the fruits of his harvests from the "holy" land. There are several elements which are distinguished concerning this land: the borders, the middle, and the beginning of the road which extends from the living arrangement to the fields. Romanian villages in the last centuries have been organized according to a system of strip fields; the properties are adjacent to one another and their borders form straight lines; the elements of the social organization of the village are recognized here. Sometimes the land itself bears the name of such and such a lineage. The farm land makes up a great space "the field" ("câmpul," "țarina"); this is where the harvests must be protected, where forgiveness is asked of the land for it having been worked and for the robbing of its produce, and where gratitude is expressed for the protection of the men who spend a great deal of their time.

It is therefore normal for many practices to take place in this area. As a general rule, the beginning of the farming and the harvest are marked by ceremonies, carried out by the peasants themselves, in part with the aid of the priest. The processions can follows the general border of the fields, retracing the steps taken by the land surveyors. The processions can stop anywhere to officiate, but two spots in particular are singled out for preference: the middle of the field and the start of the road leaving the village, that is to say, the entrance of the field. Crosses guard the latter; the forms differ according to region. In northern Transylvania, crucifixes are found which explain catholicism and which is linked to the art of central or western Europe; they are not found in areas where orthodoxy dominated. The crosses are placed in close proximity to the borders, or somewhere in the middle of the land, or they can even be placed at the exit of the village. This is the place where the priest normally stops to officiate before blessing the fields, where tables for the objects of the cult can be found. I have sometimes found crosses for the harvests next to a fountain; I have also seen them in the middle of vineyards. Special ceremonies protect the latter, strangely recalling the sacrificial ceremonies of antiquity.

Whether it is a question of magical operations or of religious processions, the same places (borders, roads, entrances, and the middle of an area) are preferred for these occasions. The same is true for ceremonies intended to bring on or stop the rain, ceremonies which mark the end of agricultural tasks, or magical operations practiced nightly by witches.

Finally, there is a distinction made concerning the high points (the summits, for example) and the various sources of water. If there is a hill, and especially there is a road that leads to the summit, a chapel or a cross is installed in this location. The high points of the territory appear to be associated with extremely ancient cults traces of which can still be found. When possible, a church (and later chapels) are built on these spots, in a place where it can dominate the dwellings. Numerous celebrations underscore the importance attached to these high areas. During certain religious celebrations, the peasants gather on the mountains, in the high mountain pasture regions, or on the summit of a hill. Not only are marriages and dances held in these areas, but contracts are also finalized here. I was able to see several of these "nedei," celebrations which have now become rare (Conea, 1940, I, chap. VII). At the northern end of Romania, in Bucovina, I saw peasants gather on a hill on Saint Elie's Day; among those present were peasants of Slavic origin from neighboring villages.

In the aquatic domain, a distinction is made between the rivers, springs, and fountains on the one hand, and the ponds on the other. Various beliefs are associated with the latter, but due to their rarity, I am mentioning them only as a point of interest. On the other hand, each village makes use of a spring whose sacred character is incontestale. Caring for or planting a tree, cleaning or constructing a fountain, harnessing a spring, these are all considered meritorious actions. By doing these things, a person is assured of having water and fruits in the afterlife, for himself and his family. The number of magical operations including the utilization of "running water," "virgin water" is impressive. Water is good, but again, you must know how to take advantage of it. The fountain from time to time talks to the "dead," in fact the soul of a child thus justifying the drownings of children. Silver coins are thrown into the water (Ciausanu, 1914, pp. 202 sq.). When water is drawn, a small amount is sprinkled on the ground to satisfy the thirst of the deceased who can be found close by. Crosses guard the fountains or the harnessed springs; they guarantee the deceased the water that they need. Often, the cross, the spring, and the tree are associated. Sometimes an image of the Virgin Mary is seen painted on an icon nailed to the trunk of an oak tree; the cult of the Virgin Mary is in fact associated to that of water and of a saved tree. In different areas of Romania or in some Balkan regions (Stahl P.H., 1965), actual altars for the cult of trees, linked to the cult of water, can be found. A special celebrations, Epiphany (*Boboteaza*), purifies the waters and assures them a sacred character for a year; the water washes away sins, illnesses, and curses.

### The Habitat

As we have seen with the territory, the settlement also has borders, entrances, roads, and fountains; moreover, it is composed of households. All around the village crosses guard the entrances and the roads, primarily at the crossroads. The English traveler, Ralph Walsh (1828, p. 183) who travelled through Romania had this to say about the presence of crosses " . . . we were instructed that we could tell if we were still in Muntenia by the wooden crosses that we were along the road. These monuments begin at the Danube and continue up to the Krapach (Carpathian) mountains. They closely resemble the same type of crosses found in Ireland, although the latter are made of stone . . . . The crosses are 10 by 12 feet, and are covered with engraved inscriptions in relief like the Greek Slovene (Cyrillic), with the monograms of Christ and the Virgin Mary, and the faces of saints. Sometimes, 10 or 12 of them are found in a row along the road and sometime one can be seen housed in a small wooden temple. Some of them have very old dates written on them. Each time that a Valaque finds himself in a unfortunate position, he makes a wish that, upon his death, a bridge, a fountain, or a cross be erected. It seems that this wish is more common than others, given the great number of monuments found along the road. When a man ends his days in a violent manner, a cross is erected where he perished in order to prevent the deceased from becoming a vampire."

If by chance, evil beings succeed in crossing the border of the village territory, they will find themselves in front of a second barrier. A document dated 1815 (Potra, 1960, doc. 566) tells us of a prince reigning in Muntenia who had marked the borders of his capital, Bucharest, with the aid of crosses whose appearance must not have differed greatly from those that I have studied throughout my research. The administrators of the town had in fact addressed a memorandum to him stating: ". . . we had formerly decided the borders of the town, and had even installed crosses in order to separate the town from the villages. . . but the inhabitants are exceeding these limits and are constructing houses and attenances outside. . ." It was therefore necessary to go "all around the town and plant crosses at the beginning of the roads which enter the area so that each person knows there marks the border of Bucharest."

In several Transylvanian villages, the crosses are installed even in the middle of the crossroad. When the funeral cortege makes its way toward the cemetery, it stops in the crossroads and the priest then reads several short prayers.

Each household has its courtyard which houses the house and the attenances, the harvests, the animals, and the domestic group itself. It must therefore be protected; numerous examples to that effect can be mentioned (Cristescu-Golopentia, 1944). I will limit myself to noting, first of all, that the courtyard has a border marked by a fence, an entrance, and a midpoint. Invisible enemies, as well as living human beings, must pass through the door. Beneficial plants or trees, whose primary quality is being green, in other words, alive, are placed in front of the entrance. The decoration of the large carriage doors, if they exist, include motifs of a magical function; a simplified outline of the tree, cross, stars, sun, or moon (Stahl, P.H., 1960). This is the third barrier, which once only a social or material one, now becomes invisible and magical. Even if the border of the village territory of even the border of the village cannot stop danger, this third barrier will also deter. Its effectiveness will be periodically reaffirmed during ceremonies when the woman make the tour of the fence two or more times. The role of the middle of the courtyard is brought to light in the Spring when the agricultural work is beginning; the cart and the oxen are placed in the middle of the courtyard and are incensed as they are turned three times before leaving for the fields. The "călușari," a group of dancers, visit the households one after the other and dance in the middle of each courtyard, which is indicated by salt and garlic. If someone dies, on burial day, before leaving the house, the people attending the services will stop in the middle of the courtyard to ask forgiveness of the deceased and to bid him goodbye and offer him a final kiss.

If all of that is not enough to keep danger away, there is still a fourth barrier, the strongest one, which is the house itself. Its construction follows rules destined to consecrate the chosen site, to assure the solidity and the luck of the people and the people it shelters, and to keep evil spirits away. The house has its own borders—the exterior walls—to which is assigned a magical role from the onset of construction when the hole is first being dug for the foundation. The construction workers, the peasants, and the priest participate in the operations. Later, once the work is completed, there is a periodic tour of the house while incensing it (Stahl, P.H., 1976, pp. 243 sq; the same, 1967).

The house has a middle which, when it is made up of a single room, coincides with the middle of that room. When there are several rooms, the middle is that of the reception room, where guests of honor and the priest are received, where the newly weds settle, and where the icons are hung. The middle of this room, which does not correspond to the actual middle of the house, is in relation to two points located at different levels: one on the floor, where men pass, and the other on the ceiling. The latter is marked by crosses, stars, and solar signs; sometimes the name of the head of the family is written there. Branches of a green willow tree or basil, brought from the church on holidays, are attached on this spot on the ceiling (if they are not placed behind the icons, they are put on the wall of the room). The main beam which crosses the ceiling in the middle is the seat of the protective decoration and beneficial plants. When the midwife cuts the umbilical cord of the newborn, after having dried it, she places it on this beam; when she comes to the house for the celebration of the first hair cut, she takes the child in her arms and riases him so that his head touches the main part of this beam; then she places the lock of hair on this beam; each operation is supposed to bring happiness. The remains of the deceased, before being buried, are placed in the middle of the room. Lastly, this is where the priest reads his prayers. The ceiling thus seems to represent, as is the case in churches, heaven, and its center, the seat of God himself; moreover, the peasants in certain Romanian regions refer to the ceiling as "heaven" ("*cerime*").

In addition, the house has certain angles that are to be avoided when sitting down. These are distinguished at the beginning of construction and are areas reserved for the setting out of food and wheat for the deceased, and where the blood of a sacrificial animal is sprinkled and its head buried together with metal money.

The construction has a summit, the rooftop. A cross, a green tree, decorated elements in wooden or clay whose form recall the tree (or even the tree topped by birds), all guard the house and assure its happiness.

Finally, the house has entrances; invisible beings (the deceased members of the family, the souls which temporarily return to the house, malicious and eerie beings) can only enter the houses through the windows or through the doors. Humans can also come with evil thoughts or bring bad luck. The entrances are therefore protected by sprinkling them with holy water or by installing on them certain plants known for the magical effectiveness; the decoration participates in this protection (crosses, the sun, the moon, stars, or a tree can be seen).

For each household there is a corresponding agricultural property, which, normally is in the form of a rectangle. Here again, there is a distinction made between the borders, protected by a stick stuck in the ground ("*potcă*"), whose top is surrounded by thatch, or by animal skulls, especially those of horses (Stahl H.H., 1934, pp. 92 sq.), attached to stakes on the fences. These skulls are especially used to protect vineyards, vegetable gardens, in other words, specialized crops. In the middle of the property, a handful of wheat, called "the priest's beard" is left after the harvest. The middle and the angles can also be the focus of magical operations carried out by the members of the domestic group and whose goal is to assure the wealth of the harvest and to appease the land.

### The Church and the Cemetery

A person who travels today in Romanian villages often sees churches, built directly in the middle of a square. But this person will often find the former village church hidden somewhere and surrounded by the cemetery. This second case is the more characteristic for the past: a church installed in the middle of a sacred place surrounded by tombs. A fence establishes the limits of the area; it has a door through which the funeral processions enter. Trees (fir or fruit trees, especially apple or plum) make the cemetery seem like a garden. In addition to this important totality, there are many customs to consider, but only several elements of nature will be discussed here to illustrate the point of this chapter.

The church is edified following rites similar to those observed for the construction of the house. The chosen site (if possible, a more elevated part of the village) is consecrated. The church itself includes limits and an entrance; the door is decorated on certain occasions with green branches, as we have seen done for houses and carriage doors. A protective decoration is represented on the flaps of the door or the frame; here we find a cross, stars, the sun, or the moon; the door of the courtyard of the church can also be decorated in similar, yet less rich, fashion.

The main section, often the only room of the church, is the naos. It is in the middle of the naos that the priest comes to recite a part of the prayers or to read the Gospels; this is also the spot where the remains of the deceased are temporarily placed; the mourning table is placed here on Good Friday and this is where the bride and groom stand during the marriage ceremony. The ceiling of the naos is its summit; the highest dome of the eastern churches, located above the center of the naos, represents heaven; God appears there, but in the form of Jesus Christ, since God does not have a human face.

In what way does the social element intervene? This subject has remained, up to the present, understudied. We know, however, that there are several ways to be seated in a church. Here is, for example, the means used in a village in southern Transylvania (Stahl, H.H., 1959, pp. 147-151); each household has a place reserved for its domestic group. The boys continue to seat themselves next to their father even after their marriage. On the other hand, the women, in a system of patrilocal life, leave their reserved place in their nature household in order to be next to their husband. In one case that I observed, still in Transylvania, in the Bihor region, a wooden church belonged to two villages; its space was divided into two parts, the front and the back; the men sat in front, the women in back, but each one either on the right or the left according to the village of which he or she was a member. When a woman from a village marries a man from the other village, she still sits in the back section but changes sides, in order to be on the same side as her husband. The seats in the church and their allocation follow the general rules concerning the transmission of property, inheritance, names, membership to one group or another.

It would be difficult to prejudge what took place in the past, in an era where lineages had an important place in social life, but this importance does seem never to have been greater than that of the household or of the village; this, for the time that historic documents can inform us. Other examples of positioning within the church with regard to position in the society can be furnished, especially those concerning Transylvania (see also Top, 1986).

A second factor, one which brings up the issue of magic, often has the opposite effect for the majority of Romania. The participants in the service are divided into two groups, the men and the women. They can seat themselves as in the case mentioned above, men in front and women in back, but they can be seen separated on the right of the church (for the men) and on the left (for women). In the princely churches, the order is even more complicated, because here is it necessary to respect very complicated hierarchy and protocol of the West; the order in succession is the prince and the prelates, seated in front of everyone, the lords, the princesses, the wives of the lords, then, if there are any places left, the petty civil servants of the court. One part of the participants remains outside. In Moldavia (Dimitrie Cantemir, 1973), this order also respects the division between men and women, which recalls the situation in peasant churches in neighboring Maramureş, where the founders of the ancient Moldavian principality came from and where the peasants thus settle in a normal manner.

Are there rules for the allocation of tombs? Here again, I am only bringing out the essential elements. The church is the most important element in the whole that it forms along with the tombs; surrounded by the cemetery (also considered as sacred) it constitutes the "middle." Families try to have their tombs located as close as possible to the church. Much thought is given to this before death, and the documents from the past which bear this out are eloquent. For example, this document coming from prince Constantin Brancoveanu which assures several important economic advantages for the priests of the church so that they can". . . serve the church night and day, all the time, pray to God for My Lordship and my deceased relatives, and all the other princes who have died before me" (Potra, 1960, doc. 110). Or, as seen in the will of a rich merchant from Bucharest, dated 1735, in which we find the entire program of a traditional burial: "And I beg all my Christian brothers to forgive me; and I myself forgive my Christian brothers. And thus, I wish with all my heart for my being to be buried, after my death, in the holy monastery of Colţea, in the church where my father and my mother are buried. And I leave thirty-three ruches and five brick stores to the holy monastery, in order to have my name and those of my parents mentioned next to the founders of the church." (Potra, 1960, doc. 250).

Princes, lords, and rich merchants thus assure themselves that their tombs will be placed in the church; sometimes they even construct a church just to be buried there and to have their name mentioned in the prayers as one of the founders. Thus they are buried in a holy place where, moreover, they can participate in all the services celebrated in the church; thanks to that and to the special prayers of the priest, access to Paradise is assured. But if there are no special economic means or holiness (the prelates can also be buried in the church), attempts are made to be buried, on the outside without a doubt, but as close to the church as possible. That is why we see the tombs of simple priests, sometimes of donors, and of people of modest means in the immediate neighborhood of the church. The farther away one gets, the more the sacred character of the place seems to dilute itself.

Every non-excommunicated Christian who has died under normal circumstances enjoys the privilege of being buried in the cementery, within the interior of the fencing. This is not the case for those who have committed suicide whose tombs are dug on the outside. This is also not the case for children who die before being baptized. In order to avoid this sad fate, sometimes even nearly lifeless newborns are baptized.

Can one recognize within the spatial organization of the tombs other criteria besides that of hierarchy and wealth? Most of the new cemeteries do not follow any rule; the deceased are buried in lines in the order that they died. But in those of the past, as I have been able to argue for the majority of the regions of Romania, a grouping by household is recognized (Stahl P.H., 1983). In several Transylvanian cemeteries there is a grouping by lineage, the bearers of the same name being buried in the same part of the cemetery; Henri H. Stahl (1958) notes this in Drăguş. More often the husband and wife are buried together; special forms of funerary crosses, having the form of double crosses or even triple ones, enable us to decode in certain regions of Muntenia the kinship of people buried together. Sometimes the old parents (if the latter have lived with their son's family) are placed in the same tomb. The children who marry found a household; they will thus have right to a new tomb. If they die before the marriage, they are buried with their parents. The daughters, after their marriage, are buried in the husband's tomb; they are therefore buried as "daughters" if they remain in their native household and as "spouses" if they are married. Pushing this thought even farther, it could be said that brothers buried together are in the same tomb not because they are brothers or spouses, but because of their being children of the couple to whom the tomb belongs.

The same grouping is found on days that are consecrated to the deceased; the relatives gather in the cemetery and, seated around a long single table, they eat on the tomb itself or next to it. The grouping is always done by households, and sometimes lineages are recognized; the women honor the memory of the deceased with their husbands, even though they may also participate in the ceremonies of their native family (Butură, 1984; Stahl, P. H., 1984).

## Paradise

In order for the description to be complete, several clarifications must be added. The church and the cemetery, in peasant folklore, seem to represent God on earth and in earthly Paradise. The church is "God's house" and the cemetery strangely recalls the garden of the Paradise. It has, in effect, the appearance of a garden; like Paradise, fruit trees are planted there as well as sacred trees (for the Romanians, the fir). A fir tree is placed on the tombs of the young people who die before marriage. Cut in the forest, its trunk is surrounded with colored wool thread and its branches are decorated with equally colored ribbons. Apples covered in silver or gold paper represent the trees and the golden fruits of Paradise; pastry birds represent souls; a pastry ladder will help the deceased climb to the seventh or ninth heaven. The entire tree is called the "tree of Paradise." Moreover, an apple tree, similar to the one planted in the center of Paradise, is planted here.

We therefore have a miniature Paradise, destined to temporarily welcome the body of the deceased (which will rise again on the Last Judgement) while their souls effectively go to Paradise if they have been just and if their living relatives help them reach there. In Paradise, they will see a world completely in gold, which has earthly pendant, but not constituted from the same noble matter. In order to appease baby Jesus, the Virgin Mary sings:

> Don't cry my son
> Don't cry my dear
> I will bring you

> Two apples
> Two pears
> All four of gold
> With the key to Paradise."
>                 (Viciu, 1914, p. 48.)

But what is the true Paradise? It is represented in wall paintings of the churches as a garden, a beautiful garden surrounded by a high wall. The trees which are represented often have the appearance of the cypress, the sacred tree of the Mediterranean regions, unkown in Romania. The explanation resides in the fact that the religious wall painting is closely related to the Byzantine tradition; artists and Greek monks frequently came north of the Danube, just as Romanian monks frequently spent part of their lives in Greek monasteries.

Paradise has a border and, therefore a door, guarded by Saint Peter. It has a middle, a place of honor occupied by the Virgin Mary. Another peasant image of the world beyond resembles Paradise, but includes pagan elements. It is called "heaven;" it is located high up, very high up, and has borders which touch the earth, there where it ends, and doors located "at the end of the world," there where the limits of heaven (called "heaven's stockings"—"*poale*") touch the earth; it is by this route that the angels can come to earth and return to heaven. It has a middle where God, surrounded by his saints, is seated at a table; on rare occasions, when heaven opens (in the middle, along the Milky Way), God looks down to see what the mortals are doing. He is seated at a table and in front of him is an apple tree, as he would put one up, decorated, in the middle of the table around which are assembled the living at the time of a ceremony organized somedays after the marriage; the guests show their hope to all be joined together in Paradise. This is the same manner in which the relatives eat together with the deceased in the cemetery, prefiguring the day when they will meet again in Paradise, because in the afterlife, the society here below must transform itself and each person will be in his household and in his village (Stahl, P. H., 1983).

A complete series of ceremonies are thus destined to guarantee familial and village unity in heaven. We therefore find from one end of my study to the other the presence of the two fundamental social units: the village and the household. Magical practices consolidate the ties between their members and assure happiness. The lineage, which has a temporary role and which lessened during the period that I studied has, perhaps for that reason, such a diminished role in customs.

Finally, I wish to underscore the recurrence of certain elements: borders, entrances, high points, the middle, and sometimes angles. The first two normally go together; the next two, the high points and the middle, often coincide. These elements are found in the social organization of the whole of the territory, in that of the whole of the civilized lands, of isolated farming parcels, in the living situation, the courtyard, the house, the church, and the unit church-cemetery. Finally they are even found in the afterlife, whose correspondence with the world below is striking.

## The "Slava"

The characteristic celebration of the social units of Yugoslavia is called the slava. "The *Slava* is a custom so essentially Serbian that the Roman Catholic Serbs also practice it. Even the Mahometans who, to conform with the precepts of their religion, had to forsake it, still know that it was their Slava, and on a certain day make offerings to the Christian churches. There is a Serbian proverb: 'There where is the Slava is the Serb'" (Georgevitch, 1917, p. 48; see also Sicard, 1943, p. 350). In Montenegro, in Herzegovina, in Dalmatia and in Bosnia, it is called *"krsno ime"* –Christian name; in northern Yugoslavia, it is called *"svetac"*–saint; it is also called *"sveti dan"*–holy day (Georgevitch, 1917, p. 48). Since the slava is related to a saint, the question is asked *"koja služis?"*–"who are you serving?" *"Ja služim sveta Nikola"*–"I am serving Saint Nicholas," or another saint (Gopčević, 1889, p. 262).

"The separate household celebrations serve to honor and reaffirm ties with matrilineal kin, almost always from a different neighborhood and often from a different village, as well as to maintain bonds of friendship with unrelated fellow villagers" (Halpern, Kerewsky-Halpern, 1972, p. 110). Each household has its own slava and its religious and magical aspects are numerous. Slobodan Zečević (1969), notes the ritual aspects attached to fruit, wheat, ritual bread, the role of the group's leader in the ritual, a role which recalls the office of the priest, and the elements with regard to the cult of the deceased. This aspect seems to him particularly important, because it evoles and glorifies the ancestors of the domestic group. Fr. Kanitz (1868, p. 260) links the cult of the Penates of antiquity with that of the cult of the domestic family (see also Trojanovitch, 1909, p. 186).

The preparations for the celebration begin well in advance, because everything is assembled with care, patiently: bread, brandy, honey, all that is needed for the preparation of an abundant meal. The house is cleaned, a cleaning which recalls that which is done for the Easter holiday; there are also other resemblances between the two celebrations, analyzed by Joel M. Halpern and Barbara Kerewski-Halpern (1972, p. 115). The dishes are brought to the church to be blessed at the same time that a list of all the names of the deceased is given to the priest so that he may read prayers for their souls (Vekhovitch, 1928, p. 18).

So many of the aspects of the slava date back to the past (Živanović, 1976, pp. 595-596), that some Christian elements have come to be added to it. The slava, even though it is the celebration of the household and its domestic group, reunites the living and the dead and coincides with the holiday of a saint; Saint George, Saint Nicholas, Saint John, the archangel Michael are among those most often mentioned (Trojanovitch, 1909, p. 185). The saint is the patron of the house, his cult is passed from one generation to the next through the boys, as well as the property. The priest comes to visit the house which is celebrating the Slava and recites prayers for the living and the deceased, especially for the males. At the time of the separation of a domestic group, the newly formed groups can continue to have their prayers said together, a sign that their relationships have remained close (Demelić, 1876, p. 27). At the time of the same separation, the trammel of the family and the icon of the patron saint of the group remain the possession of the group which inherits the house (Pavković, 1961, pp. 201-202).

The fact that that domestic group celebrates its Slava together consolidates its cohesion. To celebrate a slava together signifies being related and consequently gives rise to marriage bans. In fact, the members of a domestic group can no longer intermarry, no matter how far back their kinship links them. The foreign woman who comes from the outside to marry within a group first celebrates the slava of her native group; she will henceforth celebrate the slava of her husband's group (French, 1941, p. 51). If her husband dies, she can not marry anyone from the group because she is now kin to everyone, and must seek a husband eleswhere. "In some regions families who keep the same slava consider that therefore they are related, and do not intermarry" (Trojanovitch, 1909, p. 185; see also, Novakovitch, 1905, p. 11). It also occurs that the households of a single village celebrates their slava at the same time, in which case those involved are families having perhpas a common origin (Kajmaković, 1962, p. 158).

To organize one's own slava under the best possible conditions is a great honor. Families can bankrupt themselves because of the celebration, especially if they organize two annual slavas. The code of Prince Danilo of Montenegro, promulgated in 1885, tried to prevent this practice: "The second celebration of the patron of the family, and the presents which are used for this occasion are prohibited for the future due to the number of families that bankrupt themselves and thus become poor. . . . Once is enough, following out Servian custom (Slavic), to sanctify the holy celebration of the family, in memory of the baptism of our ancestors" (Delarue, 1862, pp. 162-163). Despite all this, these practices continued and they are even noted in recent studies (Drljača, Savković, 1973, pp. 137 sq.).

The "*domazet*" (husband who comes to live in his father-in-law's house when he has no son) celebrates his father-in-law's slava, even if he continues discreetly to celebrate his native group's slava. He celebrates the slava of father-in-law even after the death of the latter, a slava which is passed on to his own sons (Hammel, 1968, p. 22). The transmission of the slava thus follows the rules for the transmission of property. "However, it is important to note that a purchaser of a piece of property, who is not an agnate of the owners, may often celebrate their slava in addition to his own in an explicit attempt to ward off eveil" (Hammel, 1968, p. 22). At the time of the fusion of two households, the weaker adopts the slava of the stronger.

Just as their is a celebration at the level of the household, there are celebrations for the more important social units, celebrations which increase and come to be consecrated not only by the old social units, but also by newly created institutions. D. B. Rheubottom notes in the Skopska Crna Gora region, the presence of four different types of slava; that of the household, which is for the people descended from a common ancestor, those of the village, the church, and the monastery, which do not appear to him as having any relationship to lineages or another blood related group (1976, p. 19). This, however, is not the point of view shared by Sicard (1943, pp. 349 sq.) who has studied the slava of households, of the phratry–*bratstvo,* and of the tribe–*pleme;* he believes that the origin of the household and village slava can be linked to the slava of the *bratstvo.* R. M. French (1941, p. 55) notes the presence of the slava of regiments, corporations, and of schools. Iankovitch (1853, pp. 112 sq.) adds to the slava for lineages and the village, another which brings several villages together at the time of the patron saint of a church, that of the department and even that of all of Serbia.

The presence of numerous slava linked to the phratries is certain; Sicard gives a list of patron saints of the bratstva in the Rijecka Nahija and finds listed, in order of importance, Saint Nicholas, the Archangel, Saint George, Petkov dan and Ivan dan, and other less important saints. Each bratstvo has a church maintained by the members of the bratstvo (Trojanovitch, 1909, p. 175). The fact that several households have the same patron saint can signify that they are members of the same bratstvo; for example, in Herzegovina, all the domestic groups which celebrate the holiday of the "Ignat dan" are descended from the Malešević bratstvo (Sicard, 1943, p. 353).

There is a slava at the tribal level; those people celebrating it can not intermarry (Trojanovitch, 1909, p. 185), consanguinity thus playing an important role. Svetozar Tomić (1902, p. 492 sq.) describes the Drobnjak tribe and presents the patron saints of the slava; first, there is the general slava, that of Saint George, which is the slava of the entire trible to which has been added slavas which differ according to lineages. "Earlier, in the tibal commune of Drobnjak's anybody who wanted to participate had to take the general name of Drobnjak, to adopt Drobnjak slava St. George and to have a guarantee of one of the Drobnjak's that he is a constructive and good man" (Bajraktarovic, 1976, p. 113).

These three social units (household, phratry, tribe) are those which are linked to the former social structures. Each one has its celebration and also a material element which makes this unity visible; the household has the icon, the phratry a church. In Montenegro, each tribe (turned *nahija* –department) has a monastery (Karadžić, 1837, p. 68), even if there are no monks in this monastery. And since all of Montenegro is an association of tribes, a spiritual element is needed at this level in order to seal the solidarity of all the tribes; this will be the central monastery of Cetinje, with a former bishop, vladika Petar, who died in 1830 and became the national saint of Montenegro, and another bishop chief from the State. The Montenegrins take an oath by saying "By God and St. Peter," but under this name they make a distinction between Saint Peter and their bishop Petar—Peter. "I have seen men stroke their heads against his tomb and even against the door jambs of the Monastery church where he lies," affirms Mary Edith Durham (1933, p. 146). The correspondence between the social and religious structure is thus complete. At the same time it recalls that described for the Romanians of Ţara Vrancei where an icon was found at the household level, the church as the village level (the brat-stvo not existing among the Romanians) and a monastery belonging to the entire village confederation, probably formerly a tribe.

But since the village has appeared for a longtime and imposes itself more and more, it also must have spiritual elements needed to consolidate its unifying character. Nikola Pavković (1980, p. 151) considers the village as forming a religious unit which manifests itself through the village slava, called the "*zavetina*;" it is also called the "*litija*" (Stojančević, 1980, p. 35). Joseph Obrebski affirms that "The villages view themselves not only as a community of kinsmen, relatives and neighbors, but also a religious unity" (1977, p. 2). The material symbol of this unit is the village church; together with the cemetery which surrounds it, it is the most sacred point of the living situation and the place where many ceremonies take place. The territorial element is present; thus, the saint who protects the village and whose name is celebrated by the village, also protects the territory (Iankovitch, 1853, p. 102). Sometimes, the village celebration imposes itself to the detriment of the household slava which has a tendency to diminish (Kajmaković, 1959, pp. 131-133).

"Every village has its own patron saint, and the observance of the slava of the whole village is known as the *Zavetina*" (French, 1941, p. 55). A sacred tree, the "*zapis*," is normally placed at the edge of the village; its bark is marked by a cross, the Christian element this being added to the pagan element; if the tree is a fruit tree, its fruits will never be picked. "Every year at the zavetina, the trees are visited in solemn procession and the crosses upon them are renewed. The procession is headed by a man carying a large wooden cross. He is followed by the priest in full vestments bearning the Book of the Gospels, and behind the priest is a long double line of peasants with icons which they carry against their breasts as we are accustomed to see the ministers carry the books at High Mass. The procession starts from the church, if there is one, otherwise from some agreed meeting place. All this, however, happens only in the early summer. If the festival of the patron saint of the village falls between St. Peter's Day and the following Easter, the zavetina is like an ordinary slava. One of the more well-to-do inhabitants provides the *kolatch* (bread) and the *kolyvo* (boiled corn) and generally acts as *svetchar,* while many of the others who come to join the celebration bring contributions of wine and food to the banquet" (French, 1941, p. 55). Iandovitch (1853, p. 114) also describes this ceremony and adds that it is followed by a banquet organized on the spot, around a table where the priest and the leaders of the domestic groups take the first seats. Toasts follow and, by beginning with the toasts addressed to the domestic groups, they go back to toasts addressed to the lineages, to the villages, to the Serbian people, and to the king. Dances and games follow.

Among the Romanians (Vlachs) of north-eastern Serbia, (the Timoc region) many customs of an archaic nature have been maintained, including the village celebration. Slobodan Zečević (1973, pp. 43-66), who on several occasions has studied this region and this population notes, among others, the presence of the sacred tree—"*zapis*"—as a particular element. The village celebration takes place under its branches, thus acquiring the role of a sanctuary. A procession makes the tour of the village for reasons similar to those described in the magical structure of the Romanian village territory. Like the household celebration, the deceased are also honored in this celebration. The same population is presented by Petar Vlahović (1981, pp. 7-14) who adds that near the sacred tree, a lamb is sacrificed and whose blood is then sprinkled on the roots of the tree; candles are lit and the tree is decorated with flowers.

Tihomir Djordjević (1948, pp. 289 sq.) adds significant details concerning the village as a religious unit; thus, the observance of the household slava was obligatory, and those who did not celebrate their patron saint were punished, just as those who did not respect religious holidays; an entire village can be cursed by another village. Obrebski (1977, pp. 8-10) notes a person having a special function in the Macedonian villages, the "*kum*"—village sponsor. He is elected on the basis of his lineage, each lineage having its turn at this office. The sponsor takes care of relationships between the village and the religious hierarchy; he is the person who carries the village cross during ceremonies. The maintenance of the lineages within the interior of the village can be seen at the time of the commemoration of the deceased; Milenko Filipović (1946, pp. 59 sq.) describes the dining rooms and the reception rooms ("sobrašice") located near the orthodox churches in Serbia and Bosnia.

The celebration called the "*sabor*" brings together several hamlets around a parish church; it can occur on the day of the church's patron saint, or of other religious celebrations as well. Even if it seems that there are no more relationships with the related groups, in reality, these relationships have always existed because the belief in a common origin has maintained itself for a long time. The great "sabor" are organized around important churches and especially around monasteries; the people come from every region. And Iankovitch (1853, p. 117) mentions the celebration of all the Serbs called the "*sabor vidovski,*" a universal reunion; "The body of tsar Lazar being at the time in Ravanitsa, our Olympia is also there. The Serbian people, from all sides come together every year, on the day of the Battle of Kossovo," where the tzar was defeated and killed by the Ottomans.

### The Protective Divinity of the Albanian Tribes

Among the northern Albanians (whose society has been described), we regularly find each social unit doubling as a spiritual unit. Each household has its patron saint in honor of whom candles are lit; on the eve of the celebration, "the windows and the doors are left open to leave free access for the souls of the ancestors and even in certain areas, one of two seats are left vacant for them at the table" (Tirtja, 1982, p. 96). "In the houses of the wealthy Catholics in Bregmate and in Zadrime, prayer altars are found. They are the people who are most linked to the Church, to the priests. . . . In the houses of the wealthy Orthodox from the southern part of the country there is a particular corner set aside for prayers, like an altar. There is an icon of the family's protector saint, candles and silver candelabras, crosses and other religious objects" (Tirtja, 1977, p. 340). Degrand (1901, p. 30) tells that in Scutari "the young girls, even those who are veiled, could not go to the church; each wealthy dwelling had its chapel to which a priest came on Sundays to celebrate mass" (see also Hecquard, p. 339). Gopčević (1881, p. 433) affirms that the principal celebration of the Malisores (inhabitants of the mountain regions) is that of the patron of the household; here, the head of the family plays the principal role in the ritual, actively aided by his wife. The church participates in the celebration, which ends with a meal to which relatives and friends are invited.

In May, each household erects a chapel of perishable material; each evening and each morning, the leader of the domestic group recites prayers here in front of the women and children. Then, each person pulls a ticket from a sack of tickets on which is written the penitence that each one must do for the day (Hecquard, p. 339; Gopčević, 1881, p. 427).

As is the case with other populations of the region, each social unit has its patron saint and its patronal celebration. We have seen above that the former social units of the Albanians blend with those more recent ones of the village and bajrak, and sometimes mix with such and such a region. This results in the fact that often information about the celebrations present a situation which is not clear, since a single celebration can cover several social units. In Scutari, where Catholic influence is strong, there are even confraternities with their own patron saint.

For the village celebration, each household participates in whatever way it can. The people receive guests, go by cortege to church, make the tour of the building, and return home to eat. "After the *pilaf* (rice), songs celebrating the situations in which the village has found itself began" (Hecquard, p. 325; see also pp. 389-390). Contests of fighting, speed, and of target shooting take place. Sacrifices can accompany the celebrations, as noted by Eqrem Cabej for a village located in the center of Albania (1934, p. 230).

Mark Tirta (1982, p. 95) mentions for the northern and southern Albanian Christians or Islamic religious celebrations in honor of the ancestors of the lineage, *bayrak,* or region, considered as protector saints. The lineage celebrates a saint who is the protector of the lineage. Sacrifices accompany the celebrations (Tirjta, 1982, p. 97). It should be noted that when we speak of ancestors, we are always referring to men and not women, which coincides with what has been said above concerning the position of the two sexes in past Albanian society.

Valentini (1969) published several interesting documents concerning the celebrations in relation to the village, bajrak, tribe, parish, or even the "country," in reality a region inhabited by such and such a group. These celebrations (*"shejti"*) that he compares to the *"sagre"* of Italy, give rise to reunions which, for a time, dominate local social life; for example, the activities surrounding the vendettas are suspended during the days of the celebrations and the people who are "in blood" can see each other, eat together, and visit one another. "An extremely important fact about these Mountains which dominates the entire year of the mountain dwellers, is the existence of the celebrations which each village celebrates on the sacred day of the patron of the village, or of the bajrak. The Beriscia tribe or lineage celebrates the *Assunta* (Notre Dame of Assumption), the Thaci Saint Sebastian Day, the Kabasci Saint Paul's Day, and so on" (p. 21). Some people come from neighboring regions, visits are made to friends and everything occurs in an atmosphere of peace because on this day, not only does the patron saint of the region look down to see how the celebration is going, but other saints do as well (p. 22). This same document, dated 1890, insists on the ruinous character of these celebrations for the inhabitants where great quantities of food and alcoholic beverages are consumed (see also the documents numbered 18, 81, 83, 167). In order to avoid expenses, efforts are made to suppress them: "Toward the end of the mission, the leaders of the tribes gathered all the country, and, following the desire of nearly the entire population, decided to no longer celebrate more than one celebration a year with their friends, and even the latter, which was Saint Mark the Evangelist's Day, was abandoned because it comes at the time when the people are lacking in the most essential things. They begged me to announce this before the altar, and also to forbid Christians from going to visit the Turks (Moslems) on Saint George's day because the Turks would no longer come to visit the Christians" (doc. no. 224, see also doc. 244). In reality, the religious part of the celebration of the saint had not been abolished, only the ruinous banquet which accompanied it.

The groups forming a tribe can have a common church for the entire tribe, in an isolated area on a summit, away from the dwellings (Bourcart, 1921, p. 178). Each human being has an protective *"ore,"* a mythical feminine face; each social group has one as well. It is intereting to note that the ore presides over the social groups in an archaic manner, that is to say, linked by blood ties, like the household, the line, the phratry, the fis, and not the village, the quarter, the region, where this character diminishes (Sako, 1967, p. 136; see also Zojzi, 1977, p. 191). The tribe's ore decides the destiny of this tribe (Cozzi, 1914, p. 452). The face of the first ancestor of the fis was symbolized by the ore of the fis, like, for example, the ore of Shale, who lived on the summit of Rrëshell, "long like a pine, beautiful as light, bitter as a snake;" the ore of the Nakaj, who stayed on the summit of Kaki, had "a reddened face, angry to the point that a smile never appeared on her lips;" the ore of the Krasniqe, who stayed on the summit of Crijë, "blood and scatterbrained," and so forth. It is useful here to underscore the fact that the ore of the fis always stays on the highest summit of the fis' territory, in a place where she can survey all her property" (Zojzi, 1977, p. 199); and it can also be added that this is the same location where a good number of churches will later be built.

## The Chapels of Greek Lineages

If we observe the societies described for Greece, we see that in most cases, chapels dominate. In Mani, each lineage has its chapel, its priest, and sometimes it own cemetery or at least a place in the village cemetery. Churches that are common to an entire village can exist, but they are rare; for example, in one of the largest villages of the region, Vathia, there is not a central church. Its absence, compensated by the presence of lineage chapels, is an obvious sign of the local social structure, where the village plays a minor role, and the lineages dominate, lineages which are sometimes not even located in one village, but in several.

If we look at the Anoya society, the lineage remains strong, but the village also has a reality. This situation translates into the fact that at the level of the lowest living arrangement, we find village churches, attended indifferently by everyone, especially on days of celebrations which follow the religious calendar and are not based on the life of each lineage or household. On the other hand, if we go up to the level of the high mountain pastures, the pastures are divided by lineages, and each lineage has its own chapel; here, the celebrations for the patron saint of the chapel, the patron of the lineage, and the events linked to lineage life are celebrated (baptisms, marriages).

On the island of Karpathos, in the village Elympos, there is a unified village life from which the kanakares, with their superior social position, detach themselves from their fellow citizens. Consequently, we find a central village church, but where the kanakares have their reserved stalls and seats. Moreover, the kankares have chapels, near which they are buried.

The situation complicates itself if we analyze the groups of the trans-
human shepherds; there is no doubt that each household constitutes a
religious community (Campbell, 1964, p. 37) which celebrates religious
holidays together with groups forming a single "*tseligato*" (for the Sarat-
sanes of Greek expression) or a single "*fălcare*" (for the Armâns of
Romanic extraction). If each household has its icons, it is, on the other
hand, difficult to find a common church since the group changes location
continuously and because it is dispersed. Solidly built churches, an expression of social village unity, have appeared for a long time in the
solidly constructed villages of the Armâns of Pinde. Next to a central
church, they have churches consecrated to the patron saints of the shepherds; this, for example, is the case for the churches dedicated to Saint
Paraskeve, to which sometime sheep which no one touches are dedicated
(Stavrou, 1982, pp. 143 sq.).

In other regions of Greece, we also find chapels belonging to lineages,
and this is true, not only for the peasants, but the lords as well. I saw
these types of chapels on the island of Lefkas, belonging to former Vene-
tian lords; they are noted on the island of Chios, belonging to former
Genoese lords. In the description of the diocesan visit made in 1643,
after the conquest of the island by the Turks, we find the description of
various religious monuments: "We visited the fraternity of Saint George
which is located outside the city, about a mile away. . . . It is used by
both Catholics and Orthodox, and separately, in the same church, the
Latins (Catholics) have their altar and celebrate mass, and the Greeks
(Orthodox) do the same according to their custom. . . . This church was
first the private chapel of a Catholic gentleman from Chios, and was located in his garden, but having accumulated substantial debts, he was
forced to sell it and it was then purchased by a Turkish janissary. . ."
(Hofmann, 1934, p. 66). The believers meet, buy and obtain the right of
passage through the garden in order to attend church. Other similar
examples are noted in the same work (pp. 67, 68, 70, 71). In the town
of Chora Sfakion, on Crete, there are many churches and chapels which
are linked to the presence and reputation of a particular important family,
but also to people's professions (Douroudakis, 1984).

We find many other places in Greece with villages having several
chapels, situated either in the village, on the edge, or farther in the fields.
If we try to classify the membership of these cahpels, we find at least
three situations that exist. The first is that which has already been

described where the chapel belongs to a lineage; this is the case for many societies where lineages are important. Next, there are the villages where the lineages have lost their importance, and the chapels are maintained by the people of the quarter, especially by the women. It is moreover in Greece that we find a different situation; an entire village or quarter of a town, has chapels which belong to everyone. I saw some of these types of chapels, for example, in Braşov, in Romania, where the old quarter of Schei is surrounded by chapels situated on the neighboring summits; they can also be seen on the summits in the Zagori region in Greece, but their membership is not yet clear to me. Hacquet (1815, p. 21) visited the Carniola region (Krainska Deshela) and saw a similar village: "One church is not sufficient for a village; often seven, eight, or nine temples belong to the same commune. They are located on the mountains about a mile's distance, and are consecrated to different saints, but these churches are not visited more than once a year. There is no presbytery attached to these mountain churches; the priests who come there to celebrate their holy service are obliged to bring their vestments with them each time. These solemn days of celebrations are occasions of good food and rejoicing. Itinerant caterers set up under the tents and cabins of greenery. After the service, the people begin dancing and the disorder continues well into the night. . . . The foundation of these superfluous churches is a considerable burden for the people of the country. . . ."

The location on summits is found in many other places; for example, the "*nedei*" of the Romanians can be celebrated on the high mountain pastures, where no monument is constructed; they can be held around a monument constructed, as is the case for this region of the Carniola, or as we have seen for Mani. Moreover, in many of the Peloponnese areas, we find churches situated on summits belonging to one or more villages, but always visited by several villages.

Finally, in order to conclude, we can recall the case of the island of Skiros with its society where nobles (archontes), shepherds and farmers form three principal categories; each category has a church, just as each group occupies a quarter of the town.

\* \* \*

What I have stated at the beginning of the chapter has been confirmed everywhere by facts; there is an icon which signifies the spiritual unity of the household, a unity which manifests itself in numerous ways: there is a chapel for the lineage or the phratry, there is a church for the phratry or the village; lastly, there are monasteries for the broader social units. In the example of Montenegro, there is one central monastery for a tribal confederation. The ritual of the celebrations which are consecrated to them (and in which the deceased regularly participate), linked to a patron saint for each social unit would also be an interesting subject which goes beyond the scope of my study, my single goal being the argument that there is an obvious parallelism between social structure and religious organization.

This parallelism is inscribed on the territory which breaks down into as many religious and magical units as there are economic categories of land, and of pieces of property on each one of them. The magical structure of the Romanian village territory, such as it has been described above, can be observed elsewhere as well since most of the elements are found there. This is the case, for example, of the distinction between arable lands and the commonfield, between the habitat and the rest of the territory, between the summit and the plain; this is the case of the special role played by the roads, and especially by the crossroads, and by the entrances, this is also the case of the various successive magical barriers which protect a village.

# BIBLIOGRAPHY

## ABBREVIATIONS

AMET     Anuarul Muzeului Etnografic al Transilvaniei (Cluj)

ASCRS    Archives pour la Science et la Réforme Sociale (Bucare)

ASTRS    Arhiva pentru ştiinţa şi reforma socială (Bucarest)

BSRRG    Buletinul Societăţii Regale Române de Geografie (Bucarest)

CN     La Conférence Nationale des Etudes Ethnographiques. 28-30 juin 1976. (Tirana, 1977).

DCAB    Le Droit Coutumier et les Autonomies sur les Balkans et dans les Pays Voisins. Recueil de travaux. Symposium international 1-2 novembre 1971. Beograd. (Sous la redaction de Vasa Čubrilović; Belgrade, 1974).

EA     Ethnographie Albanaise (Tirana)

EKE    Epiteorisi Koinonikon Erevnon. The Greek Review of Social Sciences (Athènes)

EP     Etnoloski Pregled (Belgrade)

ESH    Ethnographia Shkiptare (Tirana)

ESL    Ethnologia Slavica (Bratislava)

GEI    Glasnik Etnografskog Instituta (Belgrade)

GEM    Glasnik Etnografskog Muzeja (Belgrade)

GMBH    Glasnik Zemaljskog Muzeja Bosni i Hercegovini (Sarajevo)

IZV    Izvestija na Etnografskija Institut s Muzei (Sofia)

REF    Revista de Etnografie şi Folclor (Bucarest)

RIEB    Revue Internationale des Etudes Balkaniques (Belgrade)

SCIA    Studii si Cercetări de Istoria Artei (Bucarest)

SR    Sociologie Românească (Bucarest)

# BIBLIOGRAPHY

ALEXAKIS, Eleft. P.
 1980   *Ta geni kai i oikogeneia stin paradosiaki koinonia tis Manis.*
        Athènes.
ALLARD, Camille.
 1864   *Souvenirs d'Orient. La Bulgarie orientale.* Paris.
ANCEL, Jacques
 1934   "L'Unité balkanique." *RIEB,* I.
*Ancheta monografică în comuna Belinţ.* Timişoara. 1938.
ANDREEV, Mihail.
 1974   "Le droit coutumier des Slaves du sud et leurs organisations
        d'autogestion pendant la domination ottomane." *DCAB.*
ANDRIĆ, Jasna
 1972   "Zadruga. Novija istraživanja, njihova svrha i rezultati." *Etno-
        loski pregled,* 10, Cetinje.
ANDROMEDAS, John N.
 1957   "Greek kinship terms in everyday use." *American Anthropolo-
        gist,* 59.
 1966   "The inner Maniat community type: a study of the local com-
        munity's changing articulation with society." *Dissertation ab-
        stracts,* 27 B, Ann Arbor.
ANGELOVA, Rašel
 1965   *Šumenski v'zroždenski k'šti.* Sofia.
 1966   "V'zroždenski k'šti ot iogozapadnite Rodopi." Académie bul-
        gare des Sciences. *Bulletin de la section de théorie et d'histoire
        de l'urbanisme et de l'architecture.* Vol. XIX.

ANTIPA, Grigore
1916　*Pescăria şi pescuitul în România.* Bucharest.
ANTONIEVIĆ, Dragoslav.
1974　"Polozai ostarelih u običajnom pravu kod Južnih Slovena."
*DCAB.*
ANTONOVICI, Ioan
1906　*Istoria comunei Bogdana din Plasa Simila, judetul Tutova.*
Bîrlad.
APOLZAN, Lucia
1943　"Sate crânguri din Munţii Apuseni." *S.R.,* V, 1-6.
ARBURE, Zamfir
1898　*Basarabia în secolul XIX.* Bucarest.
ARGENTI, Ph. P. et H. J. Ross.
1949　*The Folklore of Chois.* Cambridge.
ARON, Nicolae
1905　*Monografia comunei Galati.* Sibiu.
ARSITCH, Berisav.
1936　*La vie économique en Serbie du sud au 19-ème siècle.* Paris.
ARCHENBRENNER, Stanley Earl.
1971　*A Study of Ritual Sponsorship in a Greek Village.* University of
Minnesota, Ph.D.
1975　"Folk Model vs. actual practice; the distribution of spiritual kin
in a greek village." *Anthropological Quarterly,* 48.
ASDRACHAS, Spyros.
1981　"Quelques aspects des économies villageoises au dêbut du XIX-e
siècle." *EKE.*
BALZER, O.
1899　"O zadrudze slowianskej." *Kwartalnik historiczny.* Leopol.
BARADA, M.
1957　*Starohrvatska seoska zajednica.* Zagreb.
BARIĆ, Lorraine.
1967　"Levels of change in Yugoslav kinship." *Social Organization,*
edited by Maurice Freedman, London.
BARJAKTAROVIĆ, Mirko
1962　"Die Sippenhausgemeinschaft Osmanaj im Dorfe Djurakovac."
*Zeitschrift für Ethnologie,* LXXXV, 2.
1971　"Land Baulks among the Serbs." *ES,* 2

1972 "On some Ethnical Characteristics of Montenegrins." *ES*, 3.
1976 "Forms of Ownership as Types of Traditional Institutions in Yugoslavia." *ES*, 6.
1977 "On one Manifestation of Clan Mentality in some Balkan Peoples." *ES*, 8-9.

BAUR, Frédéric Guillaume
1778 *Mémoires historiques et géographiques sur la Valachie.* Francfort et Leipzig.

BANATEANU, Tancred
1954 "Arta populară în satele specializate din sudul raionului Beiuş, regiunea Oradea." SCIA, 1-2.
1960 "Types d'âtres dans les villages roumains d'une des régions marécageuses du Danube." *Ethnographica*, II, Brno.

BEAUBIER, Jeff.
1974 *High Life Span on the Island of Paros, Greece.* Chapel Hill.

BELLANGER, Stanislas
1846 *Le Keroutza.* Paris, 2 vol.

BELOVIĆ, Jasna
1927 *Die Sitten der Südslaven.* Dresden.

BENT, J. T.
1966 *Aegean Islands, the Cyclads, or Life among the Insular Greeks.* Chicago, reprint.

BENVENISTE, E.
1969 *Le vocabulaire des institutions indo-européennes.* Paris, 2 vol.

BEOPOULOU, Ioanna
1981 "Trikeri: mobilité et rapports d'appartenance." EKE.

BERNARD, Harvey Russell
1968 *Kalymnos: Economic and Cultural Change on a Greek Sponge Fishing Island.* Ann Arbor, University Microfilms.

BEZVICONI, Gh.
1947 *Călători ruşi în Moldova şi Muntenia.* Bucharest.

BLANC, André
1957 *La Croatie Occidentale.* Paris.

BLANQUI, M.
1845 *Voyage en Bulgarie pendant l'année 1841.* Paris.
1906-1907 "B'lgarskata čeljadna zadruga v segašno vreme." *Sbornik za umotvorenija, nauka i kniźnina*, XXII-XXIII, Sofia.

1934-1935  "Quelques remarques sur le droit coutumier bulgare pendant
           l'époque de la domination ottomane." RIEB, I.
1938       "Notes comparées sur les čorbačis chez les peuples balkaniques
           et en particulier chez les Bulgares." RIEB, III.

BOEHM, Cristopher
1962       Montenegrin Social Organization and Values. Cambridge, Harvard University.

BOGETIĆ, Ljubinka
1972       "Communautés foncières chez les peuples balkaniques de 19e
           siècle." IIe Congrès International des Etudes du Sud Est Européen. Athènes, mai. 1970. Athènes.

BOGIĆEVIĆ, Bojislav
1953       "Raboš i niegova upotreba u Bosni i Hercegovini." GMBH, VIII.

BOGIŠIĆ, Baltazar
1867       Pravni običaji u Slovena. Zagreb.
1874       Zbornik sadašnih pravnih običaja u južnih Slovena. Agram.
1884       De la forme dite "inokosna" de la famille rurale chez les Serbes
           et les Croates. Paris.

BOUÉ, Ami
1840       La Turquie d'Europe. Paris, 4 vol.

BOULAY, Juliet du
1974       Portrait of a Greek Mountain Village. Oxford.

BOURCART, J.
1921       L'Albanie et les Albanais. Paris.

BROMLEY, Julian V.
1968       The Archaic Form of the Communal Family. Moscow.
1970       "The 'sotnja' as a social cell among the Eastern and Southern
           Slavs in the Middle Ages." ESL, 1.

BUDA, Aleks
1977       "L'ethnographie albanaise et quelques-uns de ses problèmes."
           CN.

BUJOREANU, Ioan M.
1884       Pravila bisericească, 1640. Pravila lui Matei Basarab, 1652. Bucarest.

BURGEL, Guy
1965       Pobia, étude géographique d'un village crétois. Athènes.
1981       "La Grèce rurale revisitée." EKE.

BUTURA, Valer
    1978    *Etnografia poporului român.* Cluj-Napoca.
    1984    "Eglises en bois de Transylvanie. La table des ancêtres." *Etudes et documents balkinques et méditerranéens.* Paris, vol. 7.

BYRNES, Robert F. (editeur)
    1976    *Communal Families in the Balkans: the zadruga.* Notre-Dame, Indiana.

CAMPBELL, John K.
    1964    *Honour, Family and Patronage: a study of institutions and moral values in a Greek mountain community.* Oxford.

CANTEMIR, Dimitrie
    1973    *Descriptio Moldaviae.* Bucarest.

CAPETANAKIS, Sophie
    1979    *Parenté et organisation sociale à Elymbos, de Karpathos.* Paris. Doctoral dissertation, unpublished.
    1981    "Elymbos, village de Karpathos; structuration d'une société archaïsante." EKE.

CAPIDAN, Th.
    1926    *Românii nomazi. Studiu din viaţa Românilor din sudul Peninsulei Balcanice.* Cluj.
    1937    *Les Macédo-Roumains.* Bucharest.
    1942    *Macedoromânii. Etnografie, istorie, limbă.* Bucarest.

CARAMELEA, Vasile V.
    1946    *Satul Berivoeşti-Muscel. I. Obştea moşnenilor.* Câmpulung-Muscel.
    1967    "Contribution à l'étude de la forme sociale de la commune villageoisie. Méthode de restitution de ses phases." *VII-e Congrès International des Sciences Anthropologiques et Ethnologiques. Moscou, 1964.* Moscou.

CARNARVON, Earl of
    1869    *Reminiscences of Athens and the Morea.* London.

CARONNI
    1812    *Caronni in Dacia. Mie osservazioni locali, nazionali, antiquarie sui Valacchi specialmente e Zingari transilvani.* Milano.

CASTELLAN, Georges
    1967    *La vie quotidienne en Serbie au seuil de l'indépendance (1815-1839).* Paris.

CASTELLAN, Yvonne
1967 *La culture serbe au seuil de l'indépendance (1800-1840)*. Paris.
CAZACU, Petre
1906 "Locuinţele sătenilor." *Viaţa românească*, Iassy.
CARABIS, V.
1969 "O urmă de devălmaşie moşnenească." REF, XIV.
CARPINISAN, Nicoale
1897 *Monografia comunei Rahău*. Sibiu.
CHIROT, Daniel
1976 *Social Change in a Peripheral Society. The creation of a Balkan Colony*. New York.
1976 "The Romanian Communal Village; an Alternative for the Zadruga." In Byrnes, 1976.
CHIRU, Constantin
1925 *Monografia comunei Gura Foii din Judeţul Dâmboviţa*. Bucarest.
CHITU, Ion
1937 "Cum folosesc oamenii din Apele Vii pămâturile lor." SR, II, 9-10
CHIVA, Isac
1958 *Les communautés rurales. Problèmes, méthodes, exemples de recherches*. Rapports et documents de sciences sociales, no 10, UNESCO, Paris.
CHOPIN, M. et A. Ubicini
1856 *Provinces danubiennes et Roumaines*. Paris.
CIORAN, Emilia
1900 *Paul de Alep. Călăoriile patriarhului Macarie de Antiochia in Tările Române. 1653-1658*. Bucarest.
CISZEWSKI, S.
1897 *Künstliche Verwandschaft bei den Südslaven*. Leipzig.
CODRESCU, Ion
1871 *Uricariul cuprinzătoriu de hrisoave, anaforale şi alte acte din suta a XVIII si XIX*. Vol. I, Iassy.
COLAROV, Moise
1928 *Monografia circumscriptiei Pârneava a oraşului Arad. Viaţa şi obiceiurile ţăranilor români circumscripţia III*. Arad.
COLESCU, Leonida
1920 *Statistica clădirilor şi a locuinţelor din România. Intocmită pe*

*baza recensământului general al populaţiunii din 19 Decembrie 1912-1 Ianuarie 1913.* Bucarest.

COMANESCU, Iosifu

1885  *Studiu istoricu-statisticu asupra prezintelui şi trecutului Românilor din opidul Codlea.* Braşov.

COMNENE, Demetrius

1784  *Précis historique de la maison impériale des Comnènes où l'on trouve l'origine, les moeurs et les usages des maniotes.* Amsterdam

CONEA, Ion

1934  *Ţara Loviştei.* BSRRG, LIII.

1939  *Clopotiva, un sat din Haţeg.* Bucarest, 2 vol.

CONSTANTE, C. et Anton Golopentia

1943  *Românii din Timoc.* Bucarest, 3 vol.

CONSTANTINESCU-MIRCESTI, C. D.

1939  *Un sat dobrogean, Ezibei.* Bucarest.

CONSTANTINESCU-MIRCESTI, C. D. et Henri H. Stahl

1929  *Documente vrâncene.* Bucarest.

CONSTANTINIU, Florin

1972  *Relaţiile agrare din Ţara Românească în secolul al XVIII-lea.* Bucarest.

COON, Carleton S.

1950  *The Mountains of Giants. A racial and cultural study of the North Albanian mountain Ghegs.* Cambridge.

CORFUS, Ilie

1969  *L'agriculture en Valachie durant la première moitié du XIX-e siècle.* Bucarest.

COTHISEL, prêtre Constantin

1904  *Monografia comunei Certeze şi istoria bisericei greco-orientale ortodoxe române din comună.* Sibiu.

COSTA-FORU, Xenia

1936  "Quelques aspects de la vie familiale en Roumanie." ASCRS, XIII.

COULANGES, Fustel de

1943  *La cité antique.* Paris.

COUROUCLI, Maria

1981  "Changement et immobilité dans la montagne de Corfou." EKE.

COUSINERY, E. M.
  1831   *Voyage dans la Macédoine.* Paris.

COZZI, Ernesto
  1909   "Malattie, morte, funerali nelle montagne d'Albanie." *Anthropos.*
  1910   "La vendetta del sangue nelle montagne dell'Alta Albania." *Anthropos.*
  1910   A "Lo stato agricolo in Albania con speciale riguardo alle montagne di Scutari." *Revue d'Ethnographie et de Sociologie.*
  1912   "La donna albanese, con speciale riguardo al diritto consuetudinario delle Montagne di Scutari." *Anthropos.*

CRAINICEANU, Gh.
  1895   *Igiena ţăranului român.* Bucarest.

CRESIN, Roman
  1936   "Monografia comunei Şanţ." SR, I, 7-9.

CRISTESCU-GOLOPENTIA, Stefania
  1944   *Drăgus, un sat din Ţara Oltului (Făgăraş). Credinţe şi rituri magice.* Bucarest.

CRONT, Gh.
  1969   *Instituţii medievale româneşti. Infrăţirea de moşie. Jurătorii.* Bucarest.

CUISENIER, Jean
  1967   A "Systèmes de succession et de dotation en Yougoslavie et en Turquie." *L'Homme,* 3.
  1975   *Economie et parenté.* Paris-La Haye.

CVIJIĆ, Jovan
  1918   *La Péninsule Balkanique. Géographie humaine.* Paris.
  1923   "Des migrations dans les pays yougoslaves; l'adaptation au milieu." RIEB, III.

CYRILLE
  1876   *La France au Monténégro.* Paris.

ĆABEJ, Ekrem
  1934-1935   "Sitten und Gebräuche der Albaner." RIEB, I-II.
  1938   "Albaner und Slaven in Süditalien." RIEB, III.
  1966   "Albanische Volkskunde." *Süd-Ost Forschungen,* XXV.

ČIRIĆ-BOGETIĆ, Liubinka
  1966   *Komunice u Crnoj Gori u XIX i početkom veka.* Cetinje.

ČUBRILOVIĆ, Vasa (editeur)
  1974  *La droit coutumier et les autonomies sur les Balkans et dans les pays voisins. Recueil de travaux. Symposium international. 1-2 Novembre 1971. Belgrade.* Belgrade.

ČULINOVIĆ-KONSTANTINOVIĆ, Vera
  1982  "Analyse über die Stellung der Frau in der Gesellschaft und in der Familie." Dans *Ethnographia Pannonica. Die Frau in der Bauernkultur Pannoniens.* Zagreb.

DAN, Dimitrie
  1897  *Comuna Straja şi locuitorii sai. Studiu, topografic şi folkloric.* Cernăuţi, 1897.

DARESTE, Rudolphe et Albert Riviere (traducteurs)
  1892  *Code général des biens pour la principauté de Monténégro de 1888.* Paris.

DAUVILLIER, Jean et Carlo de Cleroq
  1936  *Le mariage en droit canonique oriental.* Paris.

DAVIDOIU, Ion Ilie
  1944  *Zona de tranziţie între deal şişes. Bărăştii de Cepturi-Olt. Studiu monografic.* Slatina.

DEGRAND, A.
  1901  *Souvenirs de la Haute-Albanie.* Paris.

DELARUE, Henri
  1862  *Le Monténégro.* Paris.

DEMELIĆ, Fedor
  1876  *Le droit coutumier des Slaves méridionaux.* Paris.

DENSUSIANU, Ovid.
  1915  *Graiul din Tara Haţegului.* Bucarest.

DESFEUILLES, Paul et Jacques Lassaigne.
  1937  *Les Français et la Roumanie.* Bucarest.

DIDA, Sejdi.
  1981  "Le feu dans la tradition populaire." *Culture populaire albanaise,* I.

DIDIKA, Niki.
  1977  *Vathia, un village du Mani (Péloponèse). Structures sociales archaiques.* Paris. Memoirs, unpublished.

DIONISIE ECLISIARHUL
  1934  *Conograful Ţerei Româneşti.* Craiova.

DJURDJEV, Branislav
1974   "Snačaj Crnogorskog zbora u XVII veku." DCAB.
DOBROGEANU-Gherrea, C.
1910   *Neoiobăgia. Studiu economico-sociologic al problemei noastre agrare.* Bucarest.
*Documente privind istoria României. Veacul XVI. A. Moldova. Vol. II*
1951   *(1551-1570).* Bucarest.
DOGARU, Dumitru
1937   "Năpădenii, un sat de mazili din Codru." SR, II, 7-8.
DOBROWOLSKI, K.
1961   "Die Haupttypen der Hirtenwanderungen in den Nordkarpathen vom 14. bis zum 20. Jahrhundert." Dans *Viehzucht und Hirtenleben in Ostmitteleuropa,* edited by Földes, I. Budapest. Budapest.
DOJAKA, Abaz
1972   "Ekzogamia tek shqiptarẹt." ESH, IV.
1976   "La position de la fermme en famille et en société dans la contrée de Zagorie." EA.
1977   "Aspects de développement des nouveaux liens matrimoniaux." *La conférence nationale de études ethnographiques. 20-30 juin 1976.* Tirana.
1979   "L'exogamie chez les Albanais." EA, VIII.
1980   "La rupture du mariage." EA, X.
DONCA, ION
1940   *Monografia comunei Rânzeşti, judeţul Tutova.* Bârlad.
DORDEVIC, Tihomir R.
1907   "Bigamija i poligamija kod Srba." *Srpski Kniaževni Glasnik,* 1, Belgrade.
1924   "La polyandrie chez les Slaves du sud." *Revue des Etudes Slaves,* IV, Paris.
1948   "Selo kao sud u nažem narodnom pravu." *Zbornik Filozofskog Fakulteta,* I, Belgrade.
DOURDOUDAKIS, Emmanuel
1984   "Eglises et chapelles de Chora Sfakion, Crète." *Etudes et Documents Balkaniques et Méditerranéens,* 7, Paris.
DRAGOMIR, Nicolae
1926   "Din Trecutul oierilor mărgineni din Sălişte şi comunele din

jur." *Lucrările Institutului de Geografie al Universității din Cluj.*
Cluj-Bucarest, 2nd volume.

DRAGOMIR, Silviu
1924   *Vlahii și Morlacii.* Cluj.
1959   *Vlahii din nordul peninsulei balcanice in Evul Mediu.* Bucarest.

DRAGOJILOVIĆ, Dragoliub
1971   "La župa chez les Slaves balkaniques au Moyen Age." *Balcanica*,
       II, Belgrade.

DRAŠKIĆ, Miroslav.
1973   "Specifična porodična struktura kao jedan od uslova za etnička
       mešanja i kulturno izjednačavanje stanovništva u istočnoj Srbiji."
       EP, 11.

DRIJAČA, Dušan et Dragoslava Savković.
1973   "Kučna zajednica u rasinskom selu Zlatari." E.P., 11.

DUBIĆ, Slavoljub.
1972   "A brief history of the Yugoslav peasant small-holding." Dans
       *The Yugoslav Village*, Zagreb.

DUČIĆ, Stevan.
1931   *Život i običaji plemena Kuča.* Belgarde.

DURHAM, Mary Edith.
1909   "Some Montenegrin Manners and Customs." *Journal of the
       Royal Anthropological Institute,* vol. XXXIX.
1910   "High Albania and its customs in 1908." *Journal of the Royal
       Anthropological Institute,* XXXX.
1920   "Ritual nudity in Europe." *Man.*
1923   "Some Balkan Taboos." *Man.*
1928   *Some Tribal Origins, Laws and Customs.* London.
1931   "Preservation of Pedigrees and Commemoration of Ancestors in
       Montenegro." *Man.*
1933   "The making of a Saint." *Man.*
*1935   "Bride-price in Albania." Man.*

ECONOMU N. et T. Al. Stoianovici.
1942   "O biserică moșnenească din Dâmbovnic. Găleșeștii." SR, IV,
       7-12.

ELEZI, Ismet.
1977   "Traits du droit coutumier albanais." CN.

EMERIT, Marcel

1937   *Les paysans roumains, depus le traité d'Andrinople jusqu'à la libération des terres (1829-1964).* Paris.

EMBIRICOS, A.

1975   *Vie et institutions du peuple grec sous la domination ottomane.* Paris.

*Encyclopedia of Religion and Ethics.* Edinburgh, vol. IX. 1914.

ERDELJANOVIć, J.

1926   *Stara Crna Gora. Etnička prošlost i formiranje crnogorskih plemena.* Belgrade.

ERETESCU, Constantin

1973   "Caracterul exogamic al comunităților săteşti maramureşene si unitatea folclorică a zonei." *Comunicări ştiintifice pe teme folclorice. Sighetul Marmatiei, Decembrie 1970-1971.* Baia Mare.

ERLICH, Vera St.

1940   "The southern slav patriarchal family." *Sociological Review,* 32.

1966   *Family in transition. A study of 300 yugoslav villages.* Princeton, New Jersey.

1971   "Trideset i tri godine transformiranja prodice." *Sociologija Sela,* 31-32, Zagreb.

EVAŞCU, Thomas L.

1978   "Segagea: economic and social change in a mountain village." Dans *Anuarul Muzeului Etnografic al Transilvaniei. 1978.* Cluj-Napoca, 1978.

FERMOR, P. L.

1958   *Mani, travels in southern Peloponese.* London.

FILIP, Gh.

1966   "Analiza etnografico-istorică *a unui trup de moşie."* REF, XI, 1.

FILIPOVIĆ, Milenko.

1930   "Krsno ime i slične slave u Modrić." GMBH, XLII, 2.

1946   "Porodski trpeze, kolibe ili sobašice." GMS, I.

1951   "Baptized Moslems." From the collected works of the Ethnographic Institute of the Serbian Academy of Sciences, Book 2, Belgrade.

1955   "Beleške o narodnom životu i običajima na Glasincu." GMBH, X.

1958   *Banatske Here.* Novi Sad.

1949-1950 "Rodovske trpeze, kolibe ili sobrašice." GMBH, IV-V.
1954 "Društvene i običajno-pravne ustanove u Rami." GMBH, IX.
1954 A "Levirat i sororat kod Srba, Hrvata i Arbanasa." *Rad Vojvodjanskih Muzeja.* 3, Novi Sad.
1963 "Forms and functions of ritual kinship among South Slavs." *IV-e Congrës International des Sciences Anthropologiques et Ethnologiques.* 2nd volume, Paris.
1958 "Vicarious paternity among Serbs and Croats." *Southwestern Journal of Anthropology,* 14, 2, Albuquerque.
1960 "Brak izmedju prvih rodjaka kod srpskohrvatskih muslimana." *Sociologija,* 2, Belgrade.
1965 "Symbolic adoption among the Serbs." *Ethnology,* IV, Pittsburgh.
1970 "Reciprocity in folk life. The Serbian case." *Ethnologia Europaea,* II-III, 1968-1969. Arnhem.

FIRST-DILIĆ, Ruža
1972 "Some Reflections on Social Organization of the Contemporary Farm Family in Yugoslavia." Dans *Yugoslav Village.*

FLORESCU, Florea B.
1937 "Vidra, un sat de Moţi." SR, II, 7-8.

FLORESCU, Florea, and Paul Petrescu, Paul H. Stahl
1969 *Arta populară de pe Valea Bistriţei.* Bucarest.

FÖLDES, Laszlo.
1961 *Viehzucht und Hirtenleben in Ostmitteleuropa.* Budapest.

FRASHERI, Kristo.
1977 "Remarques sur le Kanun de Skanderbeg." CN.

FRANCU, Teofil et George Candrea.
1888 *Românii din Munţii Apuseni.* Bucarest.

FREIDENBERG, M. M.
1967 "Kin Groups in Dalmatian Croatia, 11-th-16th Centuries." *Soviet Anthropology and Archeology,* 1.

FRIEDL, Ernestine.
1959 "The role of kinship in the transmission of natural culture to rural villages in mainland Greece." *American Anthropologist,* 61.
1963 *Vasilika: a village in modern Greece.* New York.

FRILEY, G. et Jovan Wlahovitj.
1876 *Le Monténégro contemporain.* Paris.

FROLEC, Vaclav.
1965 "Bolšaja semja i e zilišče v zapadnoi Bolgarii." *Sovetskaia Etnografija*, Moscow.
1966 *Die Volksarchitektur in Westbulgarien im 19. und zu Begin des 20. Jahrhundert*. Brno.
1967 "The Joint Family and its Dwelling in Western Bulgaria." Dans Lockwood, 1967.

GALIAN, Dumitru.
1903 *Monografia comunei rurale Mărăşeşci*. Focşani.

GARNETT, Lucy, M. J.
1917 *Balkan Home-Life*. London.

GAROFLID, Constantin
1943 *Agricultura veche*. Bucarest.

GASPARINI, Evel.
1973 *Il matriarcato slavo. Antropologia culturale dei protoslavi*. Firenze.

GASPAR, Mihail.
s.d. *Date monografice referitoare la Borşa Montană*. Caransebeş.

GAVAZZI, Milovan
1941 "Šišano kumstvo u Liči." *Lički kalendar, IX, za god. 1941*. Zagreb.
1955 "Die Vitalität der Wahlbruderschaft und Wahlschwesterschaft in Dalmatien." *Papers of European and Western Enthology. Stockholm, 1951*. Stockholm.
1956 "Zur ethnologischen Problematik Südosteuropas." *Actes du IVe Congrès International des Sciences Anthropologiques et Ethnologiques. Vienne 1952*. Vienne, 1956.
1957 "Die Kulturzonen Südosteuropas." *Südosteuropa Jahrbuch*, II. München.
1959 "Zur volkskundlichen Erforschung der Beziehungen des Ostalpenraumes und seiner östlichen Grenzgebiete." *Alpes Orientales*, Ljubljana.
1960 *Seljačke obitelski zadruge*. Zagreb.
1964 "Das Los der Grossfamilie auf dem Balkan." *Die Kultur Südosteuropas, ihre Geschichte und ihre Ausdrucksformen*. Südosteuropa-Schriften, VI, München.
1965 "Zadruga, Die Erfoschung der Grossfamilien Südosteuropas." *Osterreichische Osthefte*, Wien.

1970 "Vue d'ensemble sur la culture paléoslave et ses caractères gé-
néeraux." ESL, I.

1970 A *"Putovi proućavania sela Trg." Selo Trg kod Ozlija.* Belgrade.

1971 "Ein Beitrag zur kenntnis der balkan-karpatischen Kulturstro-
mungen." *Studia ethnographica et folkloristica in honorem Béla
Gunda.* Debrecen.

1976 "Die Erforschung der Mehrfamilien Südosteuropas in den letz-
ten Dezennien." Dans *Südosteuropa und Südosteuropa For-
schung,* edited by Klaus-Detlev Grothusen. Hamburg.

GADEI, A.V.

1904 *Monografia comunei rurale Bragadiru-Bulgar, din judeţul Ilfov,
plasa Sabaru.* Bucharest.

GENĆEV, Stoian

1976 "Phänomen, historische Wurzeln und Entwicklung der Tradi-
tionellen Volkstümlicher Gevatterschaft bei den Bulgaren." ESL,
6.

GEORGESCU, Valentin

1963 "Alte Albanische Rechtsgewohnheiten." *Revue des Etudes Sud-
Est Européennes,* I, 1-2, Bucharest.

1965 *Preemţiunea in istoria dreptului românesc.* Bucarest.

1967 "L'oeuvre juridique de Michel Fotino et la version roumaine du
VI-e livre de droit coutumier de son 'Manuel des lois' 1777."
*Revue des Etudes Sud-Est Européennes,* V, 1-2, Bucarest.

GEORGESCU, Valentin et Emanuela Popescu

1970 *Legislaţia agrară a Ţării Româneşti (1775-1782).* Bucarest.

GEORGIEVA, Iv., D. Moskova et L. Radeva

1971 "Rodninskite nazvaniia u naš." IXV, XIII.

GEORGOPAPADAKOS, Anastasios

1950 "I adelfopoia eis tin Manin." *Laografia,* Athens.

GEŠOV, I. E.

1887 "Zadrugata v zapadna B'lgarija." *Periodičeski spisanie na
b'lgarskoto kniževno družestvo,* Sofia.

GIURESCU, C. C.

1969 *Istoricul podgoriei Odobeştilor. Din cele mai vechi timpuri pină
la 1918.* Bucarest.

1973 *Contributii la istoria ştiinţei şi tehnicii româneşti in secolele
XV–inceputul secolul XIX.* Bucarest.

1975 *Istoria pădurii româneşti.* Bucarest.

GIURESCU, Dinu
  1962  "Anatefterul. Condica de porunci a vistieriei lui Constantin
         Brâncoveanu." *Studii şi materiale de istorie medie*, V. Bucarest.
GJEÇOV, Stefan
  1941  *Codice di Lek Dukagjini, ossia diritto conseutundinario delle
         montagne d'Albania.* Rome.
GJERGJI, Andromagi
  1963  "Gjurmë të matriarkatit në disa doke të dikurshme të jetës fa-
         *filjare."* Bulet. Univer. Shtet. Tirane, 2. Tirana.
  1970  "Transformations dans la position de la femme paysanne au
         sein de la famille." Dans *Problèmes de l'émancipation complète
         de la femme en République Populaire d'Albanie.* Tirana.
  1974  "Të dhëna mbi bujqësinë tradicionale në fshatin Pojan (Fier)."
         ESH, V.
  1976  "De l'évolution de la famille rurale contemporaine." EA.
  1979  "Différences morphologiques et artistiques des costumes popu-
         laires d'après leur fonction." EA, VIII.
  1982  "Le village, en tant qu'habitat et communautée sociale." EA,
         XII.
  1982  A "Rapport entre la structure de la famille coopératrice et l'e-
         space habité par celle-ci (Plaine de Korçe)." *Culture populaire
         albanaise*, II, 2. Tirana.
GLBOV, Glb. D.
  1961  *Turksi isvori.na istorijata na pravoto v b'lgarskite zemi.* Sofia.
GLUŠČEVIĆ, M.
  1967  "The forms of collective property in the old serbian society."
         *VII-e Congrès International des sciences Anthropologiques et
         Ethnologiques (Moscou, 3 aôut-10 aôut 1964).* Moscou, vol. IV.
GOCAN, Simion et Leontin Florian
  1939  *Monografia comunei Feiurdeni.* Cluj.
GOLOPENŢIA-ERETESCU, Sanda
  1972  "Clasificarea prin numuri." REF, XVII, pp. 145-155, 193-212.
GOPČEVIĆ, Spiridon
  1877  *Montenegro und die Montenegriner.* Leipzig.
  1881  *Oberalbanien und seine Liga.* Leipzig.
  1889  *Makedonien und Alt-Serbien.* Wien.

GOROVEI, Artur
  1976   *Literatura populară. Culegeri şi studii.* Bucarest.
GRISELINI, Francisc
  1926   *Istoria Banatului timişan.* Bucarest.
GROZDANOVA, Elena
  1974   "Les fondements économiques de la commune rurale dans les régions bulgares (XVe-XVIII-e siècles)." *Etudes Balkaniques,* I. Sofia.
GRUEV, Tudor
  1973   "O kučnim zadrugama u titovveleškom kraju," EP, 11.
GUBOGLU, Mihai
  1963   "Evliya Celebi. De la situation sociale-économique des Pays Roumains vers le milieu de XVIIe siècle." *Studia et Acta Orientalia,* IV, Bucarest.
  1967   "De la situation politique, administrative, militaire, culturelle et artistique dans les pays roumains (1651-1666)." *Studia et Acta Orientalia,* V-VI, Bucarest.
GUIDETTI, Massimo et Paul Henri Stahl
  1977   *Il sangue e la terra. Comunità di villaggio e comunità familiari nell'Europa dell'800.* Milano.
  1977-A  *Un'Italia sconosciuta. Comunità di villaggio e comunità familiari nell'Italia dell'800.* Milano.
GUNDA, Béla
  1972   "Kulturmorphologische Probleme in den Karpaten." *Ludova kultura v Karpatoch."* Bratislava.
GUŠIĆ, Marijana
  1976   "Pravni Položai ostajnice-virdinese u stočarskom društvu regi je Dinarida." *Posebna izdanija Balkanoloski Instituta,* 1. Belgrade.
GUYS
  1776   *Voyage littéraire de la Grèce.* Paris, 2 vol.
GUXHO, Naum
  1976   "La décomposition physique de la famille patriarcale à la campagne et l'influence de ce processus dans les relations familiales." EA.
HABERLANDT, Michael
  1928   *Die Völker Europas und ihre Volkstumliche Kultur.* Stuttgart.

HACQUET
  1815  *L'Illyrie et la Dalmatie, ou moeurs, usages et coutumes de leurs habitants et de ceux des contrées voisines.* Paris.
HAHN, J. G. von
  1854  *Albanische Studien.* Jena.
HALPERN, Joel Martin
  1956  *Social and Cultural Change in a Serbian Village.* New Haven.
  1958  *A Serbian Village.* New York.
  1969  *Bibliography on English language sources on Yugoslavia.* 2nd edition. Research Reports number 3. Department of Anthropology, Univ. of Massachusetts. Amherst.
  1972  "Town and countryside in Serbia in the nineteenth century, social and gold structure as reflected in the census of 1863." *Actes du IIe Congrès des Etudes du Sud Est Européen. Athènes, mai 1970.* Athens.
HALPERN, Joel Martin, John McKinstry et Dalip Saund
  1961  *Bibliography of Anthropological and Sociological Publications on Eastern Europe and the USSR (English language sources).* Los Angeles.
HALPERN, Joel Martin et David Anderson
  1970  "The zadruga, a century of change." *Anthropologica,* XII, 1.
HALPERN, Joel Martin et Barbara Kerewski Halpern
  1972  *A Serbian Village in Historical Perspective.* New York.
HALPERN, Joel et David Kideckel
  1983  "Anthropology of Eastern Europe." *Ann. Rev. Anthrop.*
HAMMEL, Eugene A.
  1957  "Serbo-Croatian Kinship Terminology." *Kroeber Anthropological Society. Papers,* no. 16. Berkeley.
  1968  *Alternative social structures and ritual relations in the Balkans.* New Jersey.
  1972  "The zadruga as process." Dans Laslett, Wall, 1972.
  1976  "Some medieval evidence on the Serbian zadruga: a preliminary analysis of the Chrysobulls of Dečani." Dans Byrnes, 1976.
  1977  "Reflections on the zadruga." ESL, 7.
HASLUCK, Margaret
  1933  "Bride Price in Albania. A Homeric Parallel." *Man.*
  1935  "Bride Price in Albania." *Man,* no. 102.

1939 "Couvade in Albania." *Man,* no. 18.

1954 *The Unwritten Law in Albania.* Cambridge.

HANDMAN, Marie Elisabeth

1981 "De la soumission à l'indépendance. Le statut de la femme dans un village du Pelion." EKE.

1983 *La violence et la ruse. Hommes et femmes dans un village grec.* Aix-en-Provence.

HAȘDEU, Bodgan Petriceicu

1884 *Ultima cronică din epoca Fanarioților.* Bucarest.

1892 *Strat și substrat. Genealogia popoarelor balcanice.* Bucarest.

HAUFE, Helmut

1937 "Rușetu-Brăila, un sat din câmpia românească. Structura socială." SR, II, 7-8.

HAXHIHASANI, Qemal

1977 "Le sujet du mariage dans notre Chansonnier des Preux." CN.

HAXHIU, Friqiri

1977 "La tradition populaire de l'aide sociale et son évolution." CN.

HACIU, Anastase N.

1936 *Aromânii.* Bucarest.

HECQUARD, Hyacinthe

1862 *Histoire et description de la Haute Albanie ou Guégarie.* Paris.

HEROVANU, Elena M.

1936. *Cotnarii.* Bucarest.

HERSENI, Traian

1941 *Probleme de sociologie pastorală.* Bucarest.

HOBHOUSE, J. C.

1813 *A Journey through Albania and other Provinces of Turkey in Europe and Asia, to Constantinople, during the years 1809 and 1810.* London.

HOFMANN, Giorgio

1934 "Vescovati cattolici della Grecia." *Orientalia Christiania,* XXX-IV, 1. Roma.

HORECKI, Paul

1969 *Southeastern Europe. A guide to basic publications.* Chicago and London.

IANKOVITCH et GROUITCH

1853 *Slaves du Sud, ou le peuple serbe avec les Croates et les Bulgares. Aperçu de leur vie historique, politique et sociale.* Paris.

ILESIĆ, Svetozar.
1950   *Sistemi poljske rasdelitve na Slovenskem.* Ljubljana. Académie
       Slovène des Sciences et des Arts.

IONESCU, Cornelia
1937   "Ungurenii de la Vaideeni-Vâlcea." SR, II, 11-12.

IONESCU DE LA BRAD, Ion
1866   *Agricultura română din judeţiulu Dorohoiu.* Bucarest.
1868   *Agricultura română din judeţul Mehedinţi.* Bucarest.

IONICA, Ion I.
1943   "Cadres de vie régionale roumaine." ASCRS, XVI, 1-4.

IORDACHE, Gh.
1977   "Unitate si diversitate socio-etnografică. Craiova.

IORGA, Nicolae
1906   *Scrisori şi inscriptii ardelene şi maramureşene. I. Scrisori din ar-
       hiva Grecilor Sibiului, din arhiva protopopiei neunite a Făgă-
       raşului şi din alte locuri.* Bucarest.
1906-A *Negoţul şi meşteşugurile in trecutul românesc.* Bucarest.
1914   *Histoire des Etats Balkaniques à l'époque moderne.* Bucarest.
1922   *Formes byzantines et réalités balkaniques.* Bucarest.
1924   *Histoire des Etats Balkaniques jusqu'en 1924.* Bucarest.
1929   *Le caractère commun des institutions du sud-est europén.* Paris.
1929-A *La création religieuse du sud-est européen.* Paris.
1930   *Anciens documents de droit roumain.* I-er volume. Paris-Bucarest.
1935   *Byzance après Byzance. Continuation de l'histoire de la vie by-
       zantine.* Bucarest.

IRIMIE, Cornel
1956   *Pivele şi vâltorile din Mărginimea Sibiului şi de pe valea Sebe-
       şului.* Sibiu.

ISLAMI, Hivzi
1981   "L'extension et le nombre des Albanais." *Culture Populaire Al-
       banaise,* I.

ISPIRESCU, Petre
1882   *Legendele sau basmele Românilor.* Bucarest.

ISTRIA, Dora d'
1859   *Les femmes en Orient.* I-er volume, "La Péninsule Orientale."

JACOBEIT, Wolfgang
1961   *Schafhaltung und Schäfer in Zentraleuropa bis zum Beginn des
       20. Jahrhundert.* Berlin.

JANJIĆ, Stjepan
  1967  "Porodična zadruga u istočnoj Hercegovini." GMBH, XXII.
HIREĆEK, H.
  1866  Des Recht in Böhmen und Mahren. Prague.
  1912  Staat und Gesellschaft im mittelalterlichen Serbien. Vienne.
JIVAN, Josef
  1937  "Un sat expansiv, Căianul Mic din Someş. Regimul proprie-
         tăţii." SR, II, 9-10.
  1938  "Evolutia propietăţilor in comuna Şanţ." SR, III.
  1939  "Problema pădurilor composesorale din Transilvania-Banat."
         SR, IV.
KADLEC, Karl
  1898  Rodinny nedil cili zadruha v pravu slovanskem. Prague.
  1905  "Ueber die Arbeitgenossenschaften im slavischen Recht." Zeit-
         schrift für Vergleichende Rechtswissenschaft, vol. XVII. Stutt-
         gart.
KAJMARKOVIĆ, Radmila
  1959  "Etnolosko folkloristička ispitivanja u Neumu i okolini. Krsno
         ime." GMBH, XIV.
  1962  "Narodni običaji." GMS, XVII.
KALEŠI, Hasan
  1974  "Turski pokušaji za revidiranie zakonika Leke Dukadjini i ukid-
         anie autonomje albanskih plemena u XIX veku." DCAB.
KALONAROU, Petrou P.
  1868  Serbien. Leipzig.
  1882  La Bulgarie danubienne et le Balkan. Etudes de voyage (1860-
         1880). Paris.
KARADZIĆ, Vuk Stefanović
  1837  Montenegro und die Montenegriner. Stuttgart.
KARANOVIĆ, Milan
  1929-1930 "Nekolike velike porodnice zadruge u Bosni i Hercegovini."
         GMBH, XLI, 2 ei XLII, 2.
  1932  "Krsno ime i Zavještina u Zmijanju." GMBH, XLIV.
  1933  "Janj i slavljenje Krsnog imena u njemi." GMBH, XLV, 2.
KRASTRATIN, Qazim
  1955  "Some sources on the unwritten law in Albania." Man, no. 134.
KAVADIAS, G.
  1965  Pasteurs nomades méditerranéens. Les Saracatsans de Grèce. Paris

KAYSER, Bernard
1964 *Géographie humaine de la Grèce*. Paris.

KELLNER, Heidrum
1972 "Die Albanische Minderheiten in Italien." *Albanische Forschungen*, X. Wiesbaden.

KERECSZENY, Edith
1982 "Die Einfügung der jungen Frau in der Grossfamilie innerhalb der Kroatischen Dörfer an der Mur." *In Ethnographia Pannonica. Die Frau in der Bauernkultur Pannoniens.* Zagreb.

KEREWSKI-HALPERN, Barbara et Joel M. Halpern
1977 *Selected papers on a Serbian village. Social structure as reflected by history. Demography and oral tradition.* Research Report no. 17, Department of Anthropology, University of Massachusetts, Amherst.

KITSIDIS, H.
1952 "Ai Ipeirotiki koinonites." *Ipeirotiki Estia,* 1.

KOGALNICEANU, Michail
1872-1874 *Cronicele României sau Letopiseţele Moldaviei şi Valahiei.* Bucharest, 3 vol., 2nd edition.

KOLEVA, T.
1964 "Žensko i detski-gurbetčiistvo (isčiläk) v Razlozko i Blagoevgradsko prez 1856-1912 g.". IZV, VII.

KOLEVA, Elena
1972 "Calendriers en bois. Raboches en Bulgaria." ESL, III.

KÖNIG, Judith
1971 *Die "Vereinigte Staaten" von Levkas. Ethnographie einer griechische Gemeinde.* Berne.

KONSULOVA, N. D.
1915 *Die Grossfamilie in Bulgarien.* Erlangen.

KOSTALLARI, Androkli
1972 "Moi shtrirjeb e shtresëzimin e së drejtës kanunore në Shkipëri dhe mbi disa ceshtje gë lidhen me studimin e saj e me organizim e luftës kundër mbeturinave të së vjetrës." ESH, IV.

KOSTIĆ, Cvetko
1958 "Oblici naših porodica." GEI, VII.
1976 "Dinamica della famiglia e della proprietà terriera nei villaggi jugoslavi." *Quaderni storici,* 33, Ancona.

KOSTOV, St. L. et E. Peteva
1935  *La vie rustique et l'art paysan dans les environs de Sofia.* Sofia.
KOSVEN, M. O.
1964  "Who is the godfather." *Soviet Anthropology and Archeology,* II.
KOVAČEVIČOVA, Sona
1970  "Deux civilisations de même racine." *Ethnologia Europaea,* II-III, Arnhem.
KOŽUKAROV, Georgi
1966  "Narodnata k'šta v dolinite na rekite Struma i Mesta prez vtorata polovina na XIX v." *Izvestija na sekciata za teorija i istorija na gradoustroistvoto i arhitekturata,* XIX. Sofia, B'lgarska Akademija na naukite.
KOUTSILIERIS, Anargirou G.
1960  "Gamilia etima tis Manis," *Laografia,* XIX.
KRASNIQI, Mark
1950-1960  "Šiptarska porodična zadruge u Kosovsko-Metohijskoj oblasti." *Glasnik Muzeja Kosove i Metohije,* IV-V. Priština.
1971  "Communita di famiglie e di beni presso gli Albanesi in Jugoslavia." *Actes du premier congrès international des études balkaniques et sud-est européennes,* VII, Sofia.
1974  "Disa problemetë evolucionit të familjes shkiptare në Kosovë." *Gjurmime albanologijke.* Prishtinë.
1979  *Jgurme e gjurmime. Studime etnografike.* Prishtinë.
1982  "La grande famille patriarcale albanaise à Kosove." EA, X.
KRAUSS, Friedrich S.
1885  *Sitte und Brauch der Südslaven: nach heimischen, gedruckten und ungedruckten Quellen.* Wien.
1908  *Slavische Volksforschungen.* Leipzig.
KR'STANOVA, Kiprijana G.
1975  "O roli 'zared' v economiceskoi obštestvennoi žizni bolgarskogo sela." IZV, XVI.
KRSTIĆ, Djurica
1982-1983  "Traces of Customary Law Institute of Montenegrin Homestead." *Balcanica,* XIII-XIV, Belgrade.
KULIŠIĆ, Spiro
1957  "Arhaično bratstvo u Crnoj Gori i Hercegovini." GMBH, XII.

1959   "Društveni i pravni običaji." GMBH, XIV.
LA CURNE de SAINTE-PALAYE
1880   *Dictionnaire historique de l'ancien langage françois.* Paris.
LANE, Rose Wilder
1923   *Peaks of Serbia.* New York.
LASLETT, Peter et Richard Wall. [Editors]
1972   *Household and family in past time.* Cambridge.
LASLETT, Peter et Marilyn Clarke
1972   "Houseful and Household in an eighteenth century Balkan City. A Tabular Analysis of the Listing of the Serbian Sector of Belgrade in 1733-1744." In Laslett and Wall, 1972.
LAUGIER, Charles H.
1910   *Sǎnǎtatea in Dolj.* Craiova.
LAVELEYE, Emile de
1886   *La péninsule des Balkans.* Paris.
1901   *De la propriété et de ses formes primitives.* Paris.
LENORMANT, F.
1866   *Turcs et Monténégrins.* Paris.
LESHCENKO, V. Ju.
1978-1979   "The postion of Women in the light of Religious-Domestic Taboos among the East Slavic Peoples in the nineteenth and early twentieth century." *Soviet Anthropology and Archeology,* XVII, 3.
LIAVAS, Lambros
1982   Contribution à l'étude des rapports entre musique et sociéte en Eubée du Nord. Paris, 1982 (Memoirs, unpublished).
LOCKWOOD, William G. (Editor).
1967   *Essays in Balkan Ethnology.* Berkeley.
1972   "Converts and consanguinity: the social organization of Moslems Slavs in Western Bosnia." *Ethnology,* 11.
1974   "Bride Theft and Social Maneuverability in Western Bosnia." *Anthropology Quarterly,* vol. 47, no. 3.
LODGE, Olive
1942   *Peasant Life in Jugoslavia.* London.
LORINT, Florica
1967   "Tradiţia moaşei de neam in Gorj." REF, XII, 2.

LORINT, Florica et C. Eretescu
1967   "Moşii in obiceiurile vieţii familiale." REF, XII, 4.
LUTOVAC, Milisav
1935   *La Metohija. Etude de géographie humaine.* Paris.
MANCIULEA, Ştefan
1942   "Articuluşul vecinătăţii din Ighişul Nou." SR, IV, 7-12.
MANDIĆ, Oleg
1952   "Bratstvo u ranosrednjevekovnoj Hrvatskoj." *Historiski Zbornik,* V, 3-4.
MANOLESCU, N.
1895   *Igiena ţăranului.* Bucarest.
MARCU, Liviu P.
1967   "The Tartar Patriarchal Community in the Dobroudja ans its Distintegration." *Revue des Etudes Sud-Est Européennes,* V, 3-4, Bucarest.
1971   "Zeitgenossische soziologische Aspekte des verstädterungsprozesses in südosteuropa. I. Typisierung der Familienstrukturen." *Revue des Etudes Sud-Est Européennes,* IX, 4.
1973   "Formes traditionnelles de la vie de famille au village de Siniţa." EP, 11.
1977   "Formes traditionnelles de jugement et de peines chez les Vlaques Balkaniques." CN.
MARINOV, Vasil
1964   *Prinos kam isučavaneto na proishoda, bita i kulturata na Karakačanite v B'lgarija.* Sofia.
MARKOVA, L. V.
1956   *Selskaja obščina u Bolgar v XIX veke.* Moscow.
1965   "Repartitional Land Tenure in the Rhodope District of Bulgaria (19th and First Quarter of 20th Centuries). *Soviet Anthropology and Archeology,* IV, 1.
MARKOVIĆ, Milan
1903   *Die serbische Hauskommunion (zadruga) und ihre Bedeutung in der Vergangenheit und Gegenwart.* Leipzig.
MARTONNE, Emmanuel de
1902   *La Valachie.* Paris.
MASLOVAROVIĆ, Dušan
1973   "Savremena porodična preraspodela radne snage u nekim ratar-

industrijskim centrima istočne Srbije i njen odraz na privredne odnose." EP, 11.

MASSON, Danièle
1982   Les femmes de Breb. Paris. Etudes et Documents Balkaniques, 4.

MAUER, Georg Ludwig von
1835   Das Griechische Volk. Heidelberg.

MEGAS, Georgiou A.
1967   "La civilisation dite balkanique. La poésie des pays des Balkans." Laografia, Athènes.
1967   Eisagogi eis tin laografian. Athens.

MEITZEN, August
1895   Siedelung und Agrarwesen der Westgermanen und Ostgermanen, Kelter, Römer, Finnen und Slaven. 4 vol., Berlin.
1983   "Communautés familiales des Slaves du Sud." Dans Etudes et Documents Balkaniques et Méditerranéens, VI, Paris.

MEÇI, Xhemal
1979   "La foire de Kabash (Pukë)." EA, IX.

MENDRAS, Henri
1961   Six villages d'Epire. Paris.

MIGNE
1853   Nouvelle Encyclopédie Théologique. Tome 37-ème. Dictionnaire d'Ethnographie moderne. Paris.

MIHAILIDOU-NOUAROU, Mihail G.
1926   Nomika etima tis nisou Karpatou tis Dodekanisou. Athens.

MIHAILESCU, Vintilă
1935   "Une carte de l'habitat rural en Roumaine." BSRRG, LIII.
1937   "L'Evolution de l'habitat rural dans les collines de la Valachie entre 1790-1900." BSRRG, LV.

MIHORDEA, Vasile
1968   Relaţii agrare din secolul al XVIII-lea in Moldova. Bucarest.

MIHORDEA, Vasile, Şerban Papacostea et Florin Constantiniu
1967   Documente privind relaţiile agrare in veacul al XVIII-lea. Ţara Românească. Bucarest.

MIHORDEA, Vasile, Ioana Constantinescu et Corneliu Istrati
1966   Documente privind relaţiile agrare in veacul al XVIII-lea. Moldova. Bucarest.

MILIĆ-KRIVODOLJANIN, Božidar
1958 "Ekonomski razvital u selu Nišićima, srez Sarajevo." GMBH, XVI.

MIJATOVICH, Chedo
1908 *Servia and the Servians.* London.

MILOJEVIĆ, Borivoje Z.
1933 *Littoral et iles dinariques dans le royaume de Jougoslavie.* Belgrade.
1939 *Les hautes montagnes dans le royaume de Yougoslavie.* Belgrade.

MILUTINOVIĆ, Vera
1958 "Ustanove i pojave društvenog života." Dans Filipović, 1958.

MIRAMBEL, André
1942-1943 "Blood vengeance (Maina) in southern Greece and among the Slavs." *Byzantion,* XVI, fasc. 2.

MITRUSHI, Llambrini
1972 "Zakon mbi lindjen e fëmijës në lalët e myzeqesë." ESH, IV.
1976 "Fiançailles et mariage chez les Lale de Muzeqe." EA.

MOSELY, Philip E.
1943 "Adaptation for survival: the Varzić zadruga." *Slavonic and East European Review,* 21.
1953 "The distribution of the zadruga within Southeastern Europe." *The Joshua Starr Memorial Volume.* Jewish Social Studies, V.

MUKA, Ali
1979 "L'habitation rurale dans la Malessie de Tirana." EA, IX.
1980 "Constructions dans les environs de Librazhd." EA, X.
1982 "Un pâté de maisons dans le village de Nrar (Tirana)." EA, XII.
1982-A "L'habitation d'une famille rurale dans la Malessie de Tirana (Petit-Shëngjin)." *Culture populaire albanaise,* II.

MUSSET, Danielle
1981 *Le mariage à Moişeni, Roumaine.* Paris. Etudes et Documents Balkaniques, 3.

MUSTE, Nicolae
1874 *Letopisetul Moldovei (1662-1729).* Dans Michail Kogălniceanu, "Cronicele României sau letopiseţele Moldaviei şi Valahiei," vol. III, Bucarest, 1874.

MOTOMANCEA, Aurelian
1973 "Structura-familială şi gradul de inrudire la populaţia din satul Nucşoara-Hunedoara." AMET, 1971-1973; Cluj, 1973.

NECULCE, Ion

1955    *Letopiseţul Ţării Moldovei.* Bucarest.

NENIŢESCU, Ioan

1895    *De la Românii din Turcia europeană. Studiu etnic şi statistic asupra Armânilor.* Bucarest.

NICOPOULOS-SIKE, Yvonne

1977    *Les costumes de Skiros.* Paris (Memoirs, unpublished).

NIEDERLE, Lubor

1926    *Manuel de l'antiquité slave.* Paris, 2 vol.

NIKOLIĆ, Vidosava

1958    "Srpska porodična zadruga u metohijskim selima." GEI, 7.

NISTOR, Cotul

1938    "Despre secretul din comuna ˌ Sant. Limitarea nasterilor." SR, III, 4-6.

NOE, Constantin

1938    "Celnicii şi fălcarea. O instituţie milenară a Aromânilor nomazi." SR, III, 1-3.

NOPCSA, Franz

1910    *Aus Sala und Klementi. Albanische Wanderungen.* Sarajevo.

1932    "Topographie und Stames Organisation in Nordalbanien." *Festschrift für Carl Ühlig.* Ohrigen.

NOVA, Koço

1972    "Pozita e guras sipas së drejtës zakonore të Labërise." ESH, IV.

1977    "La condition de la femme d'après le droit coutumier." CN.

1981    "Ndërtimi dhe veprimtaria e gjykatave të shtetit shkiptar në vitet 1912-1939." *Studime Historike,* XXXV (XVIII), 3, Tirana.

NOVAKOVITCH, D.

1905    *La zadruga. Les communautes familiales chez les Serbes.* Paris.

OBREBSKI, Joseph

1977    *Ritual and Social Structure in a Macedonian Village.* International area studies program, University of Massachusetts, Amherst.

ONIANS, R. B.

1951    *The Origins of European Thought about the Body, the Mind, the Soul, the Wold, Time and Faith.* Cambridge.

OLINESCU, Teodor.

1944    *Mitologie românească.* Bucarest.

PAMFILE, Tudor

1913   *Agricultura la Români. Studiu etnografic.* Bucarest.

1915   *Cerul şi podoabele lui după credinţele poporului român.* Bucarest.

1920   *Frăţia de cruce şi alte inrudiri sufleteşti la Români.* Bârlad.

PANAITESCU, P. N.

1946   *Răbojul, studiu de istorie economică şi socială la Români.* Bucarest.

PANTAZOPOULOS, Nikolas I.

1967   *Church and Law in the Balkan Peninsula during the Ottoman Rule.* Thessaloniki.

PANTELIĆ, Nikola

1962   "Selo i porodica." GEM, 25.

1966   "Selo, srodstvo i porodica." GEM, 28-29.

1972   "Snahačestvo in Serbia and its Origin." ESL, III.

PANTELIĆ, Nikola et Nikola Pavković

1964   "Selo i neki oblici društvenog života." GEM, 27.

PAPACOSTEA, Şerban

1971   *Oltenia sub stăpânirea austriacă (1718-1739).* Bucarest.

PAPADOPOULOS, Théodore

1970   *Présupposition historique d'une ethnographie des peuples du sud-est européen.* Corapport pour le II-ème Congrès International des études du sud-est européen. Athènes, 1970.

PAPASTATHIS, Charalambos

1974   "L'église et le droit coutumier aux Balkans pendant la domination ottomane." DCAB.

PATRICIU, Em. I.

1935   *Monografia comunei Smulţi din judeţul Covurlui.* Bârlad.

PAUL de ALEP

       See CIORAN.

PAVKOVIĆ, Nikola

1961   "Selo i zadruga u Livanskom Polju." GMS, XV-XVI.

1962   "Društvene i obićajne pravne ustanove u Imljanima." GMS, XVII.

1972   *Pravo prece kupovine u običajnom pravu Srba i Hrvata.* Belgrade.

1980   "Društvena organizacija." GEM, 44.

1986 "Le mariage matrilocal et la société patrilocale de la Yougoslavie." *Etudes et Documents Balkaniques et Méditerranéens,* 10, Paris.

PAUNEL, Eugen I.

1935 "Călătoria din 1769 a stegarului Johann Friedel, dealungul malului bănăţean al Dunării." *Arhivele Olteniei.* Craiova.

PECHOUX, P. Y.

1968 "Les paysans de la rive orientale du bas Nestos (Thrace grecque)." *Etudes Rurales,* 29, Paris.

1969 *Les paysans de la rive orientale du Bas Nestos (Thrace greque).* Athènes.

PECHOUX, Pierre-Yves, B. Kayser, Michel Sivignon

1971 *Exode rural et attraction urbaine en Grèce.* Athènes.

PENELEA, Georgeta

1973 *Les foires de la Valachie pendant la période 1774-1848.* Bucarest.

PERISTIANY, J. G. (Editeur)

1966 *Honour and Shame. The values of Mediterranean Society.* London.

1968 *Contributions to Mediterranean Sociology.* The Hague.

1976 *Mediterranean Family Structures.* Cambridge-London-New York-Melbourne.

PEŠEVA, Raina

1961 "Materialen i duhoven bit na savremennogo selsko semeistvo v s. R'zevo Konare, Plovdivsko." IZV, IV.

1965 "Struktura na semeistvoto i roda v B'lgarija v kraja da XIX i načaloto na XX v." IZV, VIII.

1971 "Jožnoslavianskaia zadruga v konce XIX i načale XX vv." *Actes du premier Congrès International des Etudes Balkaniques et Sud Est Européennes,* vol. VII. Sofia.

1972 "Late patrimonial traditions in the social organization of the Slavs." ESL, 3.

PEŠIĆ-MAKSIMOVIĆ, Nadežda

1972 "Les impasses dans les villages, conséquence de la division des zadrugas." *II-e Congrès International des Etudes de Sud-Est Européen. Athènes, mai 1970,* vol. II. Athènes.

PETRESCU, Iancu
1860 "Plaiulu Loviştei din districtulu Argeşu." *Analele statistice şi economice.* Bucarest.
PETRESCU, Paul et Paul H. Stahl
1956 *Ceramica din Hurez.* Bucarest.
1957 "Inrâuririle vieţii sociale asupra arhitecturii ţărăneşti dobrogene." SCIA, 1-2.
PETRESCU, V.
1937 "Vechiul drept românesc şi indivizibilitatea lotului ţărănesc." SR, II, 4.
PETRESCU-CRAIOVA, V.
1937 "Viaţa economica a satului Işalniţa-Dolj." SR, II, 9-10.
PETROPOULOS, D. A.
1952 "I akliria eis ta etima tou ellinikou laou." ELA, 7.
PHILIPPIDES, Demetrios Agamemmon
1973 *The Vernacular Design Setting of Elymbos. A Rural Spatial System in Greece.* A dissertation submitted in partial fulfillment of the requirements for a degree of Doctor of Architecture in the University of Michigan.
PIAULT, George
1981 "L'absence vécue au village; d'ici entre l'Ailleurs et l'Autrefois." EKE.
PIRCH, Otto von
1830 *Reise in Serbien im Spätherbst 1829.* Berlin.
PITTARD, Eugène
1917 *La Roumanie. Valachie, Moldavie, Dobroudja.* Paris.
PITT-RIVERS, Julian
1963 *Mediterranean Countryman. Essays in Social Anthropology of the Mediterranean.* Paris. (Pitt-Rivers-editors).
1977 *The Fate of Sechem or the Politics of Sex. Essays in the Anthropology of the Mediterranean.* Cambridge-London-New York-Melbourne.
PODOLAK, Jan
1967 *Pastierstvo v oblasti Vysokich Tatier.* Bratislava.
POP, Mihai
1986 "Les lignages du Maramures (Transylvanie, Roumanie)." *Etudes et documents balkaniques et Méditerranéens,* 10, Paris.

POPA LISSEANU, G.
1935 *Isvoarele istoriei Românilor. Cântecul de jale de Rogerius.* Bucarest.

POPESCU, Eleonora
1937 *Consideratiuni antropologice asupra regiunii Fundulea-Ilfov.* Manuscript, Library of the Romanian Academy.

POPESCU, Ion I.
1937 *Monografia satului Malurile, judeţul Râmnicul Sărat, alcătuită in anul 1933.* Buzau.

POPOVIĆ, Vasilj
1921-1922 "Zadruga. Teorije i literatura." GMBH, XXXIV.

POPOVICI RAISKI, Natasa
1939 "Familia şi copilul intr'un sat din Neamţ (Holda)." SR, IV, 4-6.

PORTAL, Roger
1965 *Les Slaves, peuples et nations.* Paris.

Potra, George
1961 *Documente privitoare la istoria oraşului Bucureşti (1594-1821).* Bucarest.
1975 *Documente privitoare la istoria oraşului Bucureşti (1821-1848).* Bucarest.

POUQUEVILLE, F. C. H. L.
1805 *Voyage en Morée, à Constantinople et en Albanie, et dans plusieurs autres parties de l'empire Ottoman pendant les années 1798, 1800, 1801.* Paris, 3 vol.
1826 *Voyage de la Grèce.* Paris, 6 vol.

PRIE, Octavian
1934 *Un sat românesc din Ardeal in străvechile sale intocmiri şi obiceiuri.* Cluj.

PRIMOVSKI, Anastas
1975 "Razdelina sobstvenost v'rhy zemiata i plodnite d'rveta i tiahnoto naslediavane v Rodopskata oblast." IZV, XVI.

*Problèmes de l'émancipation complète de la femme en Republique Populaire d'Albanie.* Tirana.
1970

RADU, Ion
1937 "Raport asupra manifestărilor juridice din sânul familiei." Dans *Ancheta monografică a comunei Belinţ.* Timişoara.

RADULESCU, Andrei
1940　*Monografia comunei Chiojdeanca din judeţul Prahova.* Bucarest, 4th edition.

RADULESCU, Codin et prêtre Ion Răuţescu
1923　*Dragoslavele.* Câmpulung.

RADULESCU RUDARI, N.
1926　"Răboaje pentru socoteli." *Arhivele Olteniei,* Craiova.

RETEGANUL, Ion Pop
1915　Dans Densuşianu.

RIHTMAN-AUGUŠTIN, Dunja
1982　"Über die 'Subkultur' der Frauen in der slawonischen gross-familie" Dans *Ethnographia Pannonia. Die Frau in der Bauern-kultur Pannoniens.* Zagreb.

RIZA, Emin
1976　"L'habitation type Gjirokastrite (XVIII-XIXe s.)." EA.

ROBERT, Cyprien
1844　*Les Slaves de Turquie, leurs ressources, leurs tendances, leurs progrès politiques.* Paris, 2 vol.

ROVINSKI, P.
1897　*Černogorija.* Sankt Peterburg.

RUSSU, Ion I.
1959　*Limba Tracodacilor.* Bucarest.
1963　"Elemente autohtone in terminologia ocupaţiilor." AMET 1959-1961. Cluj.
1969　*Ilirii. Istoria, limba si onomastica. Romanizarea.* Bucarest.
1970　*Elemente autohtone in limba română. Substratul comun ro-mâno-albanez.* Bucarest.

SAMARIAN, Pompei
1937　*O veche monografie sanitară a Munteniei. "Topografia Ţărei Româneşti de Dr. Constantin Caracas (1800-1928).* Bucarest.

SAKO, Zihni
1967　*Chansonnier des Preux Albanais. Paris, Unesco.*
1970　"La femme dans la société albanaise d'hier et d'aujourd'hui." Dans *Problèmes de l'émancipation complète de la femme en République Populaire d'Albanie.* Tirana.

SANDERS, Irwin T.
1949　*Balkan Village.* University of Kentucky Press.

1953    "Village social organization in Greece." *Rural Sociology*, 18.

1962    *Rainbow in the Rock. The People of Rural Greece.* Cambridge.

s.d.    "Social characteristics of traditional rural societies (with special reference to southeastern Europe)." Rapport pour le III-e Congrès International des études sud-est européennes.

SASSU, Iulian A.

1929    "Istoricul comunei Inanceşme." *Analele Dobrogei,* Cernăuţi.

SAVA, Aurel

1929    *Documente putnene.* Focşani.

SAULNIER, Françoise

1980    *Anoya, un village de montagne crétois.* Paris.

1981    "Quelques aspects du changement social dans un village de montagne crétois." EKE.

SCURTU, Vasile

1966    *Termenii de inrudire in limba română.* Bucarest.

SELIMAJ, Yllka

1982    "Changements dans les rapports matrimoniaux des plaines littorales de l'Albanie du Nord." EA, XII.

SELIMI, Yllka

1981    "Coutumes de naissance à Zadrime et changements de nos jours." EA, XI.

SERAFIM, Gh.

1938    "Impărţirea pe moşii şi pe trupuri de moşie a satului Negoieşti-Mehedinţi." SR, III, 1-3.

SERRES, Marcel de

1814    *Voyage en Autriche, ou Essai statistique et géographique sur cet empire.* Paris.

SHKURTI, Spiro

1976    "Aspects économiques des laboureurs cifçis à Vuk de Saranda (1900-1944)." EA.

1979    "Les moissons. Un essai pour l'Atlas ethnographique albanais." EA, VIII.

SHPATI, Ramazan

1945    *Les aspects de l'économie albanaise.* Saint Etienne.

SICARD, Emile

1943    *La zadruga sud-slave dans l'évolution du groupe domestique.* Paris.

1943-A *La zadruga dans la littérature serbe (1850-1912).* Paris.

1947 *Problèmes familiaux chez les Slaves du sud.* Paris.

SIGHIARTEU, Elena

1926 "Monografia comunei Agrieş." *Anuarul liceului Andrei Mureş-anu din Dej.* Dej.

SIMIĆ, Andrei

1967 "The Blood Feud in Montenegro." Dans Lockwood, 1967.

SIVIGNON, Michel

1967 *Les pasteurs du Pinde septentrional.* Lyon.

SKENDI, Stavro

1975 "Mosely on the zadruga." Dans Byrnes, 1976.

STAHL, Henri H.

1929 et 1930 "Contribuţii la problema răzăşiei satului Nerej. Dreptul obişnuielnic vrâncean." ASTRS, VIII et IX.

1936 "Rudenia spirituală din năşie la Drăguş." SR, I, 7-9.

1936-A "L'organisation collective du village communautaire." ASCRS, XIII.

1937 "Ruşeţu-Brăila, un sat din câmpia românească. Regimul de proprietate agrară." SR, II, 7-8.

1939 *Nerej. Un village d'une région archaique.* Bucarest, 3 vol.

1958, 1959, 1965 *Contribuţii la studiul satelor devălmaşe româneşti.* Bucarest, 3 vol.

1965 "Paysages et peuplement rural en Roumanie." *Nouvelles Etudes d'Histoire.*

1969 *Les anciennes communautés villageoises roumaines. Asservissement et pénétration capitaliste.* Bucarest-Paris, 1969.

1969-A *Controverse de istorie socială românească.* Bucarest.

1972 *Studii de sociologie istorică.* Bucarest.

1980 *Traditional Romanian Village Communities.* Cambridge University Press et Maison des Sciences de l'Homme-Paris.

1981 *Amintiri şi gânduri.* Bucarest.

1983 *Eseuri critice despre cultura populară românească.* Bucarest.

STAHL, Henri et Paul H. Stahl

1968 *Civilizatia vechilor sate românesti.* Bucarest.

STAHL, Paul H.

1958 *Planurile caselor româneşti ţărăneşti. Die Grundrisse der rumänische Bauernhäuser.* Sibiu.

1959   "La dendrolatrie dans le folklore et l'art rustique du XIXe siècle en Roumanie." *Archivio Internazionale di Etnografia e Preistoria,* II. Torino.

1960   "Porţile ţărăneşti la Români." SCIA, 2.

1960-A   "Les tailles-calendaires des paysans roumains." *Actes du IIe Congrès International des sciences anthropologiques et ethnologiques.* Paris, 2-e volume.

1965   "La dendrolatrie chez les Turcs et les Tatares de la Dobroudja." *Revue des Etudes Sud-Est Européennes,* Bucarest.

1967   "Interioare ţărăneşti din România (secolul al XIX-lea şi inceputul secolului al XX-lea)." *Studii şi comunicări. Muzeul Brukenthal 1817-1967,* 13th volume, Sibiu.

1969   "Organizarea interiorului." Dans Florescu, Petrescu, Stahl.

1973   "L'organisation magique du territoire villageois roumain." *L'Homme,* XIII, 3.

1973-A   "Le village traditionnel roumain et les coopératives agricoles collectives." *Archives Internationales de Sociologie de la Coopération et du Développement,* 34. Paris.

1973-B   "Frontières politiques et civilisations paysannes traditionnelle." *Confini e regioni. Boundaries and regions.* Trieste.

1974   "Groupe domestique, maison, maisnie. Le cas roumain." *In Memoriam Antonio Jorge Dias,* II-e volume. Lisbonne.

1975   *Ethnologie de l'Europe du Sud-Est. Une anthologie.* Paris.

1975-A   "Deux communautés villageoises en Europe du sud-est." *Eléments d'Ethnologie,* I-er volume, édité par Robert Cresswell. Paris.

1976   "Peasant House Building and its Relation to Church Building. The Romanian Case." *The Mutual Interaction of People and their Built Environment.* Edited by Amos Rapoport. The Hague-Paris.

1979   *Sociétés traditionnelles balkaniques. Contribution à l'étude des structures sociales.* Etudes et Documents Balkaniques, 1. Paris.

1978   "The Domestic Group in the Traditional Balkan Societies." *Zeitschrift für Balkanologie,* XIV, Berlin.

1979   "The Rumanian Household from the Eighteenth to the Early Twentieth Century." *Europe as a Cultural Area,* edited by tion de Jean Cuisenier. The Hague-Paris.

1981    "Les enfants et la pérennité de la maisnie. Quelques examples balkaniques." *Revue des Etudes Roumaines*, XVI, Athènes.

1981-A  *Le mariage. Recherches contemporaines sur des populations balkaniques.* Edited by P.H. Stahl. Freiburg.

1982    "Strukturat e vjetra shoqërore Shqiptare në kuadrin e shoqërive ballkanike dhe evropiane (Shek. XIX)." *Kultura popullore*, 2/1982. Tirana.

1983    "L'autre monde. Les signes de reconnaissance." *Buletinul Bibliotecii Române*, XIV. Freiburg.

1984    "Les églises en bois de Valachie. La table des ancêtres." *Etudes et documents balkanique et méditerranéens*, 7, Paris.

STAHL, Paul H. et Paul Petrescu
1964    "Construcţii ţărăneşti din Haţeg." AMET 1962-1964.

STAHL, Paul H. et Massimo Guidetti
1979    *La Radici dell'Europa. Il dibattito ottocentesco su comunità di villaggio e familiari.* Milano.

STANKOVIĆ, Bora
1918    *Nečistva krv.* Genève. Biblioteka Jugoslovenske Kniževnosti.

STAVROU, Assimina
1982    *Tissus valaques du Pinde.* Etudes et Documents Balkaniques, 5. Paris.

STANCESCU, Mircea
1938    "Un sat de foşti moşneni din câmpia românească. Poiana de lângă Ialomiţa." SR, III, 7-9.

STANCULESCU, Petre et Gh. Serafim
1943    "La foire de Vidra-Putna." ASCRS, XVI, 1-4.

STANCULESCU, Florea, A. Gheorghiu, P. H. Stahl et P. Petrescu
1957    *Arhitectura populara românească. Dobrogea.* Bucarest.

STEPHANIDES, Charalambos Stephoros
1965    *A Sociological Sketch of the Village of Megali Vrisi, Macedonia, Greece*, 1965.

STEPHANOPOLI, Dimo et Nicolo
1798    *Voyage en Grèce pendant les années V et VI (1797 et 1798).* Paris, 2 vol.

ST. CLAIR, S. G. B. et Charles A. Brophy
1869    *A Residence in Bulgaria.* London.

ST. GEORGE, Guillet de
1676    *Lacédémone ancienne et nouvelle.* Paris, 2 vol.

STOIANOVIĆ, Petar
1974 "Relations et influences réciproques entre le droit coutumier et les dispositions de lois au Monténégro." DCAB.

STOIANOVICI, T. Al.
1942 "Un funcţionar sătesc; pomojnicul." SR, IV, 7-12.

STOIANOVICH, Traian
1967 A Study in Balkan Civilisation. New York.

STOICESCU, Nicolae
1971 Cum măsurau stramoşii. Metrologia medievala pe teritoriul Romăniei. Bucarest.

STOJANČEVIĆ, Vidosava
1980 "Problèmes des changements contemporains dans les rapports de parenté traditionnels, dans la vie familiale et le mariage au villages de la Serbie." Dans Vlahović, 1980.

STOJSAVLJEVIĆ, B.
1973 Povijest sela. Hrvatska, Slavonija, Dalmacija. 1848-1918. Zagreb.

STRAUS, Adolf
1882 Bosnien. Land une Leute. Vienne.
1898 Die Bulgaren. Ethnographischen Studien. Leipzig.

STROHAL, Iv.
1905 "Zadruga u južnih slovjena." GMBHn XXI.

SUMNER-MAINE, Henry
1876 Village communities in the east and west. London.
1880 De l'organisation jurdique de la famille chez les Slaves du Sud et chez les Rajpoutes. Paris.

SWEET, Louise
1967 "Appearance and Reality; Status and Roles of Women in Mediterranean Societies." Anthropological Quarterly, 40, 3, Washington.

ŞAFARICA, Irina
1973 "Studierea familiei din perspectiva unor discipline şi teorii moderne." Dans Comunicări ştiintifice pe teme folclorice. Sighetul Marmatiei, decembrie 1970-1971. Baia Mare.

ŞTEFANELLI, T. V.
1915 Documente din vechiul ocol al Câmpulungului moldovenesc. Bucarest, 2 vol.

ŞUŢU, Nicolae
1957 Opere economice. Bucarest.

TAILLANDIER, Saint-René
  1872   *La Serbie. Kara-George et Milosch.* Paris.
TARZIU, Valeriu
  1939   *Ipoteştii; monografie.* Cernăuţi.
THOMESCU BACIU, N.
  1943   *Urzicenii.* Bucarest.
THOMO, Pirro
  1981   *Banesa fshatare e shqipërisë veriore.* Tirana.
TIKTIN, Hariton
  1903   *Rumänisch-Deutsch Wörterbuch.* Bukarest.
TIRTJA, Mark
  1980   "Aspects du culte des ancêtres et des morts ches les Albanais."
         EA, X.
TOMASIĆ, Dinko A.
  s.d.    *The Family in the Balkans.* Institute of East European Studies,
          Indiana University, Bloomington.
TOMIĆ, Svetozar
  1902   *Drobnjak.* Srpski Ethnografski Zbornik, IV, Beograd.
TOMITCH, G.
  1913   *Les Albanais en Vieille Serbie et dans le sandjak de Novi Pazar.*
         Paris.
TOURALI-TSATSOULI, Zacharoula
  1980   *Le costume traditionnel du Dodécanèse (les iles de Kassos et de
         Tilos).* Paris. Doctoral dissertation, unpublished.
TRIANTAPHYLLOU, Anna
  1983   "Quelques observations sur la vie et l'économie du village de
         Kalarytes (Grèce)." *Etudes et Documents Balkaniques et Médi-
         terranéens,* 6, Paris.
TRIFUNOVSKI, Jovan
  1973   "Kučna zadruga u selima S. R. Makedonije." EP, 11.
TROYANOVITCH, Sima
  1909   "Manners and customs." In Alfred Stead (editor), *Servia and
         the Servians,* London.
TUFAI, Muzafer
  1978   *Trois villages de Polog (Macédoine yougoslave). Contribution à
         l'étude des structures sociales, de la parenté et de l'habitat.*
         Doctoral dissertation, unpublished.

UÇI, Alfred
1970   "De certains aspects de l'évolution de la famille dans la Rép.
         Populaire d'Albanie." *Problèmes de l'émancipation complète
         de la femme en République Populaire d'Albanie.* Tirana.
ULQINI, Kahreman
1977   "Les rapports entre le bajrak, le fis et la région ethnographique."
         CN.
URBAN, Martin
1938   *Die Siedelung Südalbaniens.* Ohringen.
URECHI, Grigori
1872   *Domnii Moldovei (1354-1594).* Dans Michail Kogălniceanu,
         "Cronicele României sau letopiseţele Moldaviei şi Valahiei."
         Bucarest, 1872, 2nd edition, vol. I.
UTIEŠENOVIĆ, D. M.
1859   *Die Hauskommunionen der Südslaven.* Wien.
VACARELSKI, Christo
1969   *Bulgarische Volkskunde.* Berlin.
VALENTINI, Giuseppe
1945   "La famiglia nel diritto della tradizione albanese." *Annali
         lateranensi,* 9. Roma.
1956   *Il diritoo delle comunità nella tradizione giuridica albanese.
         Generalità.* Florence.
1969   *La legge delle montagne albanesi nelle relazioni volante.* 1880-
         1932. Florence.
VANCU, Petre
1905   *Monografia comunei Maderat (Magyarad).* Arad.
VASOVIĆ, Radosav
1935   *Pleme Vasojević.* Sarajevo.
VERNIER, Bernard
1977   "Emigration et dérèglement du marché matrimonial." *Actes de
         la recherche en sciences sociales,* juin 1977, Paris.
VERŞESCU, prêtre Gh.
1942   *Monografia comunei Tarcau, judetul Neamt.* Piatra Neamt.
VICIU, Alexiu
1914   *Colinde din Ardeal. Datini de Crăciun şi credinţe poporane.* Bu-
         carest.

VILFAN, Sergij
1974   "Samouprava i običajno pravo kod Slovenaca do početka XX veka." DCAB.

VINSKI, Zdenko
1938   *Die südslavische Grossfamilie in ihrer Beziehung zum asiatischen Grossraum.* Zagreb.

VISVISIS, J. L.
1953   "L'administration communale des Grecs pendant la domination turque." *L 'Hellénisme Contemporain.*

VITANESCU, Pavel
1937   *Monografia comunei Bălăneşti din judeţul Olt.* Bucarest.

VLAHOVIĆ, Petar (editor)
1980   *Changements dans la vie populaire en Serbie.* Belgrade.
1981   *Quelques problèmes ethnologiques de l'étude des peuples et des nationalités.* Belgrade.

VLAJINA, Milan Z.
1929   *Moba i požainica.* Belgrade.

VLAVIANOS, B.
1924   *Zur Lehre der Blutrache.* München.

VOINEA, Ion P., M. Stoian et C. Dumitrescu
1905   *Monografia comunei rurale Merenii de Sus.* Bucarest.

VOINEA, Şerban
1926   *Marxism oligarhic.* Bucarest.

VORONCA, Elena Niculiţă
1903   *Datinele şi credinţele poporului român.* Cernauţi, 3 vols.

VUČKOVIĆ, Dušan
       *Šumarstvo i lovstvo u Crnoj Gori u drogoj polovini XIX i početkom XX vijeka.* Titograd.

VUKMANOVIĆ, Jovan
1964   "Plemensko uredjenie, karakter i sudjenie narodnih glavara u Crnoj Gori." *Glasnik Etnografskog Muzeja na Cetinju,* IV.
1973   "Oblici, struktura i prava članova kučnih zajednica u Konavlima." EP, 11.

VUKOSAVLJEVIĆ, Sreten V.
1953   *Istorija seljačkog društva. I. Organizacija seljačke zemljišne svojine.* Belgrade.
1957   *Organizacija dinarskih plemena.* Belgrade.

WACE, A. I. B. and M. S. Thompson
1913    *The Nomads of the Balkans.* London.
WAGSTAFF, J. M.
1965    "The Economy of the Mani Peninsula (Greece), in the Eighteenth
        Century." *Balkan Studies,* 6. Thessaloniki.
1969    "The Study of Greek Rural Settlements. A Review of the Litte-
        rature." *Erdkunde,* XXIII.
WALCOT, P.
1970    *Greek Peasants. Ancient and Modern. A comparison of social
        and moral values.* Manchester University Press.
WALSH, P.
1828    *Voyage en Turquie et à Constantinople.* Paris.
WEBER, Georg
1968    *Beharrung und Einfügung.* Köln-Graz.
WEIGAND, Gustav
1895    *Die Aromunen.* Leipzig, 2 vol.
WHITAKER, Ian
1968    "Tribal structure and national politics in Albania." Dans *History
        and social anthropology,* edited by I. M. Lewis.
1976    "Familial roles in the extended patrilineal kin-group in northern
        Albania." Dans Peristiany, 1976.
1981    "A Sack for carrying Things: the Traditional Role of Women in
        Northern Albanian Society." *Anthropological Quarterly,* 54, 3.
WILKINSON, Gardner
1848    *Dalmatia and Montenegro.* London.
WINNER, Irene
1971    *A Slovenian Village: Zerovnica.* Providence, Rhode Island.
ZHEMAJ, Ukë
1981    "Travaux aratoires traditionnels dans le district de Kaçanik."
        EA, XI.
YRIARTE, Charles
1878    *Les bords de l'Adriatique et du Monténégro.* Paris.
*Yugoslav Village* (The)
1972    Special issue on Sociologija Sela.
ZAFEIRAKOPOULOS, D. K.
        "Maniatika etima." *Laografia,* vol. IV.

ZDRAVKOVIĆ, Ivan
1955-1957 "Jedna mahala šiptarskog sela Blase na Novo Brdy." GEI, IV-VI.
ZEČEVIĆ, Slobodan
1968-1969 "Praznik (Slava) u severoistočnoj Srbiji." GEM, 31-32.
1973 "Zavetina u severoistocnoj Srbiji." GEM, 36.
ZIVANOVIĆ, Srboljub
1976 "The Origin of the Saints Feast in Macedonia." *Man.*
ZLATEV, Todor
1955 *B'lgarskijat grad prez epohata na v'zraždaneto.* Sofia.
ZOIZI, Rrok
1956 "Mbi të drejtën kanunore të popullit shqiptar." *Buletin par shkencat shoqerore,* 2. Tirana.
1972 "Aspekte të kalimit nga familja patrarkalen në familjen e re socialiste." ESH, IV.
1976 "L'ancienne division ethnographique régionale du peuple albanais." EA.
1977 "Survivances de l'ordre du fis dans quelques micro-régions de l'Albanie.' CN.
ŽUPANIĆ, Niko
1952 "Šišano kumstvo kod jugoistočnih Slovenaca i ostalih Slovena." GEI, I.

*Plate I. Peasant house, Chiojdul Buzăului (Romania)*

*Plate II. Lineage cemetery (Apuseni Mountains, Romania)*

*Plate III. House of three Macedonian brothers (Polog plain).*
*The layout comprises three identical structures, each belonging to one brother.*

*Plate IV. Similar houses of three associated Albanian brothers located in one courtyard (Cegrane, Macedonia, Yugoslavia).*

*Plate V. Chapel, Anoya (Crete)*

*Plate VI. Kinsmen's houses and defense towers in the Central Mani plain*
*(Peloponnesus)*

## EAST EUROPEAN MONOGRAPHS

The *East European Monographs* comprise scholarly books on the history and civilization of Eastern Europe. They are published under the editorship of Stephen Fischer-Galati, in the belief that these studies contribute substantially to the knowledge of the area and serve to stimulate scholarship and research.

21. *The Crises of France's East-Central European Diplomacy, 1933-1938.* By Anthony J. Komjathy. 1976.
22. *Polish Politics and National Reform, 1775-1788.* By Daniel Stone. 1976.
23. *The Habsburg Empire in World War I.* Edited by Robert A. Kann, Bela K. Kiraly, and Paula S. Fichtner. 1977.
24. *The Slovenes and Yugoslavism, 1890-1914.* By Carole Rogel. 1977.
25. *German-Hungarian Relations and the Swabian Problem.* By Thomas Spira. 1977.
26. *The Metamorphosis of a Social Class in Hungary During the Reign of Young Franz Joseph.* By Peter I. Hidas. 1977.
27. *Tax Reform in Eighteenth Century Lombardy.* By Daniel M. Klang. 1977.
28. *Tradition versus Revolution: Russia and the Balkans in 1917.* By Robert H. Johnston. 1977.
29. *Winter into Spring: The Czechoslovak Press and the Reform Movement 1963-1968.* By Frank L. Kaplan. 1977.
30. *The Catholic Church and the Soviet Government, 1939-1949.* By Dennis J. Dunn. 1977.
31. *The Hungarian Labor Service System, 1939-1945.* By Randolph L. Braham. 1977.
32. *Consciousness and History: Nationalist Critics of Greek Society 1897-1914.* By Gerasimos Augustinos. 1977.
33. *Emigration in Polish Social and Political Thought, 1870-1914.* By Benjamin P. Murdzek. 1977.
34. *Serbian Poetry and Milutin Bojic.* By Mihailo Dordevic. 1977.
35. *The Baranya Dispute: Diplomacy in the Vortex of Ideologies, 1918-1921.* By Leslie C. Tihany. 1978.
36. *The United States in Prague, 1945-1948.* By Walter Ullmann. 1978.
37. *Rush to the Alps: The Evolution of Vacationing in Switzerland.* By Paul P. Bernard. 1978.
38. *Transportation in Eastern Europe: Empirical Findings.* By Bogdan Mieczkowski. 1978.
39. *The Polish Underground State: A Guide to the Underground, 1939-1945.* By Stefan Korbonski. 1978.
40. *The Hungarian Revolution of 1956 in Retrospect.* Edited by Bela K. Kiraly and Paul Jonas. 1978.
41. *Boleslaw Limanowski (1935-1935): A Study in Socialism and Nationalism.* By Kazimiera Janina Cottam. 1978.
42. *The Lingering Shadow of Nazism: The Austrian Independent Party Movement Since 1945.* By Max E. Riedlsperger. 1978.
43. *The Catholic Church, Dissent and Nationality in Soviet Lithuania.* By V. Stanley Vardys. 1978.
44. *The Development of Parliamentary Government in Serbia.* By Alex N. Dragnich. 1978.
45. *Divide and Conquer: German Efforts to Conclude a Separate Peace, 1914-1918.* By L. L. Farrar, Jr. 1978.
46. *The Prague Slav Congress of 1848.* By Lawrence D. Orton. 1978.
47. *The Nobility and the Making of the Hussite Revolution.* By John M. Klassen. 1978.
48. *The Cultural Limits of Revolutionary Politics: Change and Continuity in Socialist Czechoslovakia.* By David W. Paul. 1979.
49. *On the Border of War and Peace: Polish Intelligence and Diplomacy in 1937-1939 and the Origins of the Ultra Secret.* By Richard A. Woytak. 1979.
50. *Bear and Foxes: The International Relations of the East European States 1965-1969.* By Ronald Haly Linden. 1979.

51. *Czechoslovakia: The Heritage of Ages Past*. Edited by Ivan Volgyes and Hans Brisch. 1979.
52. *Prime Minister Gyula Andrassy's Influence on Habsburg Foreign Policy*. By Janos Decsy. 1979.
53. *Citizens for the Fatherland: Education, Educators, and Pedagogical Ideals in Eighteenth Century Russia*. By J. L. Black. 1979.
54. *A History of the "Proletariat": The Emergence of Marxism in the Kingdom of Poland, 1870–1887*. By Norman M. Naimark. 1979.
55. *The Slovak Autonomy Movement, 1935–1939: A Study in Unrelenting Nationalism*. By Dorothea H. El Mallakh. 1979.
56. *Diplomat in Exile: Francis Pulszky's Political Activities in England, 1849–1860*. By Thomas Kabdebo. 1979.
57. *The German Struggle Against the Yugoslav Guerrillas in World War II: German Counter-Insurgency in Yugoslavia, 1941–1943*. By Paul N. Hehn. 1979.
58. *The Emergence of the Romanian National State*. By Gerald J. Bobango. 1979.
59. *Stewards of the Land: The American Farm School and Modern Greece*. By Brenda L. Marder. 1979.
60. *Roman Dmowski: Party, Tactics, Ideology, 1895–1907*. By Alvin M. Fountain, II. 1980.
61. *International and Domestic Politics in Greece During the Crimean War*. By Jon V. Kofas. 1980.
62. *Fires on the Mountain: The Macedonian Revolutionary Movement and the Kidnapping of Ellen Stone*. By Laura Beth Sherman. 1980.
63. *The Modernization of Agriculture: Rural Transformation in Hungary, 1848–1975*. Edited by Joseph Held. 1980.
64. *Britain and the War for Yugoslavia, 1940–1943*. By Mark C. Wheeler. 1980.
65. *The Turn to the Right: The Ideological Origins and Development of Ukrainian Nationalism, 1919–1929*. By Alexander J. Motyl. 1980.
66. *The Maple Leaf and the White Eagle: Canadian-Polish Relations, 1918–1978*. By Aloysius Balawyder. 1980.
67. *Antecedents of Revolution: Alexander I and the Polish Congress Kingdom, 1815–1825*. By Frank W. Thackeray. 1980.
68. *Blood Libel at Tiszaeszlar*. By Andrew Handler. 1980.
69. *Democratic Centralism in Romania: A Study of Local Communist Politics*. By Daniel N. Nelson. 1980.
70. *The Challenge of Communist Education: A Look at the German Democratic Republic*. By Margrete Siebert Klein. 1980.
71. *The Fortifications and Defense of Constantinople*. By Byron C. P. Tsangadas. 1980.
72. *Balkan Cultural Studies*. By Stavro Skendi. 1980.
73. *Studies in Ethnicity: The East European Experience in America*. Edited by Charles A. Ward, Philip Shashko, and Donald E. Pienkos. 1980.
74. *The Logic of "Normalization:" The Soviet Intervention in Czechoslovakia and the Czechoslovak Response*. By Fred Eidlin. 1980.
75. *Red Cross, Black Eagle: A Biography of Albania's American Schol*. By Joan Fultz Kontos. 1981.
76. *Nationalism in Contemporary Europe*. By Franjo Tudjman. 1981.
77. *Great Power Rivalry at the Turkish Straits: The Montreux Conference and Convention of 1936*. By Anthony R. DeLuca. 1981.
78. *Islam Under the Double Eagle: The Muslims of Bosnia and Hercegovina, 1878–1914*. By Robert J. Donia. 1981.

79. *Five Eleventh Century Hungarian Kings: Their Policies and Their Relations with Rome.* By Z. J. Kosztolnyik. 1981.

80. *Prelude to Appeasement: East European Central Diplomacy in the Early 1930's.* By Lisanne Radice. 1981.

81. *The Soviet Regime in Czechoslovakia.* By Zdenek Krystufek. 1981.

82. *School Strikes in Prussian Poland, 1901-1907: The Struggle Over Bilingual Education.* By John J. Kulczychi. 1981.

83. *Romantic Nationalism and Liberalism: Joachim Lelewel and the Polish National Idea.* By Joan S. Skurnowicz. 1981.

84. *The "Thaw" In Bulgarian Literature.* By Atanas Slavov. 1981.

85. *The Political Thought of Thomas G. Masaryk.* By Roman Szporluk. 1981.

86. *Prussian Poland in the German Empire, 1871-1900.* By Richard Blanke. 1981.

87. *The Mazepists: Ukrainian Separatism in the Early Eighteenth Century.* By Orest Subtelny. 1981.

88. *The Battle for the Marchlands: The Russo-Polish Campaign of 1920.* By Adam Zamoyski. 1981.

89. *Milovan Djilas: A Revolutionary as a Writer.* By Dennis Reinhartz. 1981.

90. *The Second Republic: The Disintegration of Post-Munich Czechoslovakia, October 1938-March 1939.* By Theodore Prochazka, Sr. 1981.

91. *Financial Relations of Greece and the Great Powers, 1832-1862.* By Jon V. Kofas. 1981.

92. *Religion and Politics: Bishop Valerian Trifa and His Times.* By Gerald J. Bobango. 1981.

93. *The Politics of Ethnicity in Eastern Europe.* Edited by George Klein and Milan J. Reban. 1981.

94. *Czech Writers and Politics.* By Alfred French. 1981.

95. *Nation and Ideology: Essays in Honor of Wayne S. Vucinich.* Edited by Ivo Banac, John G. Ackerman, and Roman Szporluk. 1981.

96. *For God and Peter the Great: The Works of Thomas Consett, 1723-1729.* Edited by James Cracraft. 1982.

97. *The Geopolitics of Leninism.* By Stanley W. Page. 1982

98. *Karel Havlicek (1821-1856): A National Liberation Leader of the Czech Renascence.* By Barbara K. Reinfeld. 1982.

99. *Were-Wolf and Vampire in Romania.* By Harry A. Senn. 1982.

100. *Ferdinand I of Austria: The Politics of Dynasticism in the Age of Reformation.* By Paula Sutter Fichtner. 1982.

101. *France in Greece During World War I: A Study in the Politics of Power.* By Alexander S. Mitrakos. 1982.

102. *Authoritarian Politics in a Transitional State: Istvan Bethlen and the Unified Party in Hungary, 1919-1926.* By William M. Batkay. 1982.

103. *Romania Between East and West: Historical Essays in Memory of Constantin C. Giurescu.* Edited by Stephen Fischer-Galati, Radu R. Florescu and George R. Ursul. 1982.

104. *War and Society in East Central Europe: From Hunyadi to Rakoczi—War and Society in Late Medieval and Early Modern Hungary.* Edited by János Bak and Béla K. Király. 1982.

105. *Total War and Peace Making: A Case Study on Trianon.* Edited by Béla K. Király, Peter Pastor, and Ivan Sanders. 1982

106. *Army, Aristocracy, and Monarchy: Essays on War, Society, and Government in Austria, 1618-1780.* Edited by Wayne S. Vucinich. 1982.

107. *The First Serbian Uprising, 1804-1813.* Edited by Wayne S. Vucinich. 1982.

108. *Propaganda and Nationalism in Wartime Russia: The Jewish Anti-Fascist Committee in the USSR, 1941-1948.* By Shimon Redich. 1982.

109. *One Step Back, Two Steps Forward: On the Language Policy of the Communist Party of Soviet Union in the National Republics.* By Michael Bruchis. 1982.

110. *Bessarabia and Bukovina: The Soviet-Romanian Territorial Dispute.* by Nicholas Dima. 1982

111. *Greek-Soviet Relations, 1917-1941.* By Andrew L. Zapantis. 1982.

112. *National Minorities in Romania: Change in Transylvania.* By Elemer Illyes. 1982.

113. *Dunarea Noastra: Romania, the Great Powers, and the Danube Question, 1914-1921.* by Richard C. Frucht. 1982.

114. *Continuity and Change in Austrian Socialism: The Eternal Quest for the Third Way.* By Melanie A. Sully. 1982

115. *Catherine II's Greek Prelate: Eugenios Voulgaris in Russia, 1771-1806.* By Stephen K. Batalden. 1982.

116. *The Union of Lublin: Polish Federalism in the Golden Age.* By Harry E. Dembkowski. 1982.

117. *Heritage and Continuity in Eastern Europe: The Transylvanian Legacy in the History of the Romanians.* By Cornelia Bodea and Virgil Candea. 1982.

118. *Contemporary Czech Cinematography: Jiri Menzel and the History of The "Closely Watched Trains".* By Josef Skvorecky. 1982.

119. *East Central Europe in World War I: From Foreign Domination to National Freedom.* By Wiktor Sukiennicki. 1982.

120. *City, Town, and Countryside in the Early Byzantine Era.* Edited by Robert L. Hohlfelder. 1982.

121. *The Byzantine State Finances in the Eighth and Ninth Centuries.* By Warren T. Treadgold. 1982.

122. *East Central European Society and War in Pre-Revolutionary Eighteenth Century.* Edited by Gunther E. Rothenberg, Bela K. Kiraly and Peter F. Sugar. 1982.

123. *Czechoslovak Policy and the Hungarian Minority, 1945-1948.* By Kalman Janics. 1982.

124. *At the Brink of War and Peace: The Tito-Stalin Split in a Historic Perspective.* Edited by Wayne S. Vucinich. 1982.

125. *The Road to Bellapais: The Turkish Cypriot Exodus to Northern Cyprus.* By Pierre Oberling. 1982.

126. *Essays on World War I: Origins and Prisoners of War.* Edited by Peter Pastor and Samuel R. Williamson, Jr. 1983.

127. *Panteleimon Kulish: A Sketch of His Life and Times.* By George S. N. Luckyj. 1983.

128. *Economic Development in the Habsburg Monarchy in the Nineteenth Century: Essays.* Edited by John Komlos. 1983.

129. *Warsaw Between the World Wars: Profile of the Capital City in a Developing Land, 1918-1939.* By Edward D. Wynot, Jr. 1983.

130. *The Lust for Power: Nationalism, Slovakia, and The Communists, 1918-1948.* By Yeshayahu Jelinek. 1983.

131. *The Tsar's Loyal Germans: The Riga German Community: Social Change and the Nationality Question, 1855-1905.* By Anders Henriksson. 1983.

132. *Society in Change: Studies in Honor of Bela K. Kiraly.* Edited by Steven Bela Vardy. 1983.

133. *Authoritariansim in Greece: The Metaxas Regime.* By Jon V. Kofas. 1983.

134. *New Hungarian Peasants: An East Central European Experience with Collectivization.* Edited by Marida Hollos and Bela C. Maday. 1983.

DR 24 .S72 1986
Stahl, Paul H.
Household, village and
   village confederation in

DATE DUE

DR 24 .S72 1986
Stahl, Paul H.
Household, village and
   village confederation in

| DATE DUE | BORROWER'S NAME | ROOM NUMBER |
|---|---|---|
| 3/90 | Brandt reserve. | |
| | | |
| | | |
| | | |